George Frederick Maclear

The Gospel According to St. Mark

With Maps, Notes and Introduction

George Frederick Maclear

The Gospel According to St. Mark
With Maps, Notes and Introduction

ISBN/EAN: 9783337281038

Printed in Europe, USA, Canada, Australia, Japan

Cover: Foto ©Lupo / pixelio.de

More available books at **www.hansebooks.com**

The Cambridge Bible for Schools and Colleges.

GENERAL EDITOR:—J. J. S. PEROWNE, D.D.,
DEAN OF PETERBOROUGH.

THE GOSPEL ACCORDING TO

ST MARK,

WITH MAPS NOTES AND INTRODUCTION

BY

THE REV. G. F. MACLEAR, D.D.,
WARDEN OF ST AUGUSTINE'S, CANTERBURY, AND
LATE HEAD MASTER OF KING'S COLLEGE SCHOOL, LONDON.

EDITED FOR THE SYNDICS OF THE UNIVERSITY PRESS.

Cambridge:
AT THE UNIVERSITY PRESS.

London: C. J. CLAY AND SONS,
CAMBRIDGE UNIVERSITY PRESS WAREHOUSE,
AVE MARIA LANE.

1890

PREFACE
BY THE GENERAL EDITOR.

THE General Editor of *The Cambridge Bible for Schools* thinks it right to say that he does not hold himself responsible either for the interpretation of particular passages which the Editors of the several Books have adopted, or for any opinion on points of doctrine that they may have expressed. In the New Testament more especially questions arise of the deepest theological import, on which the ablest and most conscientious interpreters have differed and always will differ. His aim has been in all such cases to leave each Contributor to the unfettered exercise of his own judgment, only taking care that mere controversy should as far as possible be avoided. He has contented himself chiefly with a careful revision of the notes, with pointing out omissions, with

PREFACE.

suggesting occasionally a reconsideration of some question, or a fuller treatment of difficult passages, and the like.

Beyond this he has not attempted to interfere, feeling it better that each Commentary should have its own individual character, and being convinced that freshness and variety of treatment are more than a compensation for any lack of uniformity in the Series.

DEANERY, PETERBOROUGH.

CONTENTS.

		PAGES
I.	INTRODUCTION.	
	Chapter I. Life of St Mark........................	7—11
	Chapter II. Circumstances of the Composition of the Gospel.................................	11—16
	Chapter III. Characteristics of the Gospel...	16—20
	Chapter IV. Analysis of the Gospel............	20—26
II.	Text and Notes	27—194
III.	General Index...	195—199
IV.	Index of Words and Phrases explained	199, 200

MAP OF GALILEE.................................... *facing title*
SEA OF GALILEE .... *facing* p. 52
ENVIRONS OF JERUSALEM .... *facing* p. 120
PALESTINE IN THE TIME OF OUR SAVIOUR *at end of Volume*

"*Companion of the Saints! 'twas thine
To taste that drop of peace divine,
 When the great soldier of thy Lord
Call'd thee to take his last farewell,
Teaching the Church with joy to tell
 The story of your love restor'd.*"

"The Christian Year."   *St Mark's Day.*

INTRODUCTION.

CHAPTER I.

LIFE OF ST MARK.

1. WHEN the Saviour was about to leave the earth, His last command to His Apostles was that they should *go into all the world and preach the Gospel to every creature* (Mark xvi. 15).

2. Thus the first work, and that out of which all their other functions grew, was to proclaim as heralds the Glad Tidings of the Great Hope which had arisen for mankind, and to deliver a personal testimony to the chief facts of the Gospel History, the life, death, and resurrection of their Lord (Acts i. 21, 22, iv. 33, xi. 20, xx. 20, 21).

3. Of the way in which they did this, the narrative contained in the Acts of the Apostles gives us many instances. Two instances may be taken as examples of all; (i) the preaching of St Peter before Cornelius (Acts x. 37—43), and (ii) of St Paul in the synagogue of Antioch (Acts xiii. 23—39). It will be noticed that both these discourses contain a sketch of the outlines of the Saviour's ministry, from the Baptism of John to the world's first Easter-day, and both dwell on the historical events of His Passion and Resurrection[1].

4. Thus the teaching of the Apostles was in the first instance *oral* and not written, and out of the multitude of *things which Jesus did* (John xxi. 25), a cycle of representative facts was gradually selected[2], which formed the common groundwork of their message.

---

[1] See Professor Westcott's *Introduction to the New Testament*, p. 165, and his *Bible in the Church*, p. 57.

[2] "How few have been preserved, perhaps we can hardly realize, without reckoning up what a small number of days contribute all the incidents of the Gospels, and how little remains even in the record of those to bear witness to the labours which left *no leisure so much as to eat* (Mark vi. 31)." Westcott's *Bible in the Church*, p. 5c.

5. But in the course of time another step was taken Many, as St Luke expressly tells us (i. 1—4), endeavoured to *commit to writing* this oral Gospel[1], and to form in a *connected shape written collections* of the words and actions of our Lord

6. What they designed or endeavoured to do, was actually done under Apostolic sanction. As long, indeed, as the Twelve were still living and proclaiming the Word at Jerusalem, they were themselves "abiding witnesses to the facts which they preached," but when the time came for them to be scattered throughout the world, an anxiety arose that the Church should possess authoritative records to supply the place of the oral Gospel previously in use.

7. Hence originated the Four "Memoirs" or "Biographies" of the Saviour, which have come down to us in the Four Gospels. Of these, two, those of St Matthew and St John, were written by Apostles, close friends and contemporaries of the Saviour; two, those of St Mark and St Luke, were written by "Apostolic men," who, if they had no personal knowledge of Him, were at least the constant companions of those, who had the most intimate acquaintance with His Person and His Work.

8. The writer of the second and briefest of the Gospels was St Mark.

9. Marcus was his Latin surname. His Jewish name was John, which is the same as Johanan (*the grace of God*). We can almost trace the steps, whereby the former became his prevalent name in the Church. "*John, whose surname was Mark*" in Acts xii. 12, 25, xv. 37, becomes "*John*" alone in Acts xiii. 5, 13, "*Mark*" in Acts xv. 39, and thenceforward there is no change, Col. iv. 10; Philemon 24; 2 Tim. iv. 11.

10. The Evangelist was the son of a certain Mary, a Jewish matron of some position, who dwelt at Jerusalem (Acts xii. 12),

---

[1] The history of the original word translated Gospel deserves attention. In Classical Greek it denotes (i) *the reward given to the messenger of glad tidings* (as in Homer, *Od.* XIV. 152, 166); (ii) *the sacrifice offered up as a thank-offering for glad tidings* (Ar. *Eq.* 656); (iii) *the glad tidings themselves.* Thus the word passed into the Greek of the New Testament, where it denotes *the Glad Tidings of Jesus Christ,* i.e. the Gospel, A. S. *Gode-spell.*

and was probably born of a Hellenistic family in that city. Of his father we know nothing, but we do know that the future Evangelist was cousin[1] of Barnabas of Cyprus, the great friend of St Paul.

11. His mother would seem to have been intimately acquainted with St Peter, and it was to her house, as to a familiar home, that the Apostle repaired (A.D. 44) after his deliverance from prison (Acts xii. 12). This fact accounts for St Mark's[2] intimate acquaintance with that Apostle, to whom also he probably owed his conversion, for St Peter calls him "*his son*" (1 Pet. v. 13).

12. We hear of him for the first time in Acts xii. 25, where we find him accompanying Paul and Barnabas on their return from Jerusalem to Antioch A.D. 45. He next comes before us on the occasion of the earliest missionary journey of the same Apostles, A.D. 48, when he joined them as their "minister" (Acts xiii. 5). With them he now visited Cyprus, with which island he may have been previously acquainted, as being the native country of Barnabas. But at Perga in Pamphylia (Acts xiii. 13), when they were about to enter upon the more arduous part of their mission, he left them, and for some unexplained reason[3] returned to Jerusalem, to his mother and his home.

13. This occurred about A.D. 48. Three years afterwards, A.D. 51, the same Apostles resolved to set out on a second missionary tour. But on this occasion, in spite of the earnest desire of his kinsman to take him with them, St Paul resolutely

---

[1] The Greek word, used in Col. iv. 10, is applied to cousins german, the children, whether of two brothers, or of two sisters, or of a brother and a sister. In very late writers the word comes to be used for a "nephew." See Professor Lightfoot on Col. iv. 10.

[2] There is no solid ground for the conjecture that (*a*) the Evangelist was one of the Seventy disciples, or that (*b*) he was one of those who were offended at the saying of Christ in the synagogue of Capernaum (John vi. 53, 60) but was afterwards won back by St Peter. The theory, however, is not to be wholly rejected which would identify him with the young man, who on the night of our Lord's apprehension, followed in his light linen robe, which he left in the hands of the officers when he fled from them (Mark xiv. 51, 52, where see note).

[3] (i) Some think he simply wished to rejoin St Peter and the other Apostles, and share their labours at Jerusalem; (ii) others hold that he shrank from the *perils of rivers* and *perils of robbers* (2 Cor. xi. 26) in the interior of Asia Minor.

declined to associate himself again with one, who *"departed from them from Pamphylia, and went not with them to the work"* (Acts xv. 38). The issue was a *"sharp contention"* which resulted in the separation of St Paul from his old friend, who taking Mark with him once more repaired to Cyprus, while the great Apostle of the Gentiles, accompanied by Silas, proceeded through Syria and Cilicia (Acts xv. 39—41).

14. At this point St Luke's narrative takes leave of the Evangelist. But whatever was the cause of his vacillation, it did not lead to a final separation between him and St Paul. We find him by that Apostle's side during his first imprisonment at Rome, A.D. 61—63, and he is acknowledged by him as one of his few *"fellow-labourers unto the kingdom of God,"* who had been a *"comfort"* to him during the weary hours of his imprisonment (Col. iv. 10, 11; Philemon 24); while from the former of these passages it would also seem that St Mark contemplated a journey to Asia Minor, and that St Paul had prepared the Christians of Colossæ to give him a friendly reception (Col. iv. 10).

15. We have next traces of him in another passage of the New Testament. In 1 Pet. v. 13 occur the words, "The church that is at Babylon, elected together with you, saluteth you; *and so doth Marcus my son.*" From this we infer that he joined his spiritual father, the great friend of his mother, at Babylon, then and for some hundred years afterwards one of the chief seats of Jewish culture, and assisted him in his labours amongst his own countrymen.

16. From Babylon he would seem to have returned to Asia Minor, for during his second imprisonment, A.D. 68, St Paul writing to Timothy, charges him to bring Mark with him to Rome, on the ground that he was *"profitable unto him for the ministry"* (2 Tim. iv. 11). From this point we gain no further information from the New Testament respecting the Evangelist. It is most probable, however, that he did join the Apostle at Rome, whither also St Peter would seem to have proceeded, and suffered martyrdom along with St Paul. After the death of these two great Pillars of the Church, Ecclesiastical tradition[1]

---

[1] Eusebius, *H. E.* III. 16; Hieron. *Vir. Illust.* II. 8.

affirms that St Mark visited Egypt, founded the church of Alexandria, and died by martyrdom[1].

CHAPTER II.

CIRCUMSTANCES OF THE COMPOSITION OF THE GOSPEL.

1. When we pass from the Evangelist himself to the Gospel, which he wrote, it is natural to ask four questions. (1) *When was it written?* (2) *Where was it written?* (3) *For whom was it written?* (4) *In what language was it written?*

2. *When?* Upon this point nothing absolutely certain can be affirmed, and the Gospel itself affords us no information. The Evangelist is mentioned as a relative of Barnabas, as a *"comfort"* to St Paul, and *"profitable for the ministry."* But nothing is said of any greater distinction. We may conclude, therefore, that his Gospel was not written before A.D. 63[2]. Again we may as certainly conclude that it was not written after the destruction of Jerusalem, for it is not likely that he would have omitted to record so remarkable a fulfilment of our Lord's predictions. Hence A.D. 63—70 become our limits, but nearer than this we cannot go.

3. *Where?* As to the place, the weight of testimony is uniformly in favour of the belief that the Gospel was written and published at Rome. In this Clement, Eusebius, Jerome, Epiphanius all agree. Chrysostom indeed asserts that it was published at Alexandria, but his statement receives no confirmation, as otherwise it could not fail to have done, from any Alexandrine writer[3].

4. *For whom?* The traditional statement is that it was in-

[1] According to later legends his body was removed from Alexandria to Venice A.D. 827, which was formally placed under his protection. Hence "the Lion," the symbol of St Mark, became the standard of the Venetian Republic.
[2] The most direct testimony on this point is that of Irenæus, who says that it was after the deaths of the Apostles Peter and Paul.
[3] In modern times Storr has conjectured that St Mark wrote at Antioch. But his ground for this, a comparison of Mark xv. 21 with Acts xi. 20, is not a sufficient basis for the theory.

tended primarily for Gentiles, and especially for those of Rome. A review of the Gospel itself confirms this view. For

(i) *All reference to the Jewish Law* is omitted, and on his own authority the Evangelist makes no quotations from the Old Testament, with the exception of those in the opening verses from Mal. iii. 1, and Isaiah xl. 3[1].

(ii) *Words are explained* which would not be understood by Gentile readers; "*Boanerges*" (iii. 17); "*Talitha cumi*" (v. 41); "*Corban*" (vii. 11); "*Bartimæus*" (x. 46); "*Abba*" (xiv. 36); "*Eloi, Eloi, lama sabachthani*"[2] (xv. 34).

(iii) *Jewish usages* and other points, with which Jews only could be expected to be familiar, are elucidated. Thus we are told that "*the Jews eat not unless they wash their hands oft*" (vii. 3); that the Mount of Olives "*is over against the Temple*" (xiii. 3); that "*the Passover was killed on the first day of unleavened bread*" (xiv. 12); that "*the preparation* was *the day before the Sabbath*" (xv. 42).

(iv) Again, St Mark uses several *Latin forms*, which do not occur in the other Gospels, as *Speculator*="*a soldier of the guard*" (vi. 27); *xestes=sextarius* (vii. 4, 8); *quadrantes=a farthing* (xii. 42); *satisfacere=to content* (xv. 15, comp. Acts xxiv. 27); *Centurion* (xv. 39, 44, 45).

5. *In what language?* As to the language in which it was written, there never has been any reasonable doubt that it was written in Greek[3]. The hypothesis of a Latin original rests on no foundation. A portion of a supposed original autograph of the Evangelist is shewn in the library of St Mark's at Venice,

---

[1] That in Mark xv. 28 is by many considered as interpolated.

[2] Again, two mites are said to *make a farthing* (xii. 42), and Gehenna is explained as *unquenchable fire* (ix. 43).

[3] "For some considerable part of the first three centuries, the Church of Rome, and most, if not all the Churches of the West, were, if we may so speak, Greek religious colonies. Their language was Greek, their writers Greek, their Scriptures Greek; and many vestiges and traditions shew that their ritual, their Liturgy was Greek... All the Christian extant writings which appeared in Rome and in the West are Greek, or were originally Greek; the Epistles of Clement, the Shepherd of Hermas, the Clementine Recognitions and Homilies; the works of Justin Martyr, down to Caius and Hippolytus the author of the Refutation of All Heresies." Milman's *Latin Christianity*, I. p. 34.

but it is merely part of an ancient MS. of the Four Gospels, another fragment of which exists at Prague, and was formerly preserved at Aquileia. If the Evangelist had written in Latin, it is unaccountable that no ancient writer should have made mention of the fact.

6. On another point the testimony of the early Church is also unanimous, viz. that the Evangelist composed his Gospel under the eye and direction of St Peter. As to this fact the words of John the Presbyter as quoted by Papias[1] are explicit. "Mark," we read, "having become the interpreter of Peter, wrote accurately all that he remembered[2]; but he did not [record] in order that which was either said or done by Christ. For he neither heard the Lord nor followed Him; but afterwards, as I said, [attached himself to] Peter, who used to frame his teaching to meet the wants of his hearers, but not as making a connected narrative of the Lord's discourses." Here it is distinctly asserted that St Peter's teaching was the basis of the second Gospel.

7. Equally definite is the testimony of later writers. Thus Justin Martyr (A.D. 100—120) quotes from the present Gospel under the title of "the Memoirs of Peter[3]." Irenæus (A.D. 177—202) asserts that "after the decease of these (Peter and Paul), Mark, the disciple and interpreter of Peter, himself also handed down to us in writing the things which were preached by Peter[4]." Origen (A.D. 185—254) says still more expressly that "Mark made his Gospel as Peter guided him[5]." Clement of Alexandria (A.D. 191—202) mentions as a "tradition of the elders of former time" that when Peter had publicly preached the Word in Rome, and declared the Gospel by Inspiration, "those who were present, being many, urged Mark, as one who had followed him from a distant time and remembered what he said,

---

[1] Eusebius, *H. E.* III. 39; Routh, *Rell. Sacr.* I. 13 ff.
[2] Or "that he (Peter) mentioned." The word is ambiguous and may have either of these meanings. See Westcott's *Introd. to the Gospels*, p. 180, n.
[3] *Dial.* c. 106. See Westcott's *Hist. of N. T. Canon*, p. 103.
[4] Iren. *C. Hær.* III. 1. 1; comp. Eusebius *H. E.* V. 8. Elsewhere (III. 10. 6) Irenæus calls Mark *interpres et sectator Petri.*
[5] See Eusebius, *H. E.* VI. 25.

to record what he stated; and that he having made his Gospel, gave it to those who made the request of him¹." Tertullian again (A.D. 190—220) affirms that "the Gospel of Mark is maintained to be Peter's²;" while Jerome (A.D. 346—420) tells us that the "Gospel of Mark was composed, Peter relating, and he writing³."

8. With this testimony of the early Church before us we may conclude, not indeed that the narrative, as we have it in the second Gospel, was the Apostle's, but

> (*a*) That when the Evangelist, after separation from his master, under the guidance of the Holy Spirit, composed his Gospel, he reproduced many of the oral communications of St Peter⁴;
>
> (*b*) That to the keen memory of the Apostle, recalling scenes in which he had often borne a prominent part, and of which he was an eye-witness, we owe the graphic colouring, the picturesque touches, the minuteness of detail, which his "interpreter" reverently preserved, and faithfully enshrined in the pages of his Gospel.

9. In conformity with this view we find passages in St Mark where the Apostle is specially mentioned, while he is omitted by the other Evangelists. Thus we are told

> (1) It was St Peter who followed after our Lord in the morning after the miracles at Capernaum (Mark i. 36);
>
> (2) It was he, who drew attention to the rapid withering of the fig-tree (Mark xi. 21);
>
> (3) It was he, who with three others of the Apostles, asked our Lord as He sat on the Mount of Olives respecting the destruction of Jerusalem (Mark xiii. 3);
>
> (4) It was to him specially amongst the Apostles, to whom the angel directed that the announcement of the Resurrection should be made (Mark xvi. 7).

10. And, on the other hand, it has been thought that the

---

[1] Clem. Alex. *Fragm. Hypotyp.* p. 1016, *P.*; Eusebius *H. E.* VI. 14.
[2] *Adv. Marc.* IV. 5.
[3] "Cujus (Marci) Evangelium Petro narrante et illo scribente compositum est." Hieron. *de Vir. Ill.* CVIII.; *ad Hedib.* c. II.
[4] Papias as quoted by Eusebius, *H. E.* III. 39.

modesty of the Apostle, anxious to pass over what might specially redound to his own honour, has caused the omission of

(a) His name as the prompter of the question respecting "meats not defiling a man" (comp. Mark vii. 17 with Matt. xv. 15);

(b) His walking on the sea (comp. Mark vi. 50, 51 with Matt. xiv. 28—31);

(c) The miracle of the coin in the fish's mouth (comp. Mark ix. 33 with Matt. xvii. 24—27);

(d) His designation as the Rock, on which the Church should be built (comp. Mark viii. 29, 30 with Matt. xvi. 17—19);

(e) His being sent with another Apostle to make ready the Passover (comp. Mark xiv. 13 with Luke xxii. 8);

(f) The fact that it was for *him* especially that our Lord prayed that his faith might not "utterly fail" (Luke xxii. 31, 32).

11. As to the genuineness of the Gospel there is the strongest historical evidence in its favour. All ancient testimony makes St Mark the author of a certain Gospel, and that the Gospel, which has come down to us, is his, there is not the least real ground for doubting.

12. One section, however, has given rise to critical difficulties, viz. the concluding portion from xvi. 9—20. In this section, which is wanting in the Vatican and Sinaitic MSS.[1], it has been urged that there is a change of style:—

(a) That everything pictorial, all minute details, all formulas of rapid transition, everything, in fact, which is so characteristic of the Evangelist, suddenly cease;

(b) That brief notices of occurrences more fully described in other Gospels take the place of the graphic narrative which is so striking a feature of the rest of the Book;

(c) That no less than twenty-one words and expressions occur, which are never elsewhere used by St Mark.

---

[1] But it is found in all other Codices of weight, including A, C, D, in the Vet. Lat., Vulg., Syrr., Memph., Theb., Gothic Versions, is quoted by Irenæus, and supported by Hippolytus, Chrysostom, Augustine, and Leo the Great.

13. Various reasons have been suggested for the change of style. It has been attributed by some to the death of St Peter, by others to the outbreak of the terrible persecution under Nero, A.D. 64, and the necessity of seeking safety by flight. But at this distance of time it is useless to speculate on the causes of the change, and the two most probable solutions are

> Either (i) That the Evangelist, being prevented at the time from closing his narrative as fully as he had intended, *himself* added "in another land, and under more peaceful circumstances[1]," the conclusion which we now possess;
>
> Or (ii) That it was added by *some other hand*, shortly if not immediately afterwards, but at any rate before the publication of the Gospel itself.

CHAPTER III.

CHARACTERISTICS OF THE GOSPEL.

1. From the time and place of its composition we now pass on to the *general characteristics* of the Gospel.

2. One peculiarity strikes us the moment we open it,—the absence of any genealogy of our Lord. This is the key to much that follows. It is not the design of the Evangelist to present our Lord to us, like St Matthew, as the Messiah, "*the Son of David and Abraham*" (i. 1), or, like St Luke, as the universal Redeemer, "*the Son of Adam, which was the son of God*" (iii. 38).

3. His design is to present Him to us as *the incarnate and wonder-working Son of God, living and acting amongst men*, to portray Him in the fulness of His living energy[2].

4. The limits indeed and general character of the Work are nowhere more strikingly described than in the words of the Evangelist's own great teacher in Acts x. 36—42, when he addressed himself to Cornelius. Commencing with the Baptism of John and his announcement of the coming of One Mightier

---

[1] See Bp Ellicott's *Lectures on the Gospel History*, p. 26, n.; 383, n.
[2] Westcott's *Introduction*, p. 361.

than himself (Acts x. 37; Mark i. 7), he tells us how, at His Baptism, "*God anointed Jesus of Nazareth with the Holy Ghost and with power*" (Acts x. 38), and how after His temptation He "*went about doing good*," proving Himself Lord over man and nature, and "*healing all that were oppressed of the devil; for God was with Him*" (Acts x. 38).

5. While doing this, the Evangelist does not merely chronicle each incident, but "surrounds them with all the circumstances that made them impressive to the bystanders[1]," and constrains us to feel how deep that impression was. Thus we notice

(*a*) In i. 22, 27, ii. 12, vi. 2, how words and actions of our Lord called forth *awe and wonder* from the crowds that beheld them;

(*b*) In iv. 41, vi. 51, x. 24, 26, 32, how the same feelings were evoked in *the disciples;*

(*c*) In iii. 10, v. 21, 31, vi. 33, viii., how the multitudes *thronged* and *pressed* upon Him so that there was scarce room to stand or sit (ii. 2, iii. 32, iv. 1), or *leisure even to eat* (iii. 20, vi. 31);

(*d*) In vi. 56, how the diseased were brought to Him in numbers, and *whithersoever He entered, into villages, or cities, or country, they laid the sick in the streets, and besought Him that they might touch, if it were but the border of His garment; and as many as touched Him were made perfectly whole;* comp. i. 33, 34, iii. 10.

(*e*) In i. 23—26, iii. 11, how the unclean spirits no sooner saw Him than they fell down before Him *crying with a loud voice, Thou art the Son of God.*

6. But while the Evangelist thus brings out the divine power of Him, Who was the "Lion of the tribe of Judah," he also invites our attention in an especial manner to His *human personality.* Thus he tells us how our Lord

(*a*) Could *grieve* (vii. 34, viii. 12), could *love* (x. 21), could *feel pity* (vi. 34), could *wonder* (vi. 6), could be moved with righteous *anger* and *indignation* (iii. 5, viii. 12, 33, x. 14);

(*b*) Could be sensible of human infirmities, could *hunger* (xi. 12), could desire *rest* (vi. 31), could *sleep* (iv. 38).

[1] Kitto's *Biblical Cyclopædia*, III. p. 71, 3rd Edition.

7. Again, it is St Mark, who alone describes, on several occasions, the very position, the very gesture, the very words of his Divine Master:—

(i) Thus we are bidden to notice

(a) How He *looked round* with comprehensive gaze upon His hearers (iii. 5, 34), upon the woman with the issue of blood (v. 32), upon His disciples (x. 23), upon the scene of noisy buying and selling in the Temple (xi. 11);

(b) How He *took little children into His arms, laid His hands upon them* and blessed them (ix. 36, x. 16); how He *turned round* in holy anger to rebuke St Peter (viii. 33); how He *went before* His Apostles on the way towards Jerusalem (x. 32); how He *sat down* and *called the Twelve to Him* to instruct them in a lesson of humility (ix. 35);

(ii) Again we seem to hear (a) the very Aramaic words that fell from His lips, "*Boanerges*" (iii. 17); "*Talitha cumi*" (v. 41); "*Corban*" (vii. 11); "*Ephphatha*" (vii. 34); "*Abba*" (xiv. 36); and (b) the sighs which the sight of human misery drew forth from His compassionate breast (vii. 34, viii. 12).

8. In keeping with this trait, St Mark is careful to record minute particulars of *person*, *number*, *time*, and *place*, which are unnoticed by the other Evangelists[1]:

(a) *Person:* i. 29, "They entered into the house of *Simon and Andrew with James and John;*" i. 36, "*Simon* and they *that were with Him* followed after Him;" iii. 6, "the Pharisees took counsel *with the Herodians;*" iii. 22, "the Scribes which *came down from Jerusalem* said;" xi. 11, "He went out unto Bethany *with the Twelve;*" xi. 21, "*Peter calling to remembrance*, saith unto him;" xiii. 3, "*Peter and James and John and Andrew* asked him privately;" xiv. 65, "*the servants* did strike him with the palms of their hands;" xv. 21, "Simon, *a Cyrenian...the father of Alexander and Rufus;*" xvi. 7, "Go your way, tell his disciples *and Peter.*"

(b) *Number:* v. 13, "they were *about two thousand;*" vi. 7, "He began to send them forth, *two and two;*" vi. 40, "they

---

[1] For St Mark's use of diminutives, see note v. 23.

sat down in ranks, *by hundreds and by fifties;*" xiv. 30, "before the cock crow *twice,* thou shalt deny me *thrice.*"

(*c*) *Time:* i. 35, "in the morning...*a great while before day;*" ii. 1, "after *some days;*" iv. 35, "the same day, *when the even was come;*" vi. 2, "when *the sabbath day was come;*" xi. 11, "and now *the eventide was come;*" xi. 19, "when *even was come;*" xv. 25, "and it was *the third hour;*" xvi. 2, "*very early in the morning, the first day of the week.*"

(*d*) *Place:* ii. 13, "He went forth again *by the sea side;*' iii. 7, "Jesus withdrew Himself *to the sea;*" iv. 1, "He began again to teach *by the sea side,*" v. 20, "He began to publish *in Decapolis;*" vii. 31, "through the midst of the *coasts of Decapolis,*" xii. 41, "and Jesus sat *over against the treasury,*" xiii. 3, "He sat upon the Mount of Olives, *over against the temple;*" xiv. 68, "and he went *out into the porch;*" xv. 39, "and when the centurion, which *stood over against him,*" xvi. 5, "they saw a young man sitting *on the right side.*"

9. This minuteness and particularity of observation are reflected in the language and style of the Evangelist:—

(1) His *phrases of transition* are terse and lively: e. g. "*And straightway*" occurs about 27 times in his Gospel.

(2) He frequently prefers the *present* to the historic tense: i. 40, "there *cometh* a leper to him;" i. 44, "and *saith* unto him;" ii. 3, "they *come* unto him, bringing one sick of the palsy;" ii. 10, "He *saith* to the sick of the palsy;" ii. 17, "When Jesus heard it, He *saith* unto them;" xi. 1, "And when they came nigh to Jerusalem....He *sendeth forth* two of His disciples;" xiv. 43, "immediately, while He yet spake, *cometh* Judas;" xiv. 66, "there *cometh* one of the maids of the high priest."

(3) He often uses a *direct* instead of an *indirect form of expression;* iv. 39, "He said unto the sea, *Peace, be still;*" v. 8, "He said, *Come out of the man,* thou unclean spirit;" v. 9, "He asked him, *What is thy name?*" v. 12, "the devils besought Him saying, *Send us* into the swine;" vi. 23, "he sware unto her, *Whatsoever thou shalt ask of me, I will give it thee;*" vi. 31, "He said unto them, *Come*

ye yourselves apart;" ix. 25, "He rebuked the foul spirit, saying unto him, *Thou dumb and deaf spirit, I charge thee;*" xii. 6, "He sent him, saying, *They will reverence my son.*"

(4) For the sake of emphasis he *repeats what he has said*, and couples together words or phrases of similar import to heighten and define his meaning; i. 13, "He was *there, in the wilderness;*" i. 45, "but he went out and began to *publish it much*, and *to blaze abroad* the matter;" iii. 26, "he cannot *stand*, but *hath an end;*" iv. 8, "that sprang up and *increased; and brought forth;*" iv. 33, 34, "and *with many such parables spake He* unto them...but *without a parable spake He not* unto them;" v. 23, "that she may be *healed*, and *she shall live;*" vi. 25, "and she came in *straightway with haste;*" vii. 21, "*from within, out of the heart* of men;" viii. 15, "*the leaven* of the Pharisees, *and the leaven* of Herod;" xiv. 68, "*I know not, neither understand I* what thou sayest."

10. To sum up. "In substance and style and treatment," it has been well said, "the Gospel of St Mark is essentially a transcript from life. The course and issue of facts are imaged in it with the clearest outline. If all other arguments against the mythic origin of the Evangelic narratives were wanting, this vivid and simple record, stamped with the most distinct impress of independence and originality, totally unconnected with the symbolism of the Old Dispensation, totally independent of the deeper reasonings of the New, would be sufficient to refute a theory subversive of all faith in history. The details which were originally addressed to the vigorous intelligence of Roman hearers are still pregnant with instruction for us. The teaching, which 'met their wants' in the first age, finds a corresponding field for its action now[1]."

CHAPTER IV.

ANALYSIS OF THE GOSPEL.

The following Analysis will give a general idea of the construction of St Mark's Gospel:—

[1] Westcott's *Introduction*, p. 367.

INTRODUCTION.

PART I.

I. The Preparation:—i. 1—13.
  (α) The Baptism and Preaching of John.......i. 1—8.
  (β) The Baptism of Jesus ....i. 9—11.
  (γ) The Temptation ....i. 12—13.

Observe in this Section (i) *the conciseness of the Introduction;* (ii) *the absence of any genealogy of our Lord;* (iii) *the first use of St Mark's favourite formula of transition,* "*And straightway;*" (iv) *the graphic touch that our Lord was "with the wild beasts."*

PART II.

II. The Works of Christ in Eastern Galilee:—i. 14—vii. 23.

(A) *Section* (i)
  (α) Announcement of the Kingdom..............i. 14, 15.
  (β) Call of the first Disciples ....i. 16—20.
  (γ) Cure of the demoniac at Capernaum.........i. 21—28.
  (δ) Cure of Peter's wife's mother and others ...i. 29—34.
        Retirement to a solitary place ....i. 35.
  (ε) Tour in Galilee...................................i. 35—39.
  (ζ) Cleansing of a leper.............................i. 40—45.
        Retirement to desert places ....i. 45.
  (η) Commencement of the conflict with the ruling powers:—
    (1) The cure of the Paralytic..................ii. 1—12.
    (2) Call of St Matthew ....ii. 13—22.
    (3) The disciples pluck the ears of corn ...ii. 23—28.
    (4) Cure of the man with the withered hand iii. 1—6.
        Retirement to the Lake ....iii. 7—12.

Observe in this Section (i) *how each victory of the Redeemer is followed by a withdrawal which serves as a preparation for fresh progress;* (ii) *the causes of the opposition of the Pharisaic party,* (a) *assumption by our Lord of power to forgive sins* (ii. 6, 7), (b) *eating with publicans and sinners and neglect of law of fasting* (ii. 16—22); (c) *alleged infraction of Sabbatical rules* (ii. 23—28).

(B) *Section* (ii)
  (α) Call of the Apostles ....iii. 13—19.
  (β) Opposition of the Scribes from Jerusalem...iii. 20—30.
  (γ) The true kindred ....iii. 31—35.
  (δ) Parables of the Kingdom:
    (1) The Sower ....iv. 1—9.
    (2) Explanation of the Parable...............iv. 10—25.
    (3) The Seed growing secretly ....iv. 26—29.
    (4) The Mustard Seed ....iv. 30—34.

INTRODUCTION.

- (ε) Signs of the Kingdom:
  - (1) The stilling of the storm ....iv. 35—41.
  - (2) The Gadarene demoniac ....v. 1—20.
  - (3) The woman with the issue ....v. 25—34.
  - (4) The daughter of Jairus....................v. 21—43.
- (ζ) Rejection at Nazareth ....vi. 1—6.
  - **Retirement into the villages**......... vi. 6.

Observe in this Section (i) *the foundation of the Church by the election of the Apostles;* (ii) *the deepening of the conflict with the Pharisees;* (iii) *the issue of the opposition in unbelief.*

(C) Section (iii)
- (α) Mission of the Apostles ....vi. 7—13.
- (β) The murder of the Baptist ....vi. 14—29.
  - **Retirement to a desert place** ....vi. 31, 32.
- (γ) The feeding of the Five Thousand ....vi. 33—44.
- (δ) The walking on the sea ....vi. 45—52.
- (ε) Victories over disease in all its forms ....vi. 53—56.
- (ζ) Renewed opposition of the Pharisaic party...vii. 1—23.
  - **Retirement to the borders of Tyre and Sidon** ....vii. 24.

Observe in this Section (i) *the definite step taken in the mission of the Twelve;* (ii) *the effects of the murder of the Baptist;* (iii) *the significance of the feeding of the Five Thousand at the Season of the Passover.*

PART III.

III. **The Works of Christ in Northern Galilee:—vii. 24 –ix. 37.**

(A) Section (i)
- (α) Healing of the daughter of the Syrophœ-nician ....vii. 24—30.
- (β) Gradual healing of the deaf and dumb ......vii. 31—37.
- (γ) Feeding of the Four Thousand ....viii. 1—10.
- (δ) The Pharisees ask for a sign ....viii. 11—13.
- (ε) Warnings against the leaven of the Pharisees and of Herod ....viii. 14—21.
- (ζ) Gradual cure of the blind man ....viii. 22—26.
  - **Retirement to the neighbourhood of Cæsarea Philippi**......................viii. 27.

Observe in this Section (i) *the renewed opposition of the Pharisaic party;* (ii) *the request for a sign;* (iii) *the hope opened up for the Gentiles in the cure of the daughter of the Syrophœnician;* (iv) *the use of external means and the gradual nature of the miracles of this period.*

(B) *Section* (ii)
- (a) The solemn question, and confession of St Peter ....viii. 27—33.
- (β) *The First Clear Prediction of the Passion* ...viii. 34—ix. 1.
  Retirement to the mountain range of Hermon ....ix. 2.
- (γ) The Transfiguration ....ix. 2—13.
- (δ) The lunatic child ....ix. 14—27.
- (ε) The secret source of strength ....ix. 28, 29.
- (ζ) *Second Prediction of the Passion* ....ix. 31, 32.
- (η) The Apostles taught (a) humility, and (b) self-denial..................ix. 33—50.

Observe in this Section (i) *the importance of the crisis in the Saviour's ministry;* (ii) *the solemnity of the question addressed to the Apostles;* (iii) *the significance of the Transfiguration;* (iv) *the fulness of the material imagery employed by St Mark in describing it;* (v) *the commencement of the open announcements of the Passion.*

PART IV.

IV. **The Works of Christ in Peræa :—x. 1—31.**
- (a) The question of marriage and divorce ....x. 1—12.
- (β) The blessing of little children ....x. 13—16.
- (γ) The rich young ruler ....x. 17—22.
- (δ) The danger of riches..................x. 23—27.
- (ε) The reward of self-sacrifice ....x. 28—31.

Observe in this Section (i) *the conflict with the hierarchy even in Peræa;* (ii) *the fewness of the recorded miracles after the Transfiguration.*

PART V.

V. **The Last Journey to Jerusalem and the Passion:—x. 32—xv. 47**

(A) *Section* (i)
- (a) *Third Prediction of the Passion* ....x. 32—34.
- (β) The ambitious Apostles ....x. 35—45.
- (γ) Blind Bartimæus ....x. 46—52.
- (δ) The anointing at Bethany ....xiv. 1—10.

Observe in this Section (i) *how utterly unable the Apostles were to comprehend the idea of a suffering Messiah;* (ii) *how St Mark, like St Matthew, places the anointing at Bethany out of its true order.*

(B) *Section* (ii)

THE EVENTS OF HOLY WEEK:

(a) *Palm Sunday*
   (*a*) The Triumphal Entry ....xi. 1—11.
   (*b*) **Retirement to Bethany** ....xi. 11.

(β) *Monday*
   (*a*) The withering of the barren fig-tree ...xi. 12—14.
   (*b*) The second cleansing of the Temple ...xi. 15—18.
   (*c*) **Retirement to Bethany** ....xi. 19.

(γ) *Tuesday*
   (*a*) The lesson of the withered fig-tree......xi. 20—26.
   (*b*) The question of the deputation of the Sanhedrim and the counter question...xi. 27—33.
   (*c*) The Parable of the Wicked Husbandmen...xii. 1—12.
   (*d*) The subtle questions
      (1) Of the Pharisees; *the tribute-money* ....xii. 13—17.
      (2) Of the Sadducees; *the resurrection* xii. 18—27.
      (3) Of the Lawyer; *the importance of the Commandments* ....xii. 28—34.
   (*e*) The Lord's counter-question ....xii. 35—44.
   (*f*) Prediction of the destruction of Jerusalem and the end of the world ......xiii. 1—37.

Observe in this Section (i) *the profound impression at first produced by the Triumphal Entry;* (ii) *the difference between the first and the second cleansing of the Temple;* (iii) *the deepening of the bitter hostility of the hierarchy towards our Lord;* (iv) *His sublime composure amidst the conflict;* (v) *His unconquered and unconquerable conviction of His final triumph.*

(C) *Section* (iii)

THE EVENTS OF HOLY WEEK CONTINUED:

(a) *Wednesday*
   Seclusion at Bethany.
   Compact of the Traitor ....xiv. 1, 2.

(β) *Thursday*
   (*a*) Directions respecting the Passover ......xiv. 12—16.
   (*b*) Institution of the Holy Eucharist ......xiv. 17—26.
   (*c*) Protestations of St Peter ....xiv. 27—31.
   (*d*) The Agony in Gethsemane ....xiv. 32—42.
   (*e*) The Apprehension ....xiv. 43—50.
   (*f*) The Incident of the Young Man.........xiv. 51, 52.

(γ) *Friday*
- (a) The Jewish trial .... xiv. 53—65.
- (b) The denials by St Peter .... xiv. 66—72.
- (c) The trial before Pilate .... xv. 1—15.
- (d) The Crucifixion .... xv. 16—32.
- (e) The Death .... xv. 33—41.
- (f) The Burial .... xv. 42—47.

Observe in this Section (i) *the extreme minuteness of the instructions respecting the Last Supper;* (ii) *the expansion of the narrative into the fulness of a diary as we approach the Passion;* (iii) *the incident of the young man in the Garden recorded only by St Mark.*

PART VI.

VI. Christ's Victory over the Grave, and Ascension into Heaven: —xvi. 1—20.

(a) *Easter Eve*
The rest of Christ in the Tomb .... xvi. 1.

(β) *Easter Day*
- (1) The visit of the Holy Women .... xvi. 1—3.
- (2) The Resurrection .... xvi. 4—8.

(γ) The appearances after the Resurrection to
- (1) Mary Magdalene .... xvi. 9—11.
- (2) Two disciples .... xvi. 12, 13.
- (3) The Eleven .... xvi. 14.

(δ) The last charge and the Ascension .... xvi. 15—19.
(ε) The Session at the right Hand of God ...... xvi. 19, 20.

Observe in this Section (i) *How long the disciples hesitated before they would accept the fact of the Resurrection;* (ii) *how minute and distinct are the promises in the last charge of miraculous power;* (iii) *how the Ascension seems to form with St Mark the last of the many withdrawals of the Lord, which had alternated with so many victories;* (iv) *how the growth of the Church is traced to the continued operation of her Ascended Lord.*

NOTE I.

The Miracles of our Lord recorded by St Mark may be arranged as displaying His victorious power over

(i) *Nature.*
- (α) The Stilling of the Storm ....(iv. 35—41).
- (β) The Feeding of the Five Thousand ......(vi. 30—44).
- (γ) The Walking on the Lake ....(vi. 45—52).
- (δ) The Feeding of the Four Thousand......(viii. 1—9).
- (ε) The Withering of the Fig-Tree ....(xi. 12—14).

(ii) *The Spirit-world.*
- (α) The demon cast out in the Synagogue...(i. 23—28).
- (β) The Legion ....(v. 1—20).
- (γ) The daughter of the Syrophœnician woman.......................................(vii. 24—30).
- (δ) The lunatic boy.............................(ix. 17—29).

(iii) *Disease.*
- (α) Simon's wife's mother ....(i. 30, 31).
- (β) The Leper ....(i. 40—45).
- (γ) The Paralytic...............................(ii. 3—12).
- (δ) The Cure of the Man with the withered hand.......................................(iii. 1—5).
- (ε) The woman with the issue of blood .....(v. 25—34).
- (ζ) **The deaf and dumb man.............(vii. 31—37).
- (η) **The blind man at Bethsaida.........(viii. 22—26).
- (θ) Bartimæus ....(x. 46—52).

(iv) *Death.*
The daughter of Jairus ....(v. 21—43).

** *Miracles recorded only by St Mark.*

NOTE II.

THE PARABLES RECORDED BY ST MARK.

(i) *Parables of the Early Group, from the commencement of the Ministry to the Mission of the Seventy:*—
- (α) The Sower...(iv. 3—8).
- (β) **The Seed growing secretly..................(iv. 26—29).
- (γ) The Mustard-Seed ....(iv. 30—32).

(ii) *Parables of the Intermediate Group, from the Mission of the Seventy to the last journey towards Jerusalem:*—
None.

(iii) *Parables of the Final Group, immediately before and after the Entry into Jerusalem:*—
The Wicked Husbandmen ....(xii. 1—11).

** *Parable recorded only by St Mark.*

For this arrangement of the Parables of our Lord see Smith's *Dictionary of the Bible*, II. pp. 702, 703.

ST MARK.

1—8. *The Preaching and Baptism of John.*

THE beginning of the gospel of Jesus Christ, the Son of God; as it is written in the prophets, Behold, I send my messenger before thy face, which shall prepare thy way before thee. The voice of one crying in the wilderness, Prepare ye the way of the Lord, make his paths straight. John did baptize in the wilderness, and preach the baptism

CH. I. 1—8. THE PREACHING AND BAPTISM OF JOHN.

The object of St Mark is to relate *the official life and ministry* of our Lord. He therefore begins with His baptism, and first relates, as introductory to it, the *preaching of John the Baptist*.

1. *The beginning*] St Mark commences his Gospel suddenly and concisely. He does not begin with a genealogy of our Lord, like St Matthew, or with the history of the Infancy, as St Luke, or with the doctrine of the Eternal Word, as St John. He desires to pourtray Christ in the fulness of *His living energy*. See Introduction, pp. 16, 17.

of Jesus Christ] The Gospel of Jesus Christ denotes *the Glad Tidings concerning Jesus Christ = the Messiah*, the anointed Prophet, Priest, and King. For the meaning of the name JESUS see Matt. i. 21.

the Son of God] Contrast this with St Matt. i. 1, "*the Son of David, the Son of Abraham.*" The first Evangelist writes for Jews, the second for Gentiles.

2. *in the prophets*] The citation is from two prophets, (1) Mal. iii. 1, (2) Isai. xl. 3. Some would read here **in Isaiah the Prophet** according to certain MSS. Observe that St Mark in his own narrative quotes the Old Testament only twice, here and xv. 28. See Introduction, p. 12.

4. *the wilderness*] i. e. the dry and unpeopled region extending from the gates of Hebron to the shores of the Dead Sea. "It is a dreary waste of rocky valleys; in some parts stern and terrible, the rocks cleft and shattered by earthquakes and convulsions into rifts and gorges, sometimes a thousand feet in depth, though only thirty or forty in width...The whole district is, in fact, the slope of the midland chalk and limestone hills, from their highest point of nearly 3000 feet near Hebron, to 1000 or 1500 feet at the valley of the Dead Sea. The

5 of repentance for the remission of sins. And there went out unto him all the land of Judæa, and they of Jerusalem, and were all baptized of him in the river of Jordan, confessing 6 their sins. And John was clothed with camel's hair, and with a girdle of a skin about his loins; and he did eat 7 locusts and wild honey; and preached, saying, There cometh one mightier than I after me, the latchet of whose shoes I

Hebrews fitly call it Jeshimon (1 Sam. xxiii. 19, 24), 'the appalling desolation,' or 'horror.'"

for the remission] or **unto the remission**. See margin and comp. Matt. xxvi. 28; Luke i. 77. This remission was to be received of the Messiah. John required of *all* who came to him a change of mind and life with a view to pardon from Christ. Thus his baptism was preparatory to that of Christ.

5. *all the land*] This strong expression is peculiar to St Mark. But it is illustrated by the other Gospels. The crowds that flocked to his baptism included representatives of every class, Pharisees and Sadducees (Matt. iii. 7), tax-gatherers (Luke iii. 12), soldiers (Luke iii. 14), rich and poor (Luke iii. 10).

of Jordan] *Of* here is redundant and appositional. We use it after "town," "city," "valley." For its use after *river*, comp. "*the river* of Cydnus," Shak. *A. and C.* II. 2. 192. The word "river" does not occur in the best MSS. of Matt. iii. 6. It is used by St Mark, who writes for those who were unacquainted with the geography of Palestine.

6. *was clothed*] The Evangelist draws our attention to three points in reference to the Baptist:

(*a*) *His appearance.* He recalled the asceticism of the Essene. His raiment was of the coarsest texture, such as was worn by Elijah (2 Kings i. 8) and the prophets generally (Zech. xiii. 4). His girdle, an ornament often of the greatest richness in Oriental costume and of the finest linen (Jer. xiii. 1; Ez. xvi. 10) or cotton or embroidered with silver and gold (Dan. x. 5; Rev. i. 13, xv. 6), was of untanned leather (2 Kings i. 8), like that worn by the Bedouin of the present day.

(*b*) *His diet* was the plainest and simplest. Locusts were permitted as an article of food (Lev. xi. 21, 22). Sometimes they were ground and pounded, and then mixed with flour and water and made into cakes; sometimes they were salted and then eaten. For *wild honey* comp. the story of Jonathan, 1 Sam. xiv. 25—27.

(*c*) *His message.* (1) That the members of the Elect Nation were *all* morally unclean, and *all* needed moral and spiritual regeneration; (2) that One mightier than he was coming; (3) that He would baptize with the Holy Ghost.

7. *cometh*] present tense. With prophetic foresight the Baptist sees Him already come and in the midst.

latchet] diminutive of *latch*, like the Fr. *lacet* dim. of *lace*, comes from the Latin *laqueus* = a "noose," and means anything that catches. We now only apply latch to the catch of a door or gate. We speak of

am not worthy to stoop down and unloose. I indeed have 8
baptized you with water: but he shall baptize you with the
Holy Ghost.

9—11. *The Baptism of Jesus.*

And it came to pass in those days, that Jesus came 9
from Nazareth of Galilee, and was baptized of John in
Jordan. And straightway coming up out of the water, he 10

a "shoe-*lace*," and "lace" is radically the same word. Here it denotes
the thong or fastening by which the sandal was fastened to the foot;
comp. Gen. xiv. 23; Isai. v. 27. The office of bearing and unfastening
the sandals of great personages fell to the meanest slaves.

to stoop down] This expression is peculiar to St Mark. It is the first
of those minute details which we shall find in such abundance in his
Gospel.

9—11. THE BAPTISM OF JESUS.

9. *in those days*] i.e. towards the close of the year A. U. C. 781, or
A. D. 28, when our Lord was thirty years of age (Lk. iii. 23), the time
appointed for the Levite's entrance on "the service of the ministry"
(Num. iv. 3).

came from Nazareth] where He had grown up in peaceful seclusion, "increasing in wisdom and stature and in favour with God and
man" (Luke ii. 52), in a town unknown and unnamed in the Old Testament, situated among the hills which constitute the southern ridges
of Lebanon, just before they sink down into the Plain of Esdraelon.

baptized of] i.e. *by* John. Comp. Luke xiv. 8, "when thou art bidden *of* (=by) any man;" Phil. iii. 12, "I am apprehended *of* (=by)
Christ;" Collect for 25th Sunday after Trinity, "may *of* (=by) Thee be
plenteously rewarded."

in Jordan] Either (i) at the ancient ford near Succoth, which some
have identified with the Bethabara or rather Bethany of St John (John
i. 28); or (ii) at a more southern ford not far from Jericho, whither the
multitudes that flocked from Judæa and Jerusalem (Mark i. 5) would
have found a speedier and more convenient access. From St Matthew
we learn that (i) the purport of the Saviour's journey from Galilee was
that He might be thus baptized (Matt. iii. 13); that (ii) His Forerunner
instantly recognised His superhuman and stainless nature; that (iii) he
tried earnestly to prevent Him; that (iv) his objections were overruled
by the reply that thus it became Him to "fulfil all righteousness," i.e.
every requirement of the Law. St Luke tells us that the Baptism of
our Lord did not take place till "*all the people had been baptized*"
(Luke iii. 21).

10. *straightway*] This is St Mark's favourite connecting word, and
constantly recurs; comp. i. 12, 28, iv. 5, 15, viii. 10, ix. 15, xi. 3,
and other places.

he saw] i.e. Jesus, while engaged, as we learn from St Luke iii. 21,
in solemn prayer. We find solemn prayer preceding (i) our Lord's
Baptism, (ii) His choice of the Twelve (Luke vi. 12), (iii) His Transfiguration (Luke ix. 29), (iv) His Agony in the Garden (Matt. xxvi. 39).

saw the heavens opened, and the Spirit like a dove descend-
11 ing upon him: and there came a voice from heaven, *saying*,
Thou art my beloved Son, in whom I am well pleased.

12, 13. *The Temptation.*

12 And immediately the spirit driveth him into the wilderness.
13 And he was there in the wilderness forty days, tempted of

opened] Lit. **rent, or rending asunder,** one of St Mark's graphic
touches: see the Introduction. The same word in the original Greek
is applied to "the old garment *rending* the new piece" (Luke v. 36);
to the veil of the Temple *rent in twain* at the Crucifixion (Luke xxiii.
45); to the *rending* of the rocks at the same time (Matt. xxvii. 51); and
of the net in the Lake after the Resurrection (John xxi. 11).

11. *a voice from heaven*] The first of the three heavenly Voices to
be heard during our Lord's Ministry, viz., at (i) His Baptism; (ii) His
Transfiguration (Mark ix. 7); (iii) in the courts of the Temple during
Holy Week (John xii. 28). This Voice attested in the presence of His
Forerunner the Divine Nature of our Lord, and inaugurated His public
Ministry. The Baptism was a very important event in our Lord's
life:—

(1) Needing no purification Himself, He submitted to it as the
Head of His Body, the Church (Eph. i. 22) for all His members;

(2) He was thus by baptism, and the unction of the Holy Ghost
which followed (Matt. iii. 16; comp. Ex. xxix. 4—37; Lev. viii. 1—
30), solemnly consecrated to His office as Redeemer;

(3) He "sanctified water to the mystical washing away of sin." See
the Baptismal Office;

(4) He gave to His Church for all time a striking revelation of the
Divine Nature, the Son submitting in all lowliness to every requirement of the Law, the Father approving by a voice from heaven,
the Spirit descending and abiding upon the Son. "*I ad Jordanem,
et videbis Trinitatem.*"

12, 13. THE TEMPTATION.

12. *immediately*] See above, *v.* 10. The object of the Saviour's
first Advent was "to destroy the works of the devil" (1 John iii. 8).
His very first work, therefore, was to enter on a conflict with the great
Enemy of mankind.

driveth him] This is a stronger word than that employed by St
Matthew, who says He was *led up* (Matt. iv. 1), or by St Luke, who says
He was *led* by the Spirit (Luke iv. 1). The same word is here used as
in Matt. ix. 38, "Pray ye therefore the Lord of the harvest that He will
send forth labourers into His harvest;" in John x. 4, "when He *putteth
forth* His own sheep, He goeth before them." The word denotes the
Divine impulse of the Holy Ghost, which constrained Him to go forth
to the encounter, and hints at a rapid translation, such as that by which
Prophets and Evangelists were caught up and carried to a distance
(1 Kings xviii. 12; 2 Kings ii. 16; Acts viii. 39).

vv. 14, 15.] ST MARK, I. 31

Satan; and was with the wild beasts; and the angels ministered unto him.

14, 15. *Beginning of our Lord's Ministry.*

Now after that John was put in prison, Jesus came 14 into Galilee, preaching the gospel of the kingdom of God, and saying, The time is fulfilled, and the kingdom of God 15 is at hand: repent ye, and believe the gospel.

13. *tempted of Satan*] In Matt. iv. 1 and Luke iv. 2, He is said to have been tempted by the Devil, i. e. the "Slanderer," who slanders God to man (Gen. iii. 1—5) and man to God (Job i. 9—11; Rev. xii. 10). St Mark, who never uses this word, says He was tempted by *Satan*, i. e. "the Enemy" of God and man alike. He seems to have been permitted to tempt our Lord during the whole of the forty days, but at the end of that period to have assailed Him with increased intensity through every avenue that could allure, as afterwards in Gethsemane through every channel that could terrify and appal (Luke iv. 13).

the wild beasts] St Mark relates the Temptation very briefly, but he alone adds the graphic touch to the picture that the Saviour was "with the wild beasts," unhurt by them, as Adam was in Paradise. Comp. Daniel in the den of lions.

the angels] St Matthew records the ministry of Angels at the close as to a Heavenly Prince (Matt. iv. 11). St Mark records a ministry of the same celestial Visitants apparently *throughout the trial.*

14, 15. BEGINNING OF OUR LORD'S MINISTRY.

Between the events just described and those on which the Evangelist now enters, must be placed several recorded chiefly by St John; viz., (1) The testimony of the Baptist to Christ as *the Lamb of God* (John i. 19—34); (2) the early joining of Andrew, John, Simon, Philip and Nathanael (John i. 35—51); (3) the marriage at Cana (John ii. 1—12); (4) the first visit to Jerusalem, first cleansing of the Temple and conference with Nicodemus (John ii. 13—21, iii. 1—21); (5) the ministry with the Baptist (John iii. 22—36); (6) the imprisonment of the Baptist (Luke iii. 19, 20); (7) the return of Jesus to Galilee through Samaria, and the discourse with the woman at Jacob's well (John iv. 3—42); (8) cure of the nobleman's son at Cana (John iv. 43—54).

14. *put in prison*] The causes of the imprisonment of the Baptist are more fully related by the Evangelist ch. vi. 17—20.

came into Galilee] and commenced the great Galilean ministry. Galilee was the most northern and the most populous of the three provinces, into which the Romans had divided Palestine. It was to Roman Palestine what the manufacturing districts are to England, covered with busy towns and teeming villages, Roman custom-houses and thriving fisheries. See Stanley's *Sinai and Palestine*, pp. 375—377.

the gospel of the kingdom of God] or according to some MSS. **the Gospel of God.**

15. *The time*, i. e. the great fore-ordained and predicted time of the Messiah.

16—20. *Call of the first Four Disciples.*

16 Now as he walked by the sea of Galilee, he saw Simon and Andrew his brother casting a net into the sea: for they were 17 fishers. And Jesus said unto them, Come ye after me, and 18 I will make you to become fishers of men. And straightway 19 they forsook their nets, and followed him. And when he had gone a little farther thence, he saw James the *son* of Zebedee,

the kingdom of God] or as it is called in St Matthew *the Kingdom of the Heavens* (comp. Dan. ii. 44, vii. 13, 14, 27), denotes here *the Kingdom of grace*, the visible Church, of which our Lord described (*a*) in the parable of "the Mustard Seed" (Matt. xiii. 31, 32), its *slight and despised beginning;* (*b*) in that of "the Hidden Leaven" and the "Seed growing secretly," its *hidden and mysterious working* (Matt. xiii. 33: Mark iv. 26—29); (*c*) and again in the first two Parables its *final and assured triumph* in spite of the obstacles set forth in the Parable of "the Tares" (Matt. xiii. 24—30).

believe] Rather **believe in, repose your faith on,** the Gospel.

16—20. CALL OF THE FIRST FOUR DISCIPLES.

16. *as he walked*] The Saviour had *come down* (Luke iv. 31; John iv. 47, 51) from the high country of Galilee, and now made His permanent abode in the deep retreat of the Sea of Galilee at Capernaum "His own city" (Matt. iv. 13; Luke iv. 31), whence He could easily communicate, as well by land as by the Lake, with many important towns, and in the event of any threatened persecution retire into a more secure region.

the sea of Galilee] called (i) in the Old Testament "the Sea of Chinnereth" or "Cinneroth" (Num. xxxiv. 11; Josh. xii. 3) from a town of that name which stood on or near its shore (Josh. xix. 35), in the New (ii) "the Sea of Galilee" from the province which bordered on its western side (Matt. iv. 18; Mark vii. 31), (iii) "the Lake of Gennesaret" (Luke v. 1), (iv) "the Sea of Tiberias" (John xxi. 1), and sometimes (v) simply "the Sea" (Matt. iv. 15).

he saw Simon] whom He had already invited to His acquaintance (John i. 40—42); He now calls him to the Apostleship. The recent cure of the son of the officer in Herod's court had roused much interest at Capernaum, and many pressed upon the Saviour to *"hear the Word of God"* (Luke v. 1). It became clear, therefore, that an opportunity was offered for an active and systematic ministry in Galilee, and four of the number afterwards known as "the Twelve" were now permanently attached to the Saviour's Person, and invested with power to become "fishers of men."

a net] The net here spoken of and in Matt. iv. 18 was a *casting-net*, circular in shape, "like the top of a tent," in Latin *funda* or *jaculum*. The net spoken of in Matt. xiii. 47, 48 is the *drag-net* or *hauling-net*, the English *seine* or *sean*, sometimes half a mile in length; that alluded to in Luke v. 4—9 is the *bag-net* or *basket-net*, so constructed and worked as to enclose the fish out in deep water.

and John his brother, who also were in the ship mending their nets. And straightway he called them: and they left 20 their father Zebedee in the ship with the hired servants, and went after him.

21—28. *The Cure of the Demoniac at Capernaum.*

And they went into Capernaum; and straightway on 21 the sabbath day he entered into the synagogue, and taught. And they were astonished at his doctrine: for he taught 22 them as one that had authority, and not as the scribes.

19. *James the son of Zebedee*] Two brothers had already been called and two more were now to join them.

20. *straightway*] Notice the frequency of this formula of transition. It has occurred just before, *v.* 18.

the hired servants] The mention of these, of the two vessels employed (Luke v. 7), and the subsequent allusion to St John's acquaintance with a person in so high a position as the high priest (John xviii. 15), seem to indicate that Zebedee, if not a wealthy man, was at any rate of some position at Capernaum.

went after him] For the miraculous draught of fishes which accompanied or followed this incident see Luke v. 2—11. Observe how *gradually* the Four had been called to their new work; (1) first they were disciples of the Baptist (John i. 35); (2) then they were directed by him to *the Lamb of God* (John i. 36); (3) afterwards they were invited by our Lord to see where He dwelt (John i. 39); (4) then they became witnesses of His first miracle (John ii. 2); (5) now after a further exhibition of His power over nature they are enrolled amongst His attached followers. The still more formal call was yet to come.

21—28. THE CURE OF THE DEMONIAC AT CAPERNAUM.

21. *Capernaum*] is not mentioned in the Old Testament or the Apocrypha. It was situated on the western shore of the Lake, in "the land of Gennesaret" (Matt. xiv. 34; John vi. 17, 24), and was of sufficient size to be always called "a city" (Matt. ix. 1). It was a customs station (Matt. ix. 9; Luke v. 27), and the quarters of a detachment of Roman soldiers (Matt. viii. 9; Luke vii. 8). It was the scene of many striking incidents in the Gospel History besides that here recorded. It was at Capernaum that the Lord healed Simon's wife's mother (Matt. viii. 14); wrought the miracle on the centurion's servant (Matt. viii. 5); cured the paralytic (Matt. ix. 1); called Levi from the toll-house (Matt. ix. 9); taught His Apostles the lesson of humility from the child set in their midst (Mark ix. 35—37), and delivered the wonderful discourse respecting the "Bread of Life" (John vi. 59).

the synagogue] built for the Jews by the good centurion (Luke vii. 5).

22. *not as the scribes*] The Scribes, *Sopherîm*, first came into prominence in the time of Ezra. Their duty was to copy, read, study, explain, and "fence round" the Law with "the tradition of the

23 And there was in their synagogue a man with an un-
24 clean spirit; and he cried out, saying, Let *us* alone; what
have we to do with thee, thou Jesus of Nazareth? art
thou come to destroy us? I know thee who thou art, the
25 Holy One of God. And Jesus rebuked him, saying, Hold
26 thy peace, and come out of him. And when the unclean
spirit had torn him, and cried with a loud voice, he came

Elders" (Matt. xv. 2). The Scribes proper only lasted till the death of Simon "the Just," B.C. 300. In the New Testament they are sometimes called "lawyers" (Matt. xxii. 35), or "Doctors of the Law" (Luke v. 17). Their teaching was preeminently second-hand. They simply repeated the decisions of previous Rabbis. But our Lord's teaching was absolute and independent. His formula was not "It hath been said," but "*I say unto you.*"

23. *with an unclean spirit*] lit. **in an unclean spirit**, i. e. in his power, under his influence. St Luke describes him as having a "spirit of an unclean demon" (Luke iv. 33). He seems to have entered unobserved amongst the throng, but could not resist the spell of that Pure Presence.

24. *Let us alone*] Many MSS. omit the Greek word thus translated. Even if genuine, it appears to be rather an exclamation of horror = the Latin *vah! heu!* It is not the man who cries out so much as the Evil Spirit which had usurped dominion over him.

Jesus of Nazareth] As the angels had in songs of rapture recognised their King (Luke ii. 13, 14), so the evil spirits instantly recognise Him, but with cries of despair. They evince no hope and no submission, only inveterate hostility. They *believe and tremble* (James ii. 19). Man alone recognises not the "King in His beauty" (Is. xxxiii. 17). "He was in the world and the world was made by Him," and yet "the world knew Him not" (John i. 10).

25. *rebuked him*] Though he had borne testimony to Christ, yet his testimony is not accepted, for it was probably intended only to do harm, "to anticipate and mar His great purpose and plan." Compare the conduct of St Paul in reference to the girl possessed with the spirit of Apollo (Acts xvi. 16—18).

Hold thy peace] lit. **Be muzzled.** The same word is used by our Lord in rebuking the storm on the Lake, "Peace, *be still*" (Mark iv. 39). Wyclif translates it "wexe doumbe." The word means (1) "*to close the mouth with a muzzle*, comp. 1 Cor. ix. 9, "Thou shalt not *muzzle the mouth* of the ox that treadeth out the corn," cited here and in 1 Tim. v. 18 from Deut. xxv. 4; (2) *to reduce to silence*, as in Matt. xxii. 34, "But when the Pharisees had heard that He *had put* the Sadducees *to silence*," and 1 Pet. ii. 15, "so is the will of God, that with well doing ye may *put to silence* the ignorance of foolish men." It is also used in reference to the man who had not on the wedding garment, "*he was speechless*" (Matt. xxii. 12).

26. *had torn him*] i.e. thrown him into strong convulsions, and according to St Luke's account, *into the midst* (Luke iv. 35), comp.

out of him. And they were all amazed, insomuch that they 27 questioned among themselves, saying, What thing is this? what new doctrine *is* this? for with authority commandeth he even the unclean spirits, and they do obey him. And 28 immediately his fame spread abroad throughout all the region round about Galilee.

29—34. *The Cure of Peter's Wife's Mother and Others.*

And forthwith, when they were come out of the syna- 29 gogue, they entered into the house of Simon and Andrew, with James and John. But Simon's wife's mother lay sick 30 of a fever, and anon they tell him of her. And he came 31 and took her by the hand, and lifted her up; and immediately the fever left her, and she ministered unto them. And at even, when the sun did set, they brought unto 32 him all that were diseased, and them that were possessed with devils. And all the city was gathered together at the 33 door. And he healed many that were sick of divers dis- 34

Mark ix. 26. The first miracle recorded by St Matt. is the healing of a leper by a touch (Matt. viii. 1—4); the first miracle which St John records is the changing water into wine (John ii. 1—11); the first miracle recorded by St Mark and St Luke (iv. 33—37) is this casting out of a demon in the synagogue of Capernaum.

29—34. THE CURE OF PETER'S WIFE'S MOTHER AND OTHERS.

29. *they*] i. e. the Lord and the four disciples, whom He had already called. It was a Sabbath day, and He probably went to the Apostle's house to eat bread. Comp. Luke xiv. 1.

30. *Simon's wife's mother*] For St Paul's allusion to him as a *married man* see 1 Cor. ix. 5.

sick of a fever] a "great" or "violent fever" according to the physician St Luke. Intermittent fever and dysentery, the latter often fatal, are ordinary Arabian diseases.

31. *he came*] Observe all the graphic touches in this verse; the Lord (i) *went to* the sufferer, (ii) *took her by the hand*, (iii) *lifted her up*, and (iv) *the fever*, *rebuked* by the Lord of life (Luke iv. 39), *left her*, and (v) she began to *minister unto them*.

32. *when the sun did set*] All three Evangelists carefully record, that it was not till the sun was setting or had actually set, that these sick were brought to Jesus. The reason of this probably was (1) either that they waited till the mid-day heat was past and the cool of the evening was come, or (2) the day being the Sabbath (Mark i. 29—32), they were unwilling to violate the sacred rest of the day, and so waited till it was ended.

33. *at the door*] i. e. the door of St Peter's house, "the door so well

3—2

eases, and cast out many devils; and suffered not the devils to speak, because they knew him.

35—39. *Solitary Prayer. Tour in Galilee.*

35 And in the morning, rising up a great while before day, he went out, and departed into a solitary place, and there 36 prayed. And Simon and they that were with him followed 37 after him. And when they had found him, they said unto 38 him, All *men* seek for thee. And he said unto them, Let us go into the next towns, that I may preach there also: 39 for therefore came I forth. And he preached in their synagogues throughout all Galilee, and cast out devils.

known to him who supplied St Mark with materials for his Gospel." St Matthew connects the cures now wrought with the prophecy of Isaiah liii. 4, *Himself took our infirmities and bare our sicknesses.*

35—39. SOLITARY PRAYER. TOUR IN GALILEE.

35. *in the morning,...a great while before day*] Another graphic touch of the Evangelist. He brings the scene before our eyes. The previous day had been a long day of conflict with and victory over the kingdom of sin and death. He now retires to refresh Himself in the heaven of prayer, in communion with His Father. He prepares Himself in the desert for a second great mission of Love, this time accompanied by His first four disciples.

a solitary place] "A remarkable feature of the Lake of Gennesaret was that it was closely surrounded with desert solitudes. These 'desert places' thus close at hand on the table-lands or in the ravines of the eastern and western ranges, gave opportunities of retirement for rest or prayer. 'Rising up early in the morning while it was yet dark' or 'passing over to the other side in a boat,' He sought these solitudes, sometimes alone, sometimes with His disciples. The Lake in this double aspect is thus a reflex of that union of energy and rest, of active labour and deep devotion, which is the essence of Christianity, as it was of the Life of Him, in whom that union was first taught and shewn." Stanley's *Sinai and Palestine*, pp. 378, 379.

36. *Simon*] already with his earnest impulsiveness beginning to take the lead. Comp. Luke viii. 45, ix. 32.

followed after Him] The word in the original is very expressive and only occurs here. It denotes (i) *to follow hard upon*, (ii) *to pursue closely, to track out.* "Simon and his friends almost hunted for Him." It generally implies a hostile intent. It occurs in a good sense in the LXX. rendering of Ps. xxiii. 6, "Thy mercy shall *follow* me."

38. *towns*] rather **village-towns** or **country-towns**. The word only occurs here. His gracious Presence was not to be confined to Capernaum. Dalmanutha, Magdala, Bethsaida, Chorazin were all near at hand. For the crowded population of Galilee, see Josephus *B. J.* III. 3, 2.

40—45. *Cleansing of a Leper.*

And there came a leper to him, beseeching him, and kneeling down to him, and saying unto him, If thou wilt, thou canst make me clean. And Jesus, moved with compassion, put forth *his* hand, and touched him, and saith unto him, I will; be thou clean. And as soon as he had spoken, immediately the leprosy departed from him, and he was cleansed. And he straitly charged him, and forthwith sent him away; and saith unto him, See thou say nothing to any 40 41 42 43 44

40—45. CLEANSING OF A LEPER.

40. *there came*] Better, **there cometh**, in the present tense. See Introduction, p. 19.

a leper] One afflicted with the most terrible of all maladies, "a living death, a poisoning of the springs, a corrupting of all the humours, of life; a dissolution little by little of the whole body, so that one limb after another actually decayed and fell away." The Jews called it "the Finger of God," and emphatically "the Stroke;" they never expected to cure it (see 2 Kings v. 7). With lip covered (Ezek. xxiv. 17), and bare head (Lev. xiv. 8, 9), and rent garments, the leper bore about with him the emblems of mortality, "himself a dreadful parable of death." Compare the cases of Moses (Ex. iv. 6), Miriam (Num. xii. 10), Naaman (2 Kings v. 1), Gehazi (2 Kings v. 27).

kneeling down to him] St Mark alone describes this attitude of the leper, as also the look of compassion which beamed forth from the face of the Lord, spoken of in the next verse.

41. *and touched him*] though this act was strictly forbidden by the Mosaic Law as causing ceremonial defilement. But "HE, Himself remaining undefiled, cleansed him whom He touched; for in Him life overcame death, and health sickness, and purity defilement."

43. *And he straitly charged him*] The word thus rendered occurs in four other places; (1) Matt. ix. 30, "Jesus *straitly charged* them, saying, See that no man know it;" (2) Mark xiv. 5, "And they *murmured against* her," said of the Apostles in their indignation against Mary; (3) John xi. 33, 38, "And He *groaned* in spirit," said of our Lord at the grave of Lazarus. It denotes (1) *to be very angry* or *indignant*, (2) to *charge* or *command with sternness.*

straitly = **strictly.** Comp. Gen. xliii. 7, "The man asked us *straitly* of our state;" Josh. vi. 1, "Now Jericho was *straitly* shut up." Comp. also Shakespeare, *Richard III.* I. 1. 85, 86,

"His majesty hath *straitly* given in charge
That no man shall have private conference."

sent him away] or **put him forth.** "He would allow no lingering, but required him to hasten on his errand, lest the report of what had been done should outrun him." It is the same word in the original as in Mark i. 12.

man: but go thy way, shew thyself to the priest, and offer for thy cleansing those things which Moses commanded, for a 15 testimony unto them. But he went out, and began to publish *it* much, and to blaze abroad the matter, insomuch that Jesus could no more openly enter into the city, but was without in desert places: and they came to him from every quarter.

1—12. *The Paralytic and the Power to forgive Sins.*

2 And again he entered into Capernaum, after *some* days; 2 and it was noised that he was in the house. And straightway many were gathered together, insomuch that there was no room to receive *them*, no, not so much as about the 3 door: and he preached the word unto them. And they come unto him, bringing one sick of the palsy, which was 4 borne of four. And when they could not come nigh unto him for the press, they uncovered the roof where he was:

44. *shew thyself to the priest*] that he may attest the reality of thy cure (Lev. xiv. 3).

those things which Moses commanded] viz. (1) two birds, "alive and clean," Lev. xiv. 4, (2) cedar wood, (3) scarlet, and (4) hyssop; this was for the preliminary ceremony (Lev. xiv. 4—7). On the eighth day further offerings were to be made, (1) two he lambs without blemish, (2) one ewe lamb, (3) three tenth deals of fine flour, (4) one log of oil. If the leper was poor, he was permitted to offer one lamb and two turtledoves or two young pigeons, with one tenth deal of fine flour.

for a testimony unto them] Rather, **for a testimony against them**, i.e. against their unbelief in refusing to acknowledge our Lord to be all He claimed to be in spite of His mighty works. Comp. Mark vi. 11 with Luke ix. 5.

45. *began to publish it much*] even as others in similar circumstances found it impossible to keep silence ; comp. (1) the blind man, Matt. ix. 30, 31 ; (2) the man with an impediment of speech, Mark vii. 36.

could no more openly enter into the city] In these words we have perhaps one of the reasons why the Lord enjoined silence on the leper. A certain degree of secrecy and reserve was plainly necessary in respect to the Lord's miracles, or it would have been impossible for Him to have moved from place to place.

CH. II. 1—12. THE PARALYTIC AND THE POWER TO FORGIVE SINS.

1. *he entered*] after the subsidence of the late excitement.

the house] Either His own house, which He occupied with His mother and His brethren (Mark iii. 21), or possibly that of St Peter.

2. *about the door*] All the avenues of approach to the house were blocked up, and the courtyard or vestibule was filled.

3. *borne of four*] Notice the pictorial definiteness of the Evangelist.

4. *they uncovered the roof*] They appear (1) to have ascended to the flat roof probably by a flight of steps outside (Luke v. 19); (2) to have

and when they had broken *it* up, they let down the bed wherein the sick of the palsy lay. When Jesus saw their faith, he said unto the sick of the palsy, Son, thy sins be forgiven thee. But there were certain of the scribes sitting there, and reasoning in their hearts, Why doth this *man* thus speak blasphemies? who can forgive sins but God only? And immediately when Jesus perceived in his spirit that they so reasoned within themselves, he said unto them, Why reason ye these things in your hearts? Whether is it easier to say to the sick of the palsy, *Thy* sins be forgiven thee; or to

broken up the tiling or thin stone slabs, sometimes used at this day; (3) to have lowered the paralytic upon his bed through the opening into the presence of the Great Healer. The room was probably an upper-chamber, which often extended over the whole area of the house. For other notices of such upper-rooms compare Acts i. 13, ix. 37, xx. 8.

5. *their faith*] The faith of all, of the paralytic himself and those that bore him. The Holy One did not reject this "charitable work" of theirs in bringing him before Him, any more than He does that of those who bring infants to Him in Holy Baptism.

Son] St Luke, v. 20, gives the words thus, "*Man*, thy sins are forgiven thee." St Mark has preserved to us the tenderer word, even as St Matthew has done in his account (Matt. ix. 22).

thy sins] His sufferings may have been due to sinful excesses. Comp. the words of the Saviour to the man, who had an infirmity thirty and eight years, "Behold thou art made whole; *sin no more*, lest a worse thing come unto thee," John v. 14. At any rate his consciousness of sin was such that it was necessary to speak to his soul before healing was extended to his body. See Luke vii. 48.

be forgiven] The mood here is not optative but indicative. **Thy sins are**, or rather, **have been forgiven thee.**

6. *certain of the scribes*] During our Lord's absence from Capernaum it would seem there had arrived not only from Galilee, but even from Judæa and Jerusalem (Luke v. 17), Pharisees and lawyers, who were insidiously watching all that He did. Emissaries from the hostile party at Jerusalem, where the Lord's death had already been decreed (John v. 18), they proceeded to carry out a settled plan of collecting charges against Him and thwarting His work of mercy.

7. *blasphemies*] for the claim to forgive sins implied a distinct equality with God in respect to one of His most incommunicable attributes.

8. *in his spirit*] His soul was human, but His "Spirit" was divine, and by this divine faculty He penetrated and then revealed to them the "thoughts and counsels of their hearts," comp. Heb. iv. 12. On this peculiarly Divine faculty see 1 Sam. xvi. 7; 1 Chron. xxviii. 9; 2 Chron. vi. 30.

9. *Whether is it easier*] Observe what is here contrasted. Not, "Which is easier, to forgive sin or to raise a paralytic?" but "Which is

10 say, Arise, and take up thy bed, and walk? But that ye may know that the Son of man hath power on earth to for-
11 give sins, (he saith to the sick of the palsy,) I say unto thee, Arise, and take up thy bed, and go thy way into thine house.
12 And immediately he arose, took up the bed, and went forth before them all; insomuch that they were all amazed, and glorified God, saying, We never saw it on this fashion.

13—22. *The Call of St Matthew; the Discourse at his House.*

13 And he went forth again by the sea side; and all the mul-
14 titude resorted unto him, and he taught them. And as he passed by, he saw Levi the *son* of Alphæus sitting at the

easier, to *claim* this power or *claim* that ; *to say*, Thy sins be forgiven thee, or *to say*, Arise and walk"? as He had already said to the impotent man at the pool of Bethesda (John v. 8).

10. *that ye may know*] "By doing that which is capable of being put to the proof, I will vindicate My right and power to do that which, in its very nature, is incapable of being proved."

the Son of man] This is the first time this title occurs in St Mark, where we find it 14 times. This title is never applied by the writers of the Gospels themselves to the Eternal Son of God. Whenever it occurs, it is so applied by our Lord, and no other. There are only three exceptions to this rule, (1) where the title is used by Stephen (Acts vii. 56), and (2) by St John (Rev. i. 13, xiv. 14). During, however, the period of His sojourn here on earth, there was no title our Lord was pleased so often and so constantly to apply to Himself. Son of *a* man He was not. Son of *Man* he was. The word used in the original for "man" implies *human being*, and the expression denotes that He who was the Son of God from all Eternity became the "Son of Man" in time, the second Adam, the second Head of our race, the crown of our humanity. For the expression in the O.T. see Dan. vii. 13.

on earth] This power is not exercised, as ye think, only in heaven by God, but also by the Son of Man on earth.

11. *thy bed*] The original word thus rendered means a portable pallet, little more than a mat, used for mid-day sleep, and the service of the sick. It was of the commonest description and used by the poorest.

12. *immediately*] Observe the suddenness and completeness of the cure, and contrast it with the miracles of an Elijah (1 Kings xvii. 17—24), or an Elisha (2 Kings iv. 32—36).

before them all] Now yielding before him and no longer blocking up his path.

13—22. CALL OF ST MATTHEW; THE DISCOURSE AT HIS HOUSE.

13. *he went forth*] i.e. from the town of Capernaum to the shore of the Lake, probably through a suburb of fishers' huts and custom-houses.

vv. 15, 16.] ST MARK, II. 41

receipt of custom, and said unto him, Follow me. And he
arose and followed him. And it came to pass, that, as Jesus 15
sat at meat in his house, many publicans and sinners sat also
together with Jesus and his disciples: for there were many,
and they followed him. And when the scribes and Phari- 16
sees saw him eat with publicans and sinners, they said unto

14. *Levi*] This was probably the name by which he was known to his Jewish brethren. He may have changed his name after and in memory of his call, so that he who had before been known by the name of Levi, was now known as Matthew, or Mattathias, a favourite name amongst the Jews after the Captivity, and = *Theodore*, the "Gift of God."

son of Alphæus] Some have identified this Alphæus with Alphæus the father of St James the Less. But in the lists of the Apostles the two are never named together, like other pairs of brothers in the Apostolic body.

receipt of custom] Situated as Capernaum was at the nucleus of roads which diverged to Tyre, Damascus, Jerusalem, and Sepphoris, it was a busy centre of merchandise, and a natural place for the collection of tribute and taxes.

Follow me] Though he belonged to a class above all others hated and despised by the Jews, trebly hated where, as in the present instance, the tax-gatherer was himself a Jew, yet the Lord did not hesitate to invite him to become one of the Twelve.

and followed him] We cannot doubt that the new disciple had already listened to some of the discourses and beheld some of the wondrous miracles of Christ, so that he was now in the eyes of Him, Who read the heart, prepared for his call.

15. *sat at meat*] It is St Luke who tells us that St Matthew made "a great feast" in honour of his new Master (Luke v. 29), and to it, perhaps by way of farewell, he invited many of his old associates. This shews that he had made large sacrifices in order to follow Christ; see Neander's *Life of Christ*, p. 230.

publicans and sinners] The "publicans" properly so called were persons who farmed the Roman taxes and in later times were usually Roman knights and men of wealth and position. Those here alluded to were the inferior officers, natives of the province where the taxes were collected, called properly *portitores*. So notorious were they for rapacity and dishonesty that Suetonius (*Vit. Vesp.* 1.) tells us how several cities erected statues to Sabinus, "the honest publican;" and Theocritus in answer to the question, which were the worst kind of wild beasts, said, "On the mountains bears and lions; in cities, publicans and pettifoggers." The Jews included them in the same category with harlots and sinners; see Matt. xxi. 31, 32, xviii. 17. Observe that in his Gospel St Matthew alone styles *himself* in the list of the Apostles "the publican."

16. *they said unto his disciples*] Overawed by the miracles He had wrought and the overthrow they had lately experienced at the healing of

his disciples, How is it that he eateth and drinketh with
17 publicans and sinners? When Jesus heard it, he saith unto
them, They that are whole have no need of the physician,
but they that are sick: I came not to call the righteous, but
18 sinners to repentance. And the disciples of John and of the
Pharisees used to fast: and they come and say unto him,
Why do the disciples of John and of the Pharisees fast, but
19 thy disciples fast not? And Jesus said unto them, Can the
children of the bridechamber fast, while the bridegroom is
with them? as long as they have the bridegroom with them,
20 they cannot fast. But the days will come, when the bridegroom shall be taken away from them, and then shall they
21 fast in those days. No man also seweth a piece of new

the paralytic, and not as yet venturing on any open rupture with Him,
they vent their displeasure on His disciples. It is not likely that the
Pharisees were present at the feast, or they would have involved
themselves in the same blame. Probably they looked in while it
was in progress, and afterwards came forward to the disciples coming
out.

18. *the disciples of John*] The contrast between their Master in
prison and Jesus at the feast could not fail to be felt. Perhaps the
Pharisees had solicited them to make common cause with themselves
in this matter. Their rigorous asceticism offered various points of contact between them and the disciples of the Baptist.

used to fast] The Jews were wont to fast on Thursday because on that
day Moses was said to have re-ascended Mount Sinai; on Monday
because on that day he returned. Comp. the words of the Pharisee,
Luke xviii. 12, "I *fast twice* in the week." Perhaps this feast took
place on one of their weekly fasts.

19. *the children of the bridechamber*] i.e. the friends and companions
of the bridegroom, who accompanied him to the house of the bride for
the marriage. Comp. Judges xiv. 11.

the bridegroom] He reminds the disciples of John of the image
under which their own great Master had spoken of Him as the Bridegroom (John iii. 29), at the sound of Whose voice he rejoiced.

20. *the days will come*] The thought of death accompanies our
Lord even to the social meal, and in the now undisguised hatred of His
opponents He sees a token of what must hereafter come to pass. A dim
hint of the same kind He had already given in His saying to the Jewish
rulers, "Destroy this Temple and in three days I will raise it up" (John
ii. 19), and in His conversation with Nicodemus (John iii. 14).

taken away] The same word is used by each of the Synoptists, and
implies a violent termination of His life. The words occur nowhere
else in the New Testament. This is the first open allusion recorded by
St Mark, though probably little understood at the time, to the death,
which was so soon to separate Him from His disciples.

cloth on an old garment: else the new piece that filled it up taketh away from the old, and the rent is made worse. And no man putteth new wine into old bottles: else the new wine doth burst the bottles, and the wine is spilled, and the bottles will be marred: but new wine must be put into new bottles.

23—28. *The Disciples pluck the Ears of Corn.*

And it came to pass, that he went through the corn fields on the sabbath day; and his disciples began, as they went, to pluck the ears of corn. And the Pharisees said unto him, Behold, why do they on the sabbath day that which is not lawful? And he said unto them, Have ye

21. *new cloth*] Literally **uncarded** or **unteazled** cloth.
else] i.e. **if he do**, the new piece taketh from the old garment, and makes worse its original rents.
22. *new*] Men do not pour new, or unfermented, wine into old and worn wine-skins. "My disciples," our Lord seems to say, "are not yet strong. They have not yet been baptized into the Spirit. They need tenderness and consideration. They could no more endure severe new doctrine than an old robe could the insertion of a piece of new cloth which had never passed through the hands of the fuller." In training His disciples our Lord never took the old wine from them till they were capable of relishing the new. In Rom. xiv. we have the best practical commentary on His words.

23—28. THE DISCIPLES PLUCK THE EARS OF CORN.

23. *on the sabbath day*] St Luke tells us that this was a *"second first Sabbath"* i.e. either (1) the first Sabbath after the second day of unleavened bread ; or (2) the first Sabbath in the second year of a Sabbatical cycle ; or (3) the first Sabbath of the second month (Luke vi. 1). See Wieseler's *Chronol. Synop.* p. 353 sq.

to pluck the ears of corn] From St Matthew we learn that they were *an hungred* (Matt. xii. 1). The act described marks the season of the year. The wheat was ripe, for they would not have rubbed barley in their hands (Luke vi. 1). We may conclude therefore, the time was a week or two after the Passover, when the first ripe sheaf was offered as the firstfruits of the harvest. For the exact date of this Sabbath see Wieseler's *Chronol. Synop.* p. 225 sq.

24. *that which is not lawful*] They did not accuse them of theft, for the Law allowed what they were doing (Deut. xxiii. 25). They accused them of profaning the Sabbath. The Law of course forbade reaping and threshing on that day, but the Rabbis had decided that even to pluck corn was to be construed as reaping, and to rub it as threshing. They even forbad walking on grass as a species of threshing, and would not allow so much as a fruit to be plucked from a tree on that day. See Lightfoot, *Hor. Heb.* in Matt. xii. 2.

never read what David did, when he had need, and was an
26 hungred, he, and they that were with him? how he went
into the house of God in the days of Abiathar the high
priest, and did eat the shewbread, which is not lawful to eat
but for the priests, and gave also to them which were with
27 him? And he said unto them, The sabbath was made for
28 man, and not man for the sabbath: therefore the Son of man
is Lord also of the sabbath.

1—6. *The Man with the Withered Hand.*

3 And he entered again into the synagogue; and there
2 was a man there which had a withered hand. And they
watched him, whether he would heal him on the sabbath

25. *Have ye never read*] Rather, **Did ye never read?** With a gentle irony He adopts one of the favourite formulas of their own Rabbis, and inquires if they had never read what David their favourite hero had done when flying from Saul. He came to the high priest at Nob, and entered the Tabernacle, and ate of the hallowed bread (1 Sam. xxi. 1—9), of the "twelve cakes of fine flour" which no stranger might eat (Ex. xxix. 33).

26. *Abiathar*] In 2 Sam. viii. 17, and the parallel passage 1 Chron. xviii. 16, we find *Ahimelech* substituted for Abiathar; while in 2 Sam. xx. 25, and every other passage of the O. T., we are told it was Abiathar who was priest with Zadok in David's reign, and that he was the son of Ahimelech. Some therefore suppose that there is a clerical error here in the MSS. Others think that the loaves of shewbread belonged to Abiathar, at this time a priest (Lev. xxiv. 9), that he persuaded his father to let David have them, and gave them to him with his own hand.

CH. III. 1—6. THE MAN WITH THE WITHERED HAND.

1. *And he entered*] The narrative of St Mark here is peculiarly vivid and pictorial. He places the scene actually before us and relates it very much in the present tense. The incident occurred at Capernaum, and probably on the next Sabbath. See Luke vi. 6.

a withered hand] It is characteristic of the physician St Luke that he tells us it was his "*right* hand." It was probably not merely paralysed in the sinews, but dried up and withered, the result of a partial atrophy. Comp. 1 Kings xiii. 4, for the parallel case of Jeroboam. Such a malady, when once established, is incurable by any human art.

2. *they watched him*] The same company of Scribes and Pharisees had gathered together from Judæa, Jerusalem, and Galilee itself (Luke v. 17), to find matter of accusation against Him. They watched Him with no friendly purpose. The word itself signifies stratagem and hostility: comp. Luke xx. 20, "And they *watched* Him and sent forth spies:" Acts ix. 24, "And they *watched* the gates day and night to kill him."

day; that they might accuse him. And he saith unto the 3
man which had the withered hand, Stand forth. And he 4
saith unto them, Is it lawful to do good on the sabbath
days, or to do evil? to save life, or to kill? But they held
their peace. And when he had looked round about on them 5
with anger, being grieved for the hardness of their hearts,
he saith unto the man, Stretch forth thine hand. And he
stretched *it* out: and his hand was restored whole as the
other. And the Pharisees went forth, and straightway took 6

3. *he saith*] It would seem that the Pharisees first asked Him, "*Is it lawful to heal on the Sabbath day?*" (Matt. xii. 10). This question He answered, as was His wont (Matt. xxi. 24), by a counter-question, "*I will ask you one thing. Is it lawful on the Sabbath days to do good or to do evil? to save life or to destroy it?*"

4. *But they held their peace*] St Mark alone mentions this striking circumstance, as also what we read in the next verse, that "*He looked round about on them with anger.*"

5. *with anger*] Not merely did He look upon them, He "*looked round*" upon them, surveyed each face with "an all-embracing gaze of grief and anger." Feelings of "grief" and "anger" are here ascribed to Him, who was "very God and very Man," just as in another place we read that "He wept" before the raising of Lazarus (John xi. 35), and "slept" before He stilled the storm (Mark iv. 38), and was an hungred (Matt. iv. 2), and was "exceeding sorrowful even unto death" (Matt. xxvi. 38).

being grieved] The word here used occurs nowhere else in the New Testament, and implies "a feeling of compassion for," even in the midst of anger at, their conduct.

hardness] The word thus rendered denotes literally (1) *the process by which the extremities of fractured bones are re-united by a callus;* then (2) *callousness, hardness.* St Paul uses the word in Rom. xi. 25, saying, "I would not have you ignorant, brethren, ... *that hardness* (see margin) in part is happened to Israel;" and again in Eph. iv. 18, "Having the understanding darkened ... because of *the hardness* of their heart" (see margin again). The verb, which = "to petrify," "to harden into stone," occurs in Mark vi. 52, viii. 17; John xii. 40; 2 Cor. iii. 14.

whole as the other] This is one of the instances where our Lord may be said to have wrought a miracle *without a word*, or *the employment of any external means*. It also forms one of seven miracles wrought on the Sabbath-day. The other six were, (1) The demoniac at Capernaum (Mark i. 21); (2) Simon's wife's mother (Mark i. 29); (3) the impotent man at the pool of Bethesda (John v. 9); (4) the woman with a spirit of infirmity (Luke xiii. 14); (5) the man who had the dropsy (Luke xiv. 1); (6) the man born blind (John ix. 14).

6. *And the Pharisees went forth*] The effect of this miracle was very great. The Scribes and Pharisees were "*filled with madness.*"

counsel with the Herodians against him, how they might destroy him.

7—12. *Withdrawal of Jesus to the Lake of Gennesaret.*

7 But Jesus withdrew himself with his disciples to the sea: and a great multitude from Galilee followed him, 8 and from Judæa, and from Jerusalem, and from Idumæa, and *from* beyond Jordan, and they about Tyre and Sidon, a great multitude, when they had heard what great things he 9 did, came unto him. And he spake to his disciples, that a small ship should wait on him because of the multitude, lest

the Saviour had not merely broken their traditions, but He had put them to silence before all the people. In their blind hate they did not shrink even from joining the Herodians, the court party, and their political opponents, and taking counsel with them how they might put Him to death. As before at Jerusalem so now in Galilee this design is deliberately formed.

the Herodians] This is the first occasion on which the Herodians are mentioned. We shall meet with them again in Mark xii. 13, on the "Day of Questions" in Holy Week. Just as the partisans of Marius were called "Mariani," of Pompeius "Pompeiani," of Otho "Othoniani," so the partisans of Herod the Great and his successors were called "Herodians." The sect was rather a political than a religious body. Adopting Sadducean opinions, they held that the hopes of the Jewish nation rested on the Herods as a bulwark against Roman ambition, and almost looked to them for a fulfilment of the prophecies respecting the advent of the Messiah. They favoured the compromise between the ancient faith and later civilisation, which Herod inaugurated, and his successors endeavoured to realise. On one occasion our Lord warns his disciples against "the leaven of Herod" in close connection with "the leaven of the Pharisees" (Mark viii. 15; Luke xii. 1). Galilee being the chief centre of Christ's activity, the Pharisees from Judæa were glad on the present occasion to avail themselves of any aid from the tetrarch of this part of Palestine and his followers.

7—12. WITHDRAWAL OF JESUS TO THE LAKE OF GENNESARET.

7. *a great multitude*] Observe the wide area from which the multitude were now gathered together; the region (1) of Tyre and Sidon and Galilee in the North of Palestine; (2) of Judæa and Jerusalem in the centre, (3) of Peræa "beyond the Jordan" on the East, (4) of Idumæa in the extreme South. This is the only place where Idumæa, the country occupied by the descendants of Esau, is mentioned in the N. T. In the O. T. the name is found in Isai. xxxiv. 5, 6; Ezek. xxxv. 15, xxxvi. 5.

9. *a small ship*] The life on the sea, in the ship which was now His chief place of instruction in opposition to the synagogue, henceforth had its commencement.

they should throng him. For he had healed many; inso- much that they pressed upon him for to touch him, as many as had plagues. And unclean spirits, when they saw him, fell down before him, and cried, saying, Thou art the Son of God. And he straitly charged them that they should not make him known.

13—19. *The Calling of the Twelve Apostles.*

And he goeth up into a mountain, and calleth *unto him* whom he would: and they came unto him. And he ordained twelve, that they should be with him, and that

10. *plagues*] The word thus rendered denotes (1) *a whip* or *scourge*, and is used in this sense in Acts xxii. 24; Heb. xi. 36; (2) a *plague* or *disease of the body*. Comp. Mark v. 29, 34; Luke vii. 21.

11. *Thou art the Son of God*] In the Synagogue of Capernaum they had called Him the "Holy One of God" (Mark i. 24), they now acknowledge Him as the "Son of God" (comp. Luke iv. 41). The force of the imperfect tense in the original here is very striking, "**whenever the demons saw Him, they kept falling down before Him and saying**"......and as often as they did so, "He *straitly charged* them that they should not make Him known," i. e. as the Messiah "the Son of God."

13—19. THE CALLING OF THE TWELVE APOSTLES.

13. *And he goeth*] We have now reached an important turning-point in the Gospel History. (i) The fame of the Saviour had spread abroad in every direction throughout the land, and the current of popular feeling had set strongly in His favour. But (ii) the animosity of the ruling powers had deepened in intensity alike in Judæa and Galilee, and an active correspondence was going on between the Scribes and Pharisees in both districts respecting Him. Meanwhile (iii) He Himself had seemed to stand almost alone. A few indeed had gathered round Him as His disciples, but as yet they did not present the appearance of a regular and organized body, nor had they received a distinct commission to disseminate His doctrines. Such a body was now to be formed. Such a commission was now to be given. Accordingly He retired to the mountain-range west of the Lake, and spent the whole night in prayer to God (Luke vi. 12). The scene of His retirement and lonely vigil was in all probability the singular elevation now known as the Karûn Hattîn, or "Horns of Hattîn," the only conspicuous hill on the western side of the Lake, and "singularly adapted by its conformation both to form a place for short retirement, and a rendezvous for gathering multitudes." Then at dawn of the following day (Luke vi. 13), He *calleth unto him whom he would*] of the disciples, who had gradually gathered around Him, and when they had come to Him He selected for Himself (Luke vi. 13), and

14. *ordained twelve*] Hitherto they had been His friends and disciples in a wider sense, now He formally called them, and joined

15 he might send them forth to preach, and to have power
16 to heal sicknesses, and to cast out devils: and Simon he sur-
17 named Peter; and James the *son* of Zebedee, and John the

them in a united band, that (i) they "might be with Him" (comp. Acts i. 21), (ii) that He might "send them forth" as heralds to preach, and (iii) that they "might have power to cast out demons," for the words "*to heal sicknesses*" are omitted in some of the best MSS.

(i) *The number of the Apostles.* The number selected, answering to the twelve sons of Jacob, was small indeed as compared with the hundreds who enrolled themselves as disciples of a Hillel or a Gamaliel, and their position in life was humble and obscure, but "*the weak things of the world were to confound the things which are mighty*" (1 Cor. i. 27), and these Twelve were to be the Twelve Pillars of the Church.

(ii) *Their calling and training.* Observe that the calling and training of the Twelve was a most important part of our Lord's ministerial work. (*a*) Immediately after His Baptism and Temptation He began to prepare some of them for their future vocation (John i. 35—51); (*b*) to their training He devoted the greater part of His time and strength; (*c*) after His resurrection He continued for forty days His personal efforts for their improvement, and (*d*) at last He bestowed upon them His promised gift of the Holy Ghost.

(iii) *Their title.* The name also which He gave to them deserves attention. He named them *Apostles* (Luke vi. 13). The word thus rendered means (i) as an adjective, *despatched* or *sent forth*, (ii) as a substantive, the *actual delegate* of the person who sends him.

(*a*) In Classical Greek the word was almost entirely restricted to the meaning of a "naval expedition," a "fleet despatched on foreign service," and this meaning entirely superseded any other.

(*b*) In the Septuagint the word occurs only once, namely, in 1 Kings xiv. 6, in the sense of "a messenger," "one who has a commission from God," where Abijah says to the wife of Jeroboam, "I am a *messenger* unto thee of heavy tidings."

(*c*) With the later Jews the word was in common use, and was the title of those, who were sent from the mother city on any foreign mission, especially the collection of the tribute for the Temple service.

(*d*) Thus when He employed it to designate His immediate and most favoured disciples, "our Lord was not introducing a new term, but adopting one which from its current usage would suggest to His hearers the idea of a highly responsible mission." In Heb. iii. 1 He Himself is styled "The *Apostle* and high priest of our profession," with which compare John xvii. 18. Canon Lightfoot on the *Epistle to the Galatians*, p. 94.

16. *and Simon*] We have in the New Testament *four* lists of the Apostles: (*a*) Matt. x. 2; (*b*) Mark iii. 16; (*c*) Luke vi. 14; (*d*) Acts i. 13. The position of some of the names varies in the lists, but in all four the leaders of *the three groups* are the same, Peter, Philip, and James, the son of Alphæus, while in all four Judas Iscariot is placed last. According to St Mark's catalogue they may be arranged in three groups:

brother of James; and he surnamed them Boanerges, which
is, The sons of thunder: and Andrew, and Philip, and Bar- 18

(i) 1 Peter.   (ii) 5 Philip.   (iii) 9 James the Less.
     2 James.   6 Bartholomew—   10 Thaddæus.
     3 John.   7 Matthew.   11 Simon the Cananite.
     4 Andrew.   8 Thomas.   12 Judas Iscariot.

(*a*) *Group* i.

i. *Simon.* The name of Simeon (Acts xv. 14) or Simon, a
"hearer," the son of Jonas (John i. 42, xxi. 16), whom our Lord surnamed Peter or Cephas, *the Rock-man*, stands first in all the four lists.
He was brought up in his father's occupation, as a fisherman on the
Galilean lake, and lived originally at Bethsaida, and afterwards in
a house at Capernaum (Mark i. 21, 29). His earliest call came to him
through his brother Andrew, who told him the Messias, the "Anointed
One," had been found in the Person of the Lord (John i. 43). His second
call took place on the lake near Capernaum, where he and the other three
in this group were fishing. He is specially prominent on various occasions before the rest of the Apostles. Sometimes he *speaks in their
name* (Matt. xix. 27; Luke xii. 41); sometimes *answers when all are
addressed* (Matt. xvi. 16; Mark viii. 29); sometimes he is addressed as
principal, even among the favoured Three by our Lord Himself (Matt.
xxvi. 40; Luke xxii. 31); sometimes he is appealed to by others as *representing the rest* (Matt. xvii. 24; Acts ii. 37). After the Ascension he
assumes a position of special prominence (Acts i. 15, ii. 14, iv. 8, v. 29).

17. ii. *James the son of Zebedee* and Salome (Matt. xxvii. 56; Mark
xv. 40), a native of Bethsaida, commonly known as James "the Great,"
the first of the Apostolic body to suffer martyrdom, and the only one of
the Twelve whose death is actually recorded in the New Testament.

iii. *John*] the brother of James, who never in his Gospel calls himself by this name, but sometimes "*the disciple whom Jesus loved*" (John
xiii. 23, xix. 26), sometimes "*the other disciple*" (John xviii. 15, xx.
2, 3). To him our Lord committed the care of His earthly mother.
These brothers were surnamed by our Lord, according to St Mark,
Boanerges, i.e. "*sons of thunder*," in allusion we may believe to the
fiery intrepid zeal which marked their character. Of this feature we
have traces in Luke ix. 54; Mark ix. 38, x. 37.

18. iv. *Andrew*] a brother of St Peter (Matt. iv. 18), and like him
a native of Bethsaida, and a former disciple of the Baptist (John i. 40).
By his means his brother Simon was brought to Jesus (John i. 41). In
the lists of the Apostles given by St Matthew and St Luke he appears
second; but in St Mark and Acts i. 13, fourth. We have three notices
of him in the Gospels. (i) On the occasion of the feeding of the Five
Thousand it is he who points out the little lad with the five barley loaves
and the two fishes; (ii) when certain Greeks desired to see Jesus, it was
he in conjunction with Philip who introduced them to the Lord (John
xii. 22); (iii) together with Peter, James, and John he inquired privately
of our Lord respecting His future coming (Mark xiii. 3).

tholomew, and Matthew, and Thomas, and James the *son* of
19 Alphæus, and Thaddæus, and Simon the Canaanite, and

(*b*) *Group* ii.

v. *Philip*] He also was a native of Bethsaida and one of the earliest disciples (John i. 43). To him first of the whole circle of the Apostles were spoken the solemn words "Follow Me." It was to him the question was put "to prove him," "*Whence shall we buy bread, that these may eat?*" (John vi. 5—9); together with his friend and fellow townsman, St Andrew, he brought the inquiring Greeks to the Saviour (John xii. 20—22); it was he who asked "*Lord, shew us the Father, and it sufficeth us*" (John xiv. 8).

vi. *Bartholomew*] i. e. Bar-Tolmai, the "*Son of Tolmai*," and probably identical with Nathanael = "*gift of God.*" For (i) St John twice mentions Nathanael, never Bartholomew (John i. 45, xxi. 2); (ii) the other Evangelists all speak of Bartholomew, never of Nathanael; (iii) Philip first brought Nathanael to Jesus, and Bartholomew is mentioned by each of the Synoptic Evangelists immediately after Philip; (iv) St John couples Philip with Nathanael precisely in the same way that Simon is coupled with his brother Andrew. Respecting him, at least under the name Nathanael, we learn from the Gospels little more than (*a*) his birth-place, Cana of Galilee (John xxi. 2); (*b*) his simple, guileless character (John i. 47); and (*c*) that he was one of the seven, to whom our Lord shewed Himself by the lake of Gennesaret after His resurrection (John xxi. 2).

vii. *Matthew*] or *Levi*, whose call has just been described. See above, on ii. 14.

viii. *Thomas*] or Didymus = *a twin* (John xi. 16, xxi. 2), whose character was marked by a deep attachment to his Master and a readiness even to die with Him (John xi. 16), but at the same time by a tendency to misgiving and despondency, which made him ever ready to take the darker view of things, and to distrust other evidence than that of sight (John xiv. 5, xx. 25).

(*c*) *Group* iii.

ix. *James*] or "James the Less" (see note below, xv. 40), the son of Alphæus, so called to distinguish him from James, the son of Zebedee, mentioned above. He is probably a distinct person from James the Lord's brother (Gal. i. 19), and author of the Epistle, which bears his name.

x. *Thaddæus*] i. e. *Judas*, a brother, or possibly a son of James, bishop of Jerusalem (Acts i. 13). He was surnamed *Thaddæus* and *Lebbæus* (Matt. x. 3), which some interpret as = "*cordatus* or *animosus*" = "a man of energy and courage." He is the author of the Epistle which bears his name. Once only in the Gospels do we find any act or saying of his recorded, viz., in John xiv. 22, "*Lord, how is it that thou wilt manifest thyself unto us, and not unto the world?*"

xi. *Simon*] *the Cananite*, or *Cananæan* (Matt. x. 4), in Greek *Zelotes* (Luke vi. 15; Acts i. 13). The spelling of the English Version here is misleading. The word does not signify a native of Canaan, or

Judas Iscariot, which also betrayed him: and they went into an house.

20—30. *How can Satan cast out Satan?*

And the multitude cometh together again, so that they 20 could not so much as eat bread. And when his friends 21 heard *of it*, they went out to lay hold on him: for they said, He is beside himself. And the scribes which came 22 down from Jerusalem said, He hath Beelzebub, and by the prince of the devils casteth he out devils. And he 23

of Cana, but comes from a Chaldee or Syriac word *Kanean* or *Kaneniah*, by which the Jewish sect or faction of "the Zealots" was designated. To this sect Simon had probably belonged before his call.

19. xii. *Judas Iscariot*] sometimes called *the son of Simon* (John vi. 71, xiii. 2, 26), more generally *Iscariot*, i.e. probably "*a native of Kerioth*," a little village in the tribe of Judah (Jos. xv. 25; Jer. xlviii. 24). For the probable motives that led him to become the traitor, see note on xiv. 10.

and they went into an house] The incident here related took place after the delivery of the Sermon on the Mount, and the Saviour's second ministerial journey, an interval of a few months (?).

20—30. HOW CAN SATAN CAST OUT SATAN?

20. *the multitude cometh together again*] i.e. at Capernaum, which had now become our Lord's temporary home.

21. *when his friends*] not the Apostles, but His relatives, including "His brethren and His mother," who are noticed here as going forth, and a few verses later on as having arrived at the house where our Lord was (Mark iii. 31), or the place where the crowds were thronging Him.

He is beside himself] They deemed the zeal and daily devotion to His labour of love a sort of ecstasy or religious enthusiasm, which made Him no longer master of Himself. St Paul uses the word in this sense in 2 Cor. v. 13, "For whether we *be beside ourselves*, it is to God." Comp. the words of Festus to St Paul (Acts xxvi. 24).

22. *And the scribes*] The hostile party from Jerusalem, noticed above, consisting of Scribes and Pharisees, still lingered at Capernaum.

He hath Beelzebub] St Matthew tells us of the miracle, which was the occasion of this blasphemy, the cure of a man not only possessed with a demon, but also blind and dumb (Matt. xii. 22). Beelzebub or rather Beelzebu-*l* was the title of a heathen deity, to whom the Jews ascribed the sovereignty of the "evil spirits." (*a*) Some would connect the name with *zebûl* = habitation, so making it = *the Lord of the dwelling* (Matt. x. 25), in his character of "prince of the power of the air" (Eph. ii. 2), or of the lower world, or as occupying a mansion in the seventh heavens. (*b*) Others would connect it with *zebel* = *dung*, and so make it = *the lord of dung* or *the dung-hill*, a term of derision amongst the Jews for *the lord of idols, the prince of false gods*. This fearful blasphemy was repeated more than once. See Luke xi. 17 sq.

called them *unto him*, and said unto them in parables, How 24 can Satan cast out Satan? And if a kingdom be divided 25 against itself, that kingdom cannot stand. And if a house 26 be divided against itself, that house cannot stand. And if Satan rise up against himself, and be divided, he cannot 27 stand, but hath an end. No man can enter into a strong man's house, and spoil his goods, except he will first bind 28 the strong man; and then he will spoil his house. Verily I say unto you, All sins shall be forgiven unto the sons of men, and blasphemies wherewith soever they shall blas- 29 pheme: but he that shall blaspheme against the Holy Ghost hath never forgiveness, but is in danger of eternal damna- 30 tion: because they said, He hath an unclean spirit.

31—35. *His Mother and His Brethren come to Him.*

31 There came then his brethren and his mother, and, stand- 32 ing without, sent unto him, calling him. And the multitude sat about him, and they said unto him, Behold, thy mother

23. *How can Satan cast out Satan?*] Using an irresistible *argumentum ad hominem* He shews them the absurdity of supposing that Satan could be his own enemy. If neither kingdom, nor city (Matt. xii. 25), nor house could stand, when divided against itself, much less could the empire of the Evil One.

27. *a strong man's house*] The "strong man" is Satan; his House or Palace is this Lower world; the Stronger than the Strong is Christ, who first bound the Evil One, when He triumphed over his temptations. Comp. Luke xi. 21, 22.

28. *Verily I say unto you*] a favourite formula of our Lord's, which we often find in St John, when He would draw special attention to any of His Divine utterances.

29. *but he that shall blaspheme*] The sin, against which these words are a terrible but merciful warning, is not so much an *act*, as a *state* of sin, on the part of one, who in defiance of light and knowledge, *of set purpose* rejects, and not only rejects but *perseveres* in rejecting, the warnings of conscience, and the Grace of the Holy Spirit, who blinded by religious bigotry rather than ascribe a good work to the Spirit of Good prefer to ascribe it to the Spirit of Evil, and thus wilfully put "bitter for sweet" and "sweet for bitter," "darkness for light" and "light for darkness." Such a state if persevered in and not repented of excludes from pardon, for it is *the sin unto death* spoken of in 1 John v. 16.

31—35. HIS MOTHER AND HIS BRETHREN COME TO HIM.

31. *his brethren*] Their names, James, Joses, Simon, Judas, are given in Matt. xiii. 55 and Mark vi. 3. Some understand them to have been His literal "brethren," others think they were the sons of Cleophas and Mary, the sister and namesake of the Virgin.

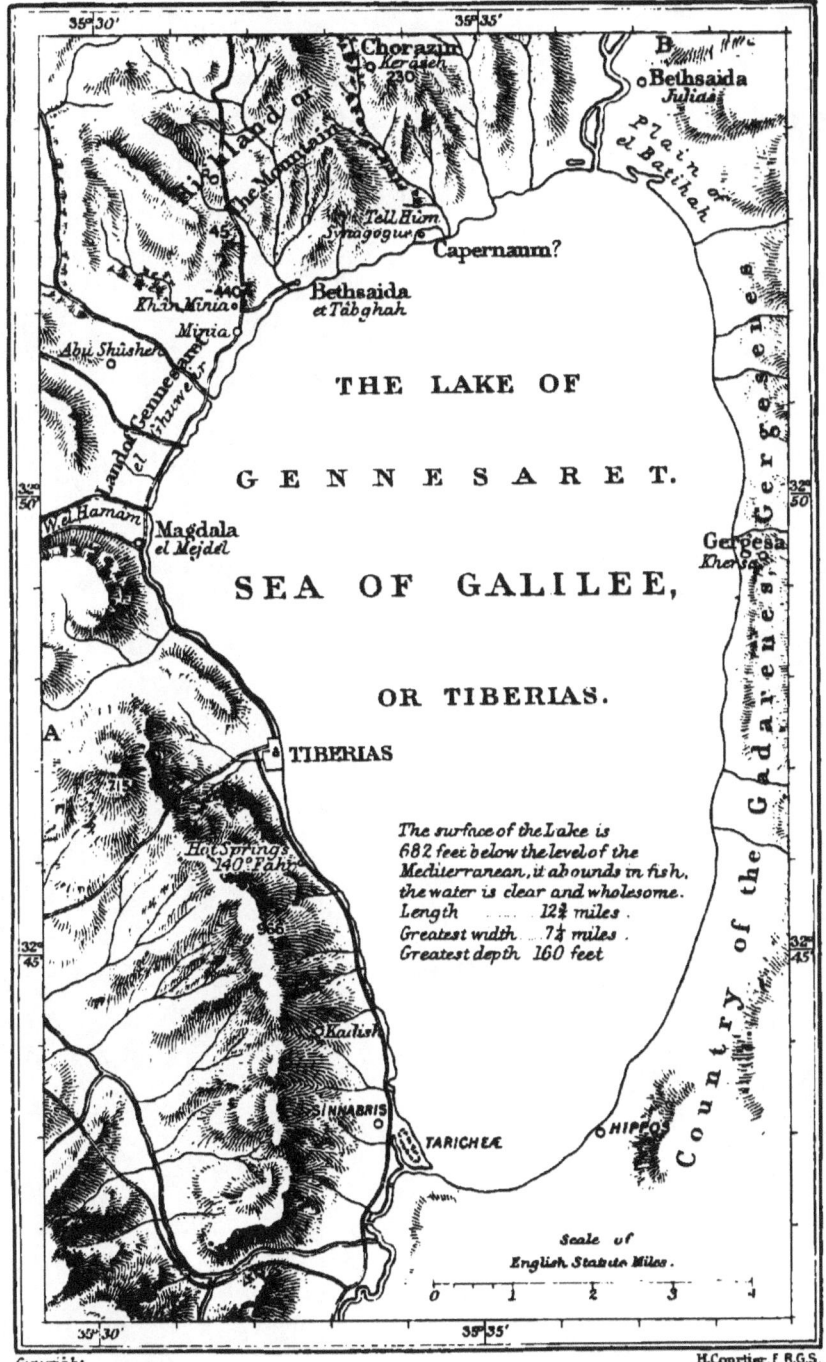

and thy brethren without seek for thee. And he answered 33
them, saying, Who is my mother, or my brethren? And he 34
looked round about on them which sat about him, and said,
Behold my mother and my brethren! For whosoever shall 35
do the will of God, the same is my brother, and my sister,
and mother.

1—9. *The Parable of the Sower.*

And he began again to teach by the sea side: and 4
there was gathered unto him a great multitude, so that he
entered into a ship, and sat in the sea; and the whole multitude was by the sea on the land. And he taught them 2

32. *seek for thee*] They had already left the place where they abode, and gone forth in quest of Him; see above, *v.* 21.

33. *Who is*] It is thought that the "brethren" wished to share in His fame, and to prove to the people their connection with Him and their influence over Him. But the tenderness of His love for His earthly mother, which He displayed so clearly upon the Cross, only brings out in stronger relief the devotion, with which He gave Himself up to the performance of the Will of His Father in heaven and the furtherance of His glory. "He despises not His Mother, He places before her His Father." Bengel.

34. *looked round*] Another graphic touch peculiar to the second Evangelist. See Introduction, p. 18. Our Lord repeated the saying here recorded on another occasion, Luke viii. 21.

CH. IV. 1—9. THE PARABLE OF THE SOWER.

1. *by the sea side*] The scenery round the Lake doubtless suggested many of the details of the Parables now delivered. (1) On the shore was the vast multitude gathered "out of every city" (Luke viii. 4); (2) from the fishing-boat the eye of the Divine Speaker would rest on (*a*) patches of undulating corn-fields with the *trodden pathway* running through them, the *rocky ground* of the hill-side protruding here and there, the large *bushes of thorn* growing in the very midst of the waving wheat, the deep loam of the *good rich soil* which distinguishes the whole of the Plain of Gennesaret descending close to the water's edge; (*b*) the mustard-tree, which grows especially on the shores of the Lake; (*c*) the fishermen connected with the great fisheries, which once made the fame of Gennesaret, plying amidst its marvellous shoals of fish, the *drag-net* or *hauling-net* (Matt. xiii. 47, 48), the *casting-net* (Matt. iv. 18; Mark i. 16), the *bag-net* and *basket-net* (Luke v. 4—9); (*d*) the women and children employed in picking out from the wheat the tall green stalks, called by the Arabs, *Zuwân* = the Greek *Zizania* = the *Lollia* of the Vulgate, the *tares* of our Version; (*e*) the countless flocks of birds, aquatic fowls by the lake-side, partridges and pigeons hovering over the rich plain. See Stanley's *Sinai and Palestine*, pp. 425—427; Thomson's *Land and the Book*, p. 402; Tristram's *Land of Israel*, p. 431.

3 many things by parables, and said unto them in his doctrine,
4 Hearken; Behold, there went out a sower to sow: and it came to pass, as he sowed, some fell by the way side, and
5 the fowls of the air came and devoured it up. And some fell on stony ground, where it had not much earth; and immediately it sprang up, because it had no depth of earth:
6 but when the sun was up, it was scorched; and because it
7 had no root, it withered away. And some fell among thorns, and the thorns grew up, and choked it, and it yielded no

2. *by parables*] (i) The Greek word thus rendered denotes (*a*) *a placing beside*, (*b*) *a comparing, a comparison*. In Hellenistic Greek it became coextensive with the Hebrew *mâshâl* = similitude. (ii) In this sense it is applied

(1) *In the Old Testament*, to—
 (*a*) *The shortest proverbs:* as 1 Sam. x. 12, "Therefore it became a *proverb*, Is Saul also among the prophets?" xxiv. 13, "As saith the *proverb* of the ancients;" 2 Chron. vii. 20, "I will make it to be a *proverb* and a byword among all nations."
 (*b*) *Dark prophetic utterances:* as Num. xxiii. 7, "And he took up his *parable* and said;" Ezek. xx. 49, "Ah Lord God! they say of me, Doth he not speak *parables?*"
 (*c*) *Enigmatic maxims:* as Ps. lxxviii. 2, "I will open my mouth in a *parable;*" Prov. i. 6, "the words of the wise and their *dark sayings*."

(2) *In the Gospels*, to—
 (*a*) *Short sayings:* as Luke iv. 23, "Ye will surely say unto me this *proverb*, Physician, heal thyself."
 (*b*) *A comparison without a narrative:* as Mark xiii. 28, "Now learn its *parable* of the fig tree" (see note in loc.).
 (*c*) *Comparisons with narratives of earthly things with heavenly*, as the Parables of our Lord.

3. *Hearken*] This summons to attention is peculiar to St Mark.

went out] The expression implies that the sower did not sow near his own house, or in a garden fenced or walled, but went forth into the open country. Thomson's *Land and the Book*, p. 82.

4. *by the way side*] i.e. on the hard footpath, or road, passing through the cultivated land.

5. *stony ground*] This must be compared with "the rock" mentioned by St Luke (viii. 6). What is meant is not a soil mingled with stones, for then there would be no hindrance to the roots striking deeply; but a thin coating of mould covering the surface of a rock, which stretched below and presented an impassable barrier to the growth of the roots.

6. *when the sun was up*] For the reference of the word thus translated to *the rising of the sun or stars* comp. Num. xxiv. 17; Is. lx. 1; Mal. iv. 2.

7. *thorns*] The "Nâbk" of the Arabs, which grows abundantly

fruit. And other fell on good ground, and did yield fruit 8
that sprang up and increased; and brought forth, some
thirty, and some sixty, and some an hundred. And he said 9
unto them, He that hath ears to hear, let him hear.

10—25. *The Explanation of the Parable.*

And when he was alone, they that were about him with the 10
twelve asked of him the parable. And he said unto them, 11
Unto you it is given to know the mystery of the kingdom of
God: but unto them that are without, all *these* things are done
in parables: that seeing they may see, and not perceive; 12

in Syria and Palestine, and of which the Crown of Thorns was probably woven.

and choked it] or as Wyclif translates it "*þornes stieded up, and strangliden* it." The seed and the thorns grew together, but the thorns gradually out-topped it, drew the moisture from the roots, and shut out the air and light, so that it pined and dwindled, and "yielded no fruit."

8. *some thirty*] St Luke says simply "*and bare fruit an hundredfold.*" St Matthew says "*some an hundred-fold, some sixty-fold, some thirty-fold.*" St Mark begins from the lowest return, and ascends to the highest. It is said of Isaac that he sowed and "*received in the same year an hundred-fold*" (Gen. xxvi. 12). Herodotus tells us that two hundred-fold was a common return in the plain of Babylon, while a kind of white maize often in Palestine returns several hundred-fold. Observe the four kinds of soil. In the first the seed did not spring up at all; in the second it sprang up, but soon withered away; in the third it sprang up and grew, but yielded no fruit; in the fourth it sprang up, grew, and brought forth fruit; and as there are three causes of unfruitfulness, so there are three degrees of fruitfulness, but only one cause of fruitfulness.

9. *He that hath ears to hear*] These solemn words are found in the three Gospels. Our Lord is recorded to have used them on *six* occasions; (1) Matt. xi. 15; (2) xiii. 43; (3) Mark iv. 9; (4) iv. 23; (5) vii. 16; (6) Luke xiv. 35. They are not found in St John's Gospel, but occur eight times in the Book of Revelation, ii. 7, 11, 17, 29, iii. 6, 13, 22, xiii. 9.

10—25. THE EXPLANATION OF THE PARABLE.

10. *And when he was alone*] St Mark here anticipates what took place after the Saviour had "*sent the multitudes away*" and "*gone into the house*" (Matt. xiii. 36).

11. *the mystery*] The word Mystery denotes (i) *a religious mystery* like those of Eleusis, into which men were initiated; (ii) *a secret* (as in 1 Cor. xv. 51); and is applied (*a*) *to the Gospel itself* (as here and in 1 Cor. ii. 7; Rom. xvi. 25; Eph. i. 9); (β) *to the various parts and truths of the Gospel* (Matt. xiii. 11; Luke viii. 10; 1 Cor. iv. 1); (iii) *to a symbolic representation* or *emblem* (Rev. xvii. 5, 7).

them that are without] Comp. 1 Cor. v. 12, 13; Col. iv. 5; 1 Thess. iv. 12.

12. *that seeing they may see, and not perceive*] At the beginning of

and hearing they may hear, and not understand; lest at any time they should be converted, and *their* sins should
13 be forgiven them. And he said unto them, Know ye not this parable? and how then will ye know all parables?
14 The sower soweth the word. And these are they by
15 the way side, where the word is sown; but when they have heard, Satan cometh immediately, and taketh away the word
16 that was sown in their hearts. And these are they likewise which are sown on stony ground; who, when they have heard
17 the word, immediately receive it with gladness; and have no root in themselves, and so endure but for a time: afterward, when affliction or persecution ariseth for the word's sake,
18 immediately they are offended. And these are they which
19 are sown among thorns; such as hear the word, and the cares of this world, and the deceitfulness of riches, and the

His ministry our Lord did not teach by Parables. "The Sermon on the Mount may be taken as the type of the 'words of grace' which He spake 'not as the Scribes.' Beatitudes, laws, promises were uttered distinctly, not indeed without similitudes, but with similitudes that explained themselves." And so He continued for some time. But His direct teaching was met with scorn, unbelief, and hardness. From this time forward "parables" entered largely into His recorded teaching, and were at once attractive and penal. (a) *Attractive*, as "instruments of education for those who were children in age or character," and offering in a striking form much for the memory to retain, and for the docile and truth-loving to learn; (b) *Penal*, as testing the disposition of those who listened to them; withdrawing the light from such as loved darkness and were wilfully blind, and protecting the truth from the mockery of the scoffer; finding out the fit hearers, and leading them, but them only, on to deeper knowledge. See Article on *Parables* in Smith's *Bible Dict.*

13. *Know ye not this parable?*] For it afforded the simplest type or pattern of a Parable.

all parables = **all My Parables.**

14. *The sower*] This is applicable to (i) Christ, who "*came forth* from the Father and was come into the world" (John xvi. 28); (ii) His Apostles; (iii) all who go forth in His Name, and with His authority. For other comparisons of the relations of the teacher and the taught to those between the sower and the soil, comp. 1 Pet. i. 23; 1 John iii. 9.

15. *Satan*] See note above, iii. 23.

17. *affliction*] The word thus translated denotes (i) *pressure*, that which presses upon or burdens the spirit; then (2) the *distress* arising therefrom. The word *tribulation* rests upon this image, coming as it does from *tribulum* = *the threshing-roller*.

lusts of other things entering in, choke the word, and it becometh unfruitful. And these are they which are sown on good ground; such as hear the word, and receive *it*, and bring forth fruit, some thirtyfold, some sixty, and some an hundred. And he said unto them, Is a candle brought to be put under a bushel, or under a bed? and not to be set on a candlestick? For there is nothing hid, which shall not be manifested; neither was any thing kept secret, but that it should come abroad. If any man have ears to hear, let him hear. And he said unto them, Take heed what ye hear: with what measure ye mete, it shall be measured to you: and unto you that hear shall more be given. For he that hath, to him shall be given: and he that hath not, from him shall be taken even that which he hath.

26—29. *The Seed growing secretly.*

And he said, So is the kingdom of God, as if a man should cast seed into the ground; and should sleep, and rise night and day, and the seed should spring and grow up, he

19. *the cares of this world*] The word rendered "cares" denotes in the original "distracting anxieties," which, as it were, "cut a man in sunder." St Luke expands the one word here employed into "cares," "riches," and "pleasures" (Luke viii. 14).

21. *Is a candle brought*] Rather, **The lamp is not brought, is it?** The article here points to the simple and indispensable furniture in every Jewish household. The original word means not a *candle* but a *lamp*. Wyclif renders it, "Wher a *lanterne* come, þat it be put vndir a bushel?"

to be put under a bushel] The original word *Modius* denotes a dry measure containing 16 sextarii, or about a peck. The English equivalent is greatly in excess of the Latin, as is noted in the margin.

a candlestick] Rather, **the lamp-stand.** "Do not suppose that what I now commit to you in secret, I would have concealed for ever; the light is kindled by Me in you, that by your ministry it may disperse the darkness of the whole world." Erasmus.

24. *with what measure ye mete*] According to the measure of your ability and diligence as hearers, ye shall receive instruction, and be enabled to preach to others.

25. *he that hath*] Comp. Matt. xiii. 12, xxv. 29; Luke viii. 18, xix. 26.

26—29. THE SEED GROWING SECRETLY.

26. *as if a man should cast seed into the ground*] This is *the only parable which is peculiar to St Mark*, and seems to take the place of "the Leaven" recorded by St Matthew (Matt. xiii. 33).

27. *spring and grow up*] We need not inquire too minutely who the Sower is, though primarily it refers to the Lord Himself. It is the

28 knoweth not how. For the earth bringeth forth fruit of herself; first the blade, then the ear, after that the full corn in 29 the ear. But when the fruit is brought forth, immediately he putteth in the sickle, because the harvest is come.

30—34. *The Parable of the Mustard Seed.*

30 And he said, Whereunto shall we liken the kingdom 31 of God? or with what comparison shall we compare it? *It is* like a grain of mustard seed, which, when it is sown in the 32 earth, is less than all the seeds that be in the earth: but when it is sown, it groweth up, and becometh greater than all herbs, and shooteth out great branches; so that the fowls

property of the seed which is intended to engage our attention, the secret energy of its own, the principle of life and growth within itself, whereby it springs up and grows.

28. *of herself*] = *of its own accord*, spontaneously. It is used of the gate of St Peter's prison *opening of its own accord* in Acts xii. 10.

first the blade] There is a law of orderly development in natural growth, so also is it in reference to spiritual growth; comp. 1 John ii. 12—14.

after that the full corn] or rather, **then** (there is) **full corn in the ear.**

29. *when the fruit is brought forth*] Literally, **when the fruit yields itself, or offers itself,** i.e. **is ripe.** The original word only occurs here in this sense. Comp. Virgil *Geo.* I. 287,

"Multa adeo gelidâ melius *se* nocte *dedere*."

the sickle] The sickle is only mentioned here and in Rev. xiv. 14, 15, "And I looked, and behold a white cloud, and upon the cloud one sat, like unto the Son of Man, having on His head a golden crown, and in His hand a *sharp sickle*." For the entire Parable comp. 1 Pet. i. 23—25.

30—34. THE PARABLE OF THE MUSTARD SEED.

30. *Whereunto shall we liken*] This method of asking a question before beginning a discourse was not unknown to the Rabbis. See the parallel in Luke xiii. 18.

31. *a grain of mustard seed*] The growth of a worldly kingdom had been already set forth under the image of a tree, and that of the kingdom of God also had been similarly compared. (See Dan. iv. 10—12; Ezek. xvii. 22, 24, xxxi. 3—9.)

in the earth] In St Matt. xiii. 31 a man is represented as taking and sowing it "*in his field*," while St Luke, xiii. 19, says "*in his garden*."

less than all the seeds] "Small as a grain of mustard seed" was a proverbial expression among the Jews for something exceedingly minute. The mustard-seed is not the least of all seeds *in the world*, but of all which the husbandman was accustomed to *sow*, and the "tree," when full grown, was larger than the other herbs in his garden.

32. *great branches*] In hot countries, as in Judæa, the mustard-tree

of the air may lodge under the shadow of it. And with 33
many such parables spake he the word unto them, as they
were able to hear *it*. But without a parable spake he not 34
unto them: and when they were alone, he expounded all
things to his disciples.

35—41. *The Stilling of the Storm.*

And the same day, when the even was come, he saith 35
unto them, Let us pass over unto the other side. And 36
when they had sent away the multitude, they took him
even as he was in the ship. And there were also with him
other little ships. And there arose a great storm of wind, 37
and the waves beat into the ship, so that it was now full.
And he was in the hinder part of the ship, asleep on a 38
pillow: and they awake him, and say unto him, Master,

attains a great size. Thomson, *Land and the Book*, p. 414, tells us he has seen it on the rich plain of Akkâr as tall as the horse and his rider. A variety of it may have been *cultivated* in the time of our Lord, which grew to an enormous size.

the fowls] The seed of the mustard-tree is a favourite food with birds. For the language comp. Ezek. xvii. 23.

35—41. THE STILLING OF THE STORM.

35. *he saith unto them*] The three Synoptic Evangelists all agree in placing the Stilling of the Storm before the healing of the possessed in the country of the Gadarenes.

the other side] After a long and exhausting day he needed retirement, and repose could nowhere be more readily obtained than in the solitude of the eastern shore.

36. *as he was*] i.e. without any preparation for the voyage. Just before the boat put off three of the listeners to His words desired to attach themselves to Him as His disciples, (1) a scribe, (2) an already partial disciple, (3) another who wished first to bid farewell to his friends at home (Matt. viii. 19—22; Luke ix. 57—62).

37. *a great storm*] The word here used is found in Luke viii. 23. The word employed in Matt. viii. 24 generally means an *earth*quake. It was one of those sudden and violent squalls to which the Lake of Gennesaret was notoriously exposed, lying as it does 600 feet lower than the sea and surrounded by mountain gorges, which act "like gigantic funnels to draw down the cold winds from the mountains." These winds are not only violent, but they come down suddenly, and often when the sky is perfectly clear. See Thomson's *Land and the Book*, p. 374; Tristram's *Land of Israel*, p. 430.

beat] Rather, **kept beating**. Comp. Matt. viii. 24.

was now full] Rather, **was already filling**, or **beginning to fill**.

38. *a pillow*] The word only occurs here. It was probably the leather cushion of the steersman. These details we learn only from St Mark.

39 carest thou not that we perish? And he arose, and rebuked the wind, and said unto the sea, Peace, be still. And 40 the wind ceased, and there was a great calm. And he said unto them, Why are ye so fearful? how is it that ye 41 have no faith? And they feared exceedingly, and said one to another, What manner of man is this, that even the wind and the sea obey him?

1—20. *The Healing of the Gadarene Demoniac.*

5 And they came over unto the other side of the sea, 2 into the country of the Gadarenes. And when he was come out of the ship, immediately there met him out of the tombs

Master] The double "*Master*," "*Master*" of St Luke (viii. 24) gives vividness to their haste and terror. The exclamation recorded by St Mark sounds more like rebuke, as though He was unmindful of their safety.

39. *rebuked the wind*] All three Evangelists record that He *rebuked* the wind (comp. Ps. cvi. 9), St Mark alone adds His distinct address to the furious elements. On *be still* see above, i. 25. Comp. Matt. viii. 26; Luke viii. 24, and note. The perfect imperative of the original implies the command that the result should be instantaneous.

the wind ceased] Lit. **grew tired.** We have the same word in Matt. xiv. 32, and again in Mark vi. 51. As a rule, after a storm the waves continue to heave and swell for hours, but here at the word of the Lord of Nature there was a "great calm."

CH. V. 1—20. THE HEALING OF THE GADARENE DEMONIAC.

1. *they came*] to the eastern shore, but not even there was the Lord destined to find peace or rest.

the Gadarenes] All three Gospels which record this miracle vary in their readings between (1) *Gadarenes*, (2) *Gergesenes*, and (3) *Gerasenes*. (a) *Gadara*, the capital of Peræa, lay S. E. of the southern extremity of Gennesaret, at a distance of about 60 stadia from Tiberias, its country being called Gadaritis, (β) *Gerasa* lay on the extreme eastern limit of Peræa, and was too far from the Lake to give its name to any district on its borders, (γ) *Gergesa* was a little town nearly opposite Capernaum, the ruined site of which is still called *Kerza* or *Gersa*. Origen tells us that the exact site of the miracle was here pointed out in his day. St Mark and St Luke using the word *Gadarenes* indicate *generally* the scene of the miracle, Gadara being a place of importance and acknowledged as the capital of the district. See Thomson's *Land and the Book*, pp. 375—378.

2. *out of the tombs*] These tombs were either natural caves or recesses hewn by art out of the rock, often so large as to be supported with columns, and with cells upon their sides for the reception of the dead. Such places were regarded as unclean because of the dead men's bones which were there (Num. xix. 11, 16; Matt. xxiii. 27). Such tombs can still be traced in more than one of the ravines on the eastern side of the Lake. Thomson's *Land and the Book*, p. 376.

a man with an unclean spirit, who had *his* dwelling among 3
the tombs; and no man could bind him, no, not with chains:
because that he had been often bound with fetters and 4
chains, and the chains had been plucked asunder by him,
and the fetters broken in pieces: neither could any *man*
tame him. And always, night and day, he was in the moun- 5
tains, and in the tombs, crying, and cutting himself with
stones. But when he saw Jesus afar off, he ran and wor- 6
shipped him, and cried with a loud voice, and said, What 7
have I to do with thee, Jesus, *thou* Son of the most high
God? I adjure thee by God, that thou torment me not. For 8
he said unto him, Come out of the man, *thou* unclean spirit.
And he asked him, What *is* thy name? And he answered, 9
saying, My name *is* Legion: for we are many. And he 10

a man] St Matthew (viii. 28) mentions two demoniacs, St Luke (viii. 27), like St Mark, only speaks of one. Probably one was better known in the country round than the other, or one was so much fiercer that the other was hardly taken any account of. "Amid all the boasted civilisation of antiquity, there existed no hospitals, no penitentiaries, no asylums; and unfortunates of this class, being too dangerous and desperate for human intercourse, could only be driven forth from among their fellow-men, and restrained from mischief by measures at once inadequate and cruel." Farrar's *Life of Christ*, I. p. 334.

no, not with chains] This is a general expression for any *bonds* confining the hands or feet. Comp. Acts xxi. 33; Eph. vi. 20; Rev. xx. 1; *fetters* were restricted to the feet.

4. *he had been often*] Each Evangelist adds something to complete the picture of the terrible visitation, under which the possessed laboured. St Matthew that he made the way impassable for travellers (viii. 28); St Luke that he was without clothing (viii. 27); St Mark that he cried night and day and cut himself with stones (v. 5).

broken in pieces] For another instance of the extraordinary muscular strength which maniacs put forth see Acts xix. 16.

6. *afar off*] St Mark alone tells us this. While, as a man, he is attracted towards the Holy One; as possessed by the Legion, he desires to withdraw from Him.

7. *What have I to do with thee?*] · Literally, **What is there between Thee and me?** What have we in common? Why interferest Thou with us?

I adjure thee] Notice the intermixture of praying and adjuring, so characteristic of demoniac possession when brought into the presence of Christ.

9. *My name is Legion*] "He had seen the thick and serried ranks of a Roman legion, that fearful instrument of oppression, that sign of terror and fear to the conquered nations." Even such, terrible in their strength, inexorable in their hostility, were the "lords many," which

besought him much that he would not send them away out
11 of the country. Now there was there nigh unto the moun-
12 tains a great herd of swine feeding. And all the devils
besought him, saying, Send us into the swine, that we may
13 enter into them. And forthwith Jesus gave them leave.
And the unclean spirits went out, and entered into the
swine: and the herd ran violently down a steep place into
the sea, (they were about two thousand;) and were choked
14 in the sea. And they that fed the swine fled, and told *it* in
the city, and in the country. And they went out to see what
15 it was that was done. And they come to Jesus, and see him
that was possessed with the devil, and had the legion, sitting,
and clothed, and in his right mind: and they were afraid.
16 And they that saw *it* told them how it befel to him that
was possessed with the devil, and *also* concerning the swine.
17 And they began to pray him to depart out of their coasts.

had dominion over him. Compare (i) the "seven demons," by whom Mary Magdalene was possessed (Luke viii. 2), (ii) the "seven other spirits" "worse than the first," which our Lord describes as taking up their abode in a man (Matt. xii. 45).

10. *out of the country*] i.e. as it is expressed in St Luke, into "the abyss of hell" (viii. 31).

11. *a great herd of swine*] The lawless nature of the country, where Jews lived mingled with Gentiles, the Evangelist denotes by the circumstance of the two thousand swine, emphasizing the greatness of the herd. If their owners were only in part Jews, who merely trafficked in these animals, still they were not justified before the Law. The territory was not altogether Jewish.

13. *down a steep place*] At *Kerza* or *Gersa*, "where there is no precipice running sheer to the sea, but a narrow belt of beach, the bluff behind is so steep, and the shore so narrow, that a herd of swine rushing frantically down, must certainly have been overwhelmed in the sea before they could recover themselves." Tristram's *Land of Israel* p. 462.

the sea] This, as we have seen above (iii. 7), was one of the names, by which the Lake of Gennesaret was called.

15. *clothed*] because, as St Luke informs us (viii. 27), before the wretched man *wore no clothes*. "On descending from the heights of Lebanon, I found myself," writes Warburton, "in a *cemetery*... The silence of the night was now broken by *fierce yells and howlings*, which I discovered proceeded from *a naked maniac*, who was fighting with some wild dogs for a bone." *The Crescent and the Cross*, II. 352.

17. *to depart out of their coasts*] Many were doubtless annoyed at the losses they had already sustained, and feared greater losses might follow. "And their prayer was heard: He did depart; He took them

And when he was come into the ship, he that had been pos- 18
sessed with the devil prayed him that he might be with him.
Howbeit Jesus suffered him not, but saith unto him, Go 19
home to thy friends, and tell them how great things the Lord
hath done for thee, and hath had compassion on thee. And 20
he departed, and began to publish in Decapolis how great
things Jesus had done for him: and all *men* did marvel.

21—24. *The Petition of Jairus.*

And when Jesus was passed over again by ship unto the 21
other side, much people gathered unto him: and he was
nigh unto the sea. And, behold, there cometh one of the 22
rulers of the synagogue, Jairus by name; and when he saw

at their word; and let them alone" (cf. Exod. x. 28, 29). Trench *on the Miracles*, p. 177.

18. *And when he was come...*] Rather, **when He was in the act of stepping into the ship.**

that he might be with him] Either (i) in a spirit of deepest gratitude longing to be with his Benefactor, or (ii) fearing lest the many enemies, from whom he had been delivered, should return. Comp. Matt. xii. 44, 45.

19. *and tell them*] On others (comp. Matt. viii. 4; Luke viii. 56) after shewing forth towards them His miraculous power, He enjoined silence; on this man He enjoined publicity. He appoints him to be a living memorial of His own saving Power, and so to become the first great preacher in the half-heathen district.

20. *Decapolis*] When the Romans conquered Syria, B.C. 65, they rebuilt, partially colonized, and endowed with peculiar privileges "ten cities," the country which was called Decapolis. All of them lay, with the exception of Scythopolis, East of the Jordan, and to the East and South-East of the Sea of Galilee. They were (but there is some variation in the lists), 1 Scythopolis, 2 Hippos, 3 Gadara, 4 Pella, 5 Philadelphia, 6 Gerasa, 7 Dion, 8 Canatha, 9 Abila, 10 Capitolias. The name only occurs three times in the Scriptures, (*a*) here; (*b*) Matt. iv. 25, and (*c*) Mark vii. 31; but it seems to have been also employed to denote a large district extending along both sides of the Jordan.

21—24. THE PETITION OF JAIRUS.

21. *unto the other side*] i.e. the western side of the Lake, near Capernaum.

22. *the rulers of the synagogue*] Each synagogue had a kind of Chapter or College of Elders, presided over by *a ruler*, who superintended the services, and possessed the power of excommunication. From this place, e.g., compared with Acts xiii. 15, it would appear that some synagogues had several rulers.

Jairus by name] It is but rarely we know the *names* of those who were the objects of the Saviour's mercy. He afterwards probably was

23 him, he fell at his feet, and besought him greatly, saying, My little daughter lieth at the point of death: *I pray thee*, come and lay thy hands on her, that she may be healed; 24 and she shall live. And *Jesus* went with him; and much people followed him, and thronged him.

25—34. *The Healing of the Woman with an Issue of Blood.*
25 And a certain woman, which had an issue of blood twelve 26 years, and had suffered many things of many physicians, and had spent all that she had, and was nothing bettered, but rather 27 grew worse, when she had heard of Jesus, came in the press 28 behind, and touched his garment. For she said, If I may 29 touch but his clothes, I shall be whole. And straightway the fountain of her blood was dried up; and she felt in *her*

one of those who came to the Lord pleading for the centurion at Capernaum (Luke vii. 3). The aid he then asked for another, he now craves for himself, but under the pressure of a still greater calamity.

23. *My little daughter*] His *"only daughter,"* Luke viii. 42. The use of diminutives is characteristic of St Mark. Here we have "little daughter;" in *v.* 41 "damsel," or *"little maid;"* in vii. 27, "dogs= *"little dogs," "whelps;"* in viii. 7, *a few "small fishes;"* in xiv. 47, *his ear*, literally *"a little ear."* She was about 12 years of age, Lk. viii. 42.

at the point of death] The original word here used is one of the frequent Latinisms of St Mark. See Introduction. She lay a dying (Luke viii. 42), and all but gone when he left her, the sands of life ebbing out so fast, that he could even say of her that she was "dead" (Matt. ix. 18), at one moment expressing himself in one language, at the next in another.

24. *thronged him*] The word thus rendered only occurs here and at *v.* 31.

25—34. THE HEALING OF THE WOMAN WITH AN ISSUE OF BLOOD.

25. *a certain woman*] "Such overflowing grace is in Him, the Prince of Life, that as He is hastening to the accomplishing of one work of His power, He accomplishes another, as by the way." Trench, p. 188.

an issue of blood] Her malady was especially afflicting (Lev. xv. 19—27), for not only did it unfit her for all the relationships of life, but was popularly regarded as the direct consequence of sinful habits.

28. *his garment*] The law of Moses commanded every Jew to wear at each corner of his *tallith* a fringe or tassel of blue, to remind them that they were God's people (Num. xv. 37—40; Deut. xxii. 12). "Two of these fringes usually hung down at the bottom of the robe, while one hung over the shoulder where the robe was fastened round the person." Those who wished to be esteemed eminently religious were wont to make broad, or "enlarge the borders of their garments" (Matt. xxiii. 5).

29. *of that plague*] On this word see above, note on iii. 10.

body that she was healed of that plague. And Jesus, immediately knowing in himself that virtue had gone out of him, turned him about in the press, and said, Who touched my clothes? And his disciples said unto him, Thou seest the multitude thronging thee, and sayest thou, Who touched me? And he looked round about to see her that had done this thing. But the woman fearing and trembling, knowing what was done in her, came and fell down before him, and told him all the truth. And he said unto her, Daughter, thy faith hath made thee whole; go in peace, and be whole of thy plague.

35—43. *The Raising of the Daughter of Jairus.*

While he yet spake, there came from the ruler of the synagogue's *house certain* which said, Thy daughter is dead: why troublest thou the Master any further? As

30. *Who touched my clothes?*] He who with the eye of His Spirit saw Nathanael under the fig tree (John i. 47, 48), recognised at once (Mark v. 30) the magnetic touch of faith however weak and trembling (Luke viii. 46). "Many throng Him, but only one touches Him." "Caro premit, fides tangit," says St Augustine.

32. *he looked round*] Another proof of St Mark's graphic power. The tense in the original is still more expressive. It denotes that He **kept on looking all round**, that His eyes **wandered over** one after the other of the many faces before Him, till they fell on her who had done this thing.

33. *fearing and trembling*] She may have dreaded His anger, for according to the Law (Lev. xv. 19) the touch of one, afflicted as she was, caused ceremonial defilement until the evening.

told him] i.e. probably all the particulars we find in verses 25, 26, and this before all the people (Luke viii. 47).

34. *Daughter*] Our Lord is recorded to have addressed no other woman by this title. It calmed all her doubts and fears.

go in peace] This is not merely "go with a blessing," but *abi in pacem, enter into peace,* "as the future element in which thy life shall move," and *be whole of thy plague. Be* = esto perpetuo. "Post longam miseriam, beneficium *durabile.*" Bengel.

35—43. THE RAISING OF THE DAUGHTER OF JAIRUS.

35. *why troublest thou the Master?*] Or as, literally rendered, it is in St Luke's Gospel (viii. 49), "*trouble not the Master any further.*" The word, here translated "*trouble,*" one which is used here and here alone by St Mark and St Luke (except Luke vii. 6), denotes properly (1) *to flay:* then (2) *to fatigue* or *to worry,* often with a more particular allusion to fatiguing with the length of a journey.

soon as Jesus heard the word that was spoken, he saith unto
37 the ruler of the synagogue, Be not afraid, only believe. And
he suffered no man to follow him, save Peter, and James, and
38 John the brother of James. And he cometh to the house of
the ruler of the synagogue, and seeth the tumult, and them
39 that wept and wailed greatly. And when he was come in, he
saith unto them, Why make ye this ado, and weep? the damsel
40 is not dead, but sleepeth. And they laughed him to scorn.
But when he had put them all out, he taketh the father and
the mother of the damsel, and them that were with him, and
41 entereth in where the damsel was lying. And he took the
damsel by the hand, and said unto her, Talitha cumi; which
42 is, being interpreted, Damsel, I say unto thee, arise. And
straightway the damsel arose, and walked; for she was *of the*

36. *heard*] Perhaps according to a better reading, "*overheard.*"
The very instant the Lord heard the message, He hastens to reassure
the ruler with a word of confidence and encouragement.

37. *save Peter, and James, and John*] This is the first time we
hear of an election within the election. "That which He was about to
do was so great and holy that those three only, the flower and crown of
the Apostolic band, were its fitting witnesses." The other occasions
when we read of such an election were equally solemn and significant,
(1) the Transfiguration (Matt. xvii. 2); and (2) the Agony in the
Garden of Gethsemane (Matt. xxvi. 37).

38. *them that wept*] These were the hired mourners, chiefly
women; whose business it was to beat their breasts (Luke viii. 52), and
to make loud lamentations at funerals; comp. 2 Chron. xxxv. 25; Jer. ix.
17, 18; Amos v. 16. The Rabbinic rule provided for the poorest
Israelite at least two flute-players, and one mourning woman. "A
Ruler of the Synagogue, bereaved of his only child, may well have been
prodigal in the expression of his grief."

39. *but sleepeth*] Comp. His words in reference to Lazarus (John xi.
11). The Lord of life takes away that word of fear, "*She is dead,*"
and puts in its room that milder word which gives promise of an
awakening, "*She sleepeth.*"

41. *Talitha cumi*] = "**Little Maid, arise.**" Doubtless St Peter, who
was now present, often recalled the actual words used on this memorable
occasion by our Lord, and told them to his friend and kinsman St
Mark. So it is the same Evangelist, who preserves the very word,
which our Lord used, when He opened the eyes of the blind man,
Ephphatha (vii. 34). The mention of these words goes to prove that in
ordinary life our Lord availed Himself of the popular Aramaic dialect.

42. *And immediately her spirit came again and she arose straightway*
(Luke viii. 55), and *began to walk*. There is no struggle, no effort on
His part, Who is "*the Resurrection and the Life*" (John xi. 25); we
read of no "crying unto the Lord," or "stretching himself upon the

age of twelve years. And they were astonished with a great astonishment. And he charged them straitly that no man 43 should know it; and commanded that something should be given her to eat.

1—6. *Christ is despised at Nazareth.*

And he went out from thence, and came into his own 6 country; and his disciples follow him. And when the sab- 2 bath day was come, he began to teach in the synagogue: and many hearing *him* were astonished, saying, From whence hath this *man* these things? and what wisdom *is* this which is given unto him, that even such mighty works are

child three times" as in the case of Elijah at Sarepta (1 Kings xvii. 21); He "lieth not upon the child, or putteth his mouth upon her mouth, and his eyes upon her eyes, and his hands upon her hands" as in the case of Elisha (2 Kings iv. 34). He speaks but a word and instantly He is obeyed.

a great astonishment] The word thus rendered denotes sometimes (1) *a trance*, as in Acts x. 10, "but while they made ready, he (St Peter) fell into *a trance;"* and Acts xxii. 17, "while I prayed in the temple, I was in *a trance*," with which comp. 2 Cor. xii. 23 (ii) *amazement, awe,* as in Luke v. 26, "and *amazement* seized all;" Mark xvi. 8, "*trembling and amazement* seized them;" Acts iii. 10, "and they were filled *with wonder and amazement.*" Here it points to a very extremity of astonishment.

43. *something should be given her to eat*] At once to strengthen the life thus wonderfully restored, and to prove that she was no spirit, but had really returned to the realities of a mortal existence.

CH. VI. 1—6. CHRIST IS DESPISED AT NAZARETH.

1. *his own country*] that is, Nazareth. From this time forward He ceased to have His abiding residence at Capernaum, although He still assembled His disciples on passing occasions. This visit to Nazareth is recorded only by St Matthew and St Mark.

2. *he began to teach in the synagogue*] For his former visit here see Luke iv. 16 sq. The conduct of His hearers on this occasion did not betray the frantic violence exhibited at His first visit.

mighty works] Rather, **powers.** This is one of the four names given by the Evangelists to the miracles which the Lord was pleased to work while incarnate here on earth. They are called:

(α) "*Wonders,*" a term never used alone, but always in conjunction with other names. They are continually styled "signs and wonders," or "signs" or "powers" alone, but never "wonders" alone. By this word the effect of astonishment, which the work produces on the beholder, is transferred to the work itself. The word only occurs once in St Mark, in xiii. 22, and there it is in conjunction with "signs."

(β) "*Signs,*" as being tokens and indications of something beyond

5—2

3 wrought by his hands? Is not this the carpenter, the son of Mary, the brother of James, and Joses, and of Juda, and

themselves, of the near presence and working of God, the seals and credentials of a higher power. The word is an especial favourite with St John, though in our Version "sign" too often gives place to the vaguer "miracle," to the great detriment of the true meaning and force of the word. It occurs three times in St John, twice in St Mark, xvi. 17, xvi. 20 alone, and once in conjunction with "wonders," xiii. 22.

(γ) "*Powers,*" that is of God, coming into and working in this world of ours. As in the "wonder" the effect is transferred and gives a name to the cause, so here the cause gives its name to the effect. The word occurs four times in St Mark: v. 30 (A. V. *virtue*), vi. 2, vi. 14, ix. 39. In our Version it is rendered sometimes "*wonderful works*" (Matt. vii. 22), sometimes "*mighty works*" (Matt. xi. 20; Mark vi. 14; Luke x. 13), and still more frequently "*miracles*" (Acts ii. 22, xix. 11; Gal. iii. 5), thus doing away with a portion of its force.

(δ) "*Works.*" This is a significant term very frequently used by St John. With him miracles are the natural form of *working* for Him, whose *Name is Wonderful* (Isaiah ix. 6), and Who therefore doeth "works of wonder." Comp. John vi. 28, vii. 21, x. 25, 32, 38, xiv. 11, &c. See Abp. Trench *on the Parables,* Introd.

3. *Is not this the carpenter?*] Save in this one place, our Lord is nowhere Himself called "the Carpenter." According to the custom of the Jews, even the Rabbis learnt some handicraft. One of their proverbs was that "he who taught not his son a trade, taught him to be a thief." Hence St Paul learnt to "labour with his own hands" at the trade of a tent-maker (Acts xviii. 3; 1 Thess. ii. 9; 1 Cor. iv. 12). "In the cities the carpenters would be Greeks, and skilled workmen; the carpenter of a provincial village could only have held a very humble position, and secured a very moderate competence." Farrar's *Life of Christ,* 1. 81.

the brother of James, and Joses...] The four "brothers" here mentioned, and "the sisters," whose names are nowhere recorded, were in all probability the children of Clopas and Mary, the sister and namesake of the blessed Virgin, and so the "cousins" of our Lord. (Compare Matt. xxvii. 56 with Mark xv. 40 and John xix. 25.) Joseph would seem to have died at some time between A.D. 8 and A.D. 26, and there is no reason for believing that Clopas was alive during our Lord's ministry. It has been suggested, therefore, that the two widowed sisters may have lived together, the more so as one of them had but one son, and He was often taken from her by His ministerial duties. Three other hypotheses have been formed respecting them: (1) that they were the children of Joseph by a former marriage; (2) that they were the children of Joseph and Mary; (3) that Joseph and Clopas being brothers, and Clopas having died, Joseph raised up seed to his dead brother, according to the Levirate law.

Simon? and are not his sisters here with us? And they were offended at him. But Jesus said unto them, A prophet is 4 not without honour, but in his own country, and among his own kin, and in his own house. And he could there do no 5 mighty work, save that he laid his hands upon a few sick folk, and healed *them*. And he marvelled because of their 6 unbelief. And he went round about the villages, teaching.

7—13. *Mission of the Twelve.*

And he called *unto him* the twelve, and began to send 7 them forth by two and two; and gave them power over unclean spirits; and commanded them that they should take 8 nothing for *their* journey, save a staff only; no scrip, no

4. *A prophet is not without honour*] He repeats to them once more almost the same proverb which He before uttered in their hearing and from the same place (Luke iv. 24).
5. *no mighty work*] Literally, **no power**. He performed some miracles, but not all He would have done, because of their deep-seated unbelief. His miraculous power was not magical. It was an influence which required and presupposed *faith*.
6. *he marvelled*] Our Lord does not marvel at other human things generally, but He does marvel on the one hand, at faith, when, as in the case of the centurion, it overcomes in its grandeur all human hindrances, and, on the other, at unbelief, when it can, in the face of numerous Divine manifestations, harden itself into a wilful rejection of Himself. He now seems to have left Nazareth never to return to it, or preach in its synagogue, or revisit the home, where He had so long toiled as the village Carpenter.

he went round about] On the evening of the day of His rejection at Nazareth, or more probably on the morrow, our Lord appears to have commenced a short circuit in Galilee, in the direction of Capernaum.

7—13. MISSION OF THE TWELVE.

7. *he called*] Rather, **He calleth unto Him.**

two and two] St Mark alone records this. They were sent forth probably in different directions on a tentative mission, to make trial of their powers, and fit them for a more extended mission afterwards. Their election had taken place in the solitude of a mountain range, their first mission occurred amidst the busy towns and villages of Galilee.

8. *and commanded them*] Now follows a brief summary of the charge, which the Lord proceeded to give them on this occasion, and which is recorded at far greater length by St Matthew, x. 5—42.

save a staff] They were to go forth with their staff as they had it at the time, but they were not (Matt. x. 10) to "*seek*," or "*procure one carefully*" for the purposes of this journey. The "staff" in Matt. x. 10, depends on "acquire not" or "provide not for yourselves" in verse 9.

9 bread, no money in *their* purse: but *be* shod with sandals;
10 and not put on two coats. And he said unto them, In what place soever ye enter into an house, there abide till ye depart
11 from that place. And whosoever shall not receive you, nor hear you, when ye depart thence, shake off the dust under

no scrip] Scrip, from Sw. skråppa, denotes a "wallet" or "small bag." Comp. 1 Sam. xvii. 40, "And (David) took his staff in his hand and chose him five smooth stones, and put them in a shepherd's bag which he had, even in a *scrip.*" It was so called, perhaps, because it was designed to hold scraps, trifling articles, scraped off as it were from something larger. It was part of the pilgrim's or traveller's equipage : comp. *Piers Ploughman's Vis.* 3573;

"I seigh nevere palmere
With pyk ne with *Scrippe,*'

and Shakespeare, *As you like it*, III. 2. 171,

"Though not with bag and baggage, yet with *scrip* and scrippage."

The scrip of the Galilean peasants was of leather, "the skins of kids stripped off whole, and tanned by a very simple process," used especially to carry their food on a journey, and slung over their shoulders (Thomson's *Land and the Book*, p. 355).

no money] "There was no departure from the simple manners of the country in this. At this day the farmer sets out on excursions, quite as extensive, without a *para* in his purse, and a modern Moslem prophet of Tarshîsha thus sends forth his apostles over this identical region. No traveller in the East would hesitate to throw himself on the hospitality of any villager." Thomson's *Land and Book*, p. 346.

9. *be shod with sandals*] That is, they were to take no other shoes with them for travelling "than their ordinary sandals of palm-bark." So now "the Galilean peasants wear a coarse shoe, answering to the sandal of the ancients, but never take two pair with them."

two coats] That is, they were not to take with them a change of raiment.

10. *there abide*] "When a stranger arrives in a village or an encampment, the neighbours, one after another, must invite him to eat with them. There is a strict etiquette about it, involving much ostentation and hypocrisy: and a failure in the due observance of this system of hospitality is violently resented, and often leads to alienation and feuds among neighbours. It also consumes much time, causes unusual distraction of mind, leads to levity, and everyway counteracts the success of a spiritual mission. The Evangelists...were sent, not to be honoured and feasted, but to call men to repentance, prepare the way of the Lord, and proclaim that the kingdom of heaven was at hand. They were, therefore, first to seek a becoming habitation to lodge in, and there abide until their work in that city was accomplished." *The Land and the Book*, p. 347.

11. *the dust under your feet*] For instances of the carrying out of this command, compare the conduct of St Paul at Antioch in Pisidia,

your feet for a testimony against them. Verily I say unto you, It shall be more tolerable for Sodom and Gomorrha in the day of judgment, than for that city. And they went out, 12 and preached that men should repent. And they cast out 13 many devils, and anointed with oil many that were sick, and healed *them*.

14—29. *The Murder of John the Baptist.*

And king Herod heard *of him;* (for his name was spread 14 abroad:) and he said, That John the Baptist was risen from the dead, and therefore mighty works do shew forth themselves in him. Others said, That it is Elias. And 15 others said, That it is a prophet, or as one of the prophets.

Acts xiii. 51, and at Corinth, Acts xviii. 6. The action must be regarded as symbolical of a complete cessation of all fellowship, and a renunciation of all further responsibility. It was customary with Pharisees when they entered Judæa from a Gentile land, to do this in token of renunciation of all communion with heathenism; those who rejected the Apostolic message were to be looked upon as those who placed themselves beyond the pale of fellowship and communion.

13. *anointed with oil*] St Mark alone mentions this anointing as the method, whereby the healing of the sick was effected. Though not expressly ordered, it was doubtless implied in the injunction to "heal the sick" (Matt. x. 8). The prophet Isaiah (i. 6) alludes to the use of oil for medicinal purposes, and we find this form of cure prescribed thirty years later than this Gospel, by St James in his general Epistle (v. 14). It was much used by the Jews for curative purposes, and thus supplied at once a fitting symbol and an efficient means in these miraculous cures wrought by the Apostles. For the use of the symbolical media by our Lord Himself comp. Mark viii. 23; John ix. 6.

14—29. THE MURDER OF JOHN THE BAPTIST.

14. *And king Herod heard of him*] This first missionary journey of the Apostles was but short, and they would seem to "have returned to Capernaum as early as the evening of the second day," Bp. Ellicott's *Gospel History*, p. 196. This Herod was Herod Antipas, to whom, on the death of Herod the Great, had fallen the tetrarchy of Ituræa and Peræa. He is here called "king," or "prince," in the ancient and wide sense of the word. St Matt. (xiv. 1), and St Luke (ix. 7), style him more exactly "the tetrarch."

his name] It is peculiar to St Mark that he connects the watching observation of Herod Antipas with the work of Christ as extended by the preaching and miracles of His Apostles.

was risen from the dead] Herod's guilty conscience triumphed over his Sadducean profession of belief that there is no resurrection. Comp. Matt. xvi. 6; Mark viii. 15.

16 But when Herod heard *thereof*, he said, It is John, whom I
17 beheaded: he is risen from the dead. For Herod himself
had sent forth and laid hold upon John, and bound him in
prison for Herodias' sake, his brother Philip's wife: for he
18 had married her. For John had said unto Herod, It is not
19 lawful for thee to have thy brother's wife. Therefore Herodias had a quarrel against him, and would have killed him;

16. *It is John*] The words in the original, according to the best MSS., are very striking. **John whom I** (=*I myself;* the pronoun "has the emphasis of a guilty conscience") **beheaded—this is he—he is risen.** Josephus confirms the account of these forebodings when he tells us that after the utter defeat of Herod Antipas by Aretas, the people regarded it as a righteous retribution for the murder of John (Jos. *Ant.* XVIII. 5. 1, 2).

17. *For Herod*] St Mark now proceeds more fully than the first Evangelist to relate the circumstances of the murder of the Baptist.

for Herodias' sake] During one of his journeys to Rome, Herod Antipas had fallen in with Herodias the wife of his brother Herod Philip, a son of Herod the Great and Mariamne, who was living there as a private person. Herodias was not only the sister-in-law, but the niece of Antipas, and already had a daughter who was grown up. Herod himself had long been married to the daughter of Aretas, Emîr of Arabia Petræa, but this did not prevent him from courting an adulterous alliance with Herodias, and she consented to become his wife, on condition that the daughter of the Arabian prince was divorced. But the latter, suspecting her husband's guilty passion, did not wait to be divorced, and indignantly fled to the castle of Machærus, and thence to her father's rocky fortress at Petra, who forthwith assembled an army to avenge her wrongs, and defeated Herod in a decisive battle (Jos. *Ant.* v. 1).

18. *For John had said*] Herod was probably on his way to meet his father-in-law, when he first encountered the Baptist, who, in the presence of the Galilean king, proved himself no "reed shaken by the wind" (Luke vii. 24), but boldly denounced the royal crimes (Luke iii. 19), and declared the marriage unlawful. For this outspoken faithfulness he was flung into prison, probably in the castle of Machærus or "the Black Fortress," which Herod's father had built in one of the most abrupt wâdys to the east of the Dead Sea, to overawe the wild Arab tribes of the neighbourhood. Though originally in the possession of Aretas, Herod had probably seized the fortress after the departure of his first wife to her father's stronghold at Petra (Jos. *Ant.* XVIII. 5. 2).

19. *had a quarrel*] or as it is rendered in the margin, "*had an inward grudge*" against him. The word here translated "had a quarrel" occurs in Luke xi. 53, where we have rendered it, "and the Pharisees began to *urge Him vehemently*," and in Gen. xlix. 23, where the dying Jacob says of Joseph, "The archers sorely grieved him, and shot at him, and *hated* him." It denotes literally (1) to "hold" or "keep fast within one;" then (2) to "lay up" or "cherish

but she could not: for Herod feared John, knowing that he 20
was a just man and an holy, and observed him; and when
he heard him, he did many things, and heard him gladly.
And when a convenient day was come, that Herod on his 21
birthday made a supper to his lords, high captains, and chief
estates of Galilee; and when the daughter of the said Hero- 22
dias came in, and danced, and pleased Herod and them

wrath" against another. Comp. Herod. I. 118, VI. 119. In Tyndale
and Cranmer's Versions it is rendered "laid waite for him," in the
Rhemish, "sought all occasion against him."

would have killed] The word in the original is much stronger, and
denotes that she **had a settled wish** to kill him. Some Versions read
"*she sought*" or "*kept seeking*" means to kill him.

20. *observed him*] Rather, as in the margin, **kept him**, i.e. **kept
him safe** from her machinations. The original word occurs in Matt.
ix. 17, and Luke v. 38, "they put new wine into new bottles, and both
are preserved."

when he heard him] The Greek here is still more emphatic; "and
when he heard him, he **used to do many things**, and **used to
listen to him gladly**." Not once or twice but many times Herod
sent for his lonely prisoner, even as Felix sent for St Paul (Acts xxiv.
26), and listened to him as he reasoned with him of righteousness,
temperance, and judgment to come, and not only listened, but *listened
gladly*; nay more, he "did many things;" many things, but not "*the
thing*." He would not put away his unlawful wife.

21. *a convenient day*] i.e. a suitable day for her fell designs.

on his birthday] In imitation of the Roman emperors, the Herodian
princes kept their birthdays with feasting and revelry and magnificent
banquets. Wieseler, however, considers the word denotes a feast cele-
brating Herod's accession, but this is more than doubtful. Birthday
festivals were one sample of foreign habits introduced into Palestine
and spread there by the Herodians.

made a supper] probably at Machærus or some neighbouring palace.

lords, high captains] or "*chiliarchs*." The words here used denote
servants of the state, civil and military.

chief estates] This term denotes men of high rank, and includes the
Galilæan nobles generally. Comp. Fuller *Ch. Hist.* v. iii. 28, "God
never gave grace nor knowledge of Holy Scripture to any *great estate*
or rich man." State is also employed in the same way. Thus Adams
says (Nichol's *Puritan Divines*), "Sin deals with her guests as that
bloody prince that, having invited many great *states* to a solemn feast."

22. *the daughter of...Herodias*] Her name was Salome, and she
afterwards married (1) Philip the tetrarch of Trachonitis, her paternal
uncle, and (2) Aristobulus, the king of Chalcis. "A luxurious feast of
the period was not regarded as complete unless it closed with some
gross pantomimic representation; and doubtless Herod had adopted
the evil fashion of his day. But he had not anticipated for his guests
the rare luxury of seeing a princess—his own niece, a granddaughter of

that sat with him, the king said unto the damsel, Ask of me
23 whatsoever thou wilt, and I will give *it* thee. And he sware
unto her, Whatsoever thou shalt ask of me, I will give *it*
24 thee, unto the half of my kingdom. And she went forth,
and said unto her mother, What shall I ask? And she said,
25 The head of John the Baptist. And she came in straightway
with haste unto the king, and asked, saying, I will that thou
give me by and by in a charger the head of John the Bap-
26 tist. And the king was exceeding sorry; *yet* for his oath's

Herod the Great and of Mariamne, a descendant, therefore, of Simon the High Priest, and the great line of Maccabæan princes—a princess, who afterwards became the wife of a tetrarch, and the mother of a king—honouring them by degrading herself into a scenic dancer." Farrar's *Life of Christ*, I. 391.

23. *unto the half of my kingdom*] Compare the words of Ahasuerus (i.e. Xerxes) to Esther: "What is thy petition, queen Esther? and it shall be granted thee : and what is thy request? and it shall be performed, *even to the half of the kingdom*" (Esther v. 3, vii. 2).

'**24.** *The head of John the Baptist*] Herodias saw that her hour was come. No jewelled trinket, no royal palace, no splendid robe, should be the reward of her daughter's feat—"Ask," said she, "for the head of John the Baptizer."

25. *straightway with haste*] Observe the ready alacrity, with which she proved herself a true daughter of her mother.

by and by] i.e. "*immediately.*" Comp. Matt. xiii. 21, "when tribulation or persecution ariseth because of the word, *by and by* he is offended;" Luke xvii. 7, "which of you, having a servant plowing or feeding cattle, will say unto him *by and by?*" xxi. 9, "but the end is not *by and by.*" In all these instances the expression has its old meaning of "at once," "immediately." Thus Edward IV. is reported to have said on his death-bed, "I wote not whether any prechers' woordes ought more to moue you than I that is goyng *by and by* to the place that they all preche of," Hall, Ed. v. fol. 116; "Men dare not give the name of emperor to any other, for he punisheth his offender and traitor *by and by;* but they dare give the name of God to others, because He for repentance suffereth the offenders ;" Homily *Against Idolatry*, pt. iii.

a charger] = "*a large dish*," or "*platter.*" This word only occurs here and in the parallel, Matt. xiv. 8. It comes from the Fr. *charger* and O. E. *charge*="to load;" hence it means "that on which anything is laid, a dish," as the Hebrew word thus rendered (Num. vii. 13, &c.) is elsewhere given (Exod. xxv. 29). Thus Fuller says of Oswald, king of Northumberland, when he was told that a number of poor people were at his gate, that he commanded "not onely that the meat set before him should be given them, but also that the large *Silver-Charger* holding the same should be broken in pieces and (in want, perchance, of present coin) parted betwixt them :" *Ch. Hist.* II. ii. 76.

26. *exceeding sorry*] The Greek word thus translated is very

sake, and for their sakes which sat with him, he would not reject her. And immediately the king sent an executioner, 27 and commanded his head to be brought: and he went and beheaded him in the prison, and brought his head in a 28 charger, and gave it to the damsel: and the damsel gave it to her mother. And when his disciples heard *of it*, they 29 came and took up his corpse, and laid it in a tomb.

30—44. *Return of the Twelve. Feeding of the Five Thousand.*

And the apostles gathered themselves together unto Jesus, 30 and told him all things, both what they had done, and what they had taught. And he said unto them, Come ye your- 31 selves apart into a desert place, and rest a while: for there were many coming and going, and they had no leisure so much as to eat. And they departed into a desert place by 32

strong, and denotes very great grief and sorrow. It is used of (1) the rich young ruler, "when he heard this, he was *very sorrowful*," Luke xviii. 23; (2) of our Lord Himself in the Garden of Gethsemane, "My soul is *exceeding sorrowful*, even unto death," Matt. xxvi. 38; Mark xiv. 34.

27. *an executioner*] Literally, **a soldier of the guard.** The word *Speculator* denotes (1) *a looker-out, spy, scout;* (2) *a special adjutant, soldier of the guard.* These scouts formed a special division in each legion; but under the emperors a body bearing this name was specially appointed to guard the emperor and execute his commands (Tac. *Hist.* I. 24, 25; II. 11; Suet. *Claud.* xxxv.). Hence they were often employed as special messengers in seeking out those who were proscribed or sentenced to death (Seneca, *de Ira* I. 16). In the earlier English Versions the word is rendered "hangman," but this term describes a mere accident of his office. The use of a military term, compared with Luke iii. 14, is in accordance with the fact that Herod was at this time making war on Aretas (Jos. *Antiq.* XVIII. 5. 1).

29. *laid it in a tomb*] and then "*went and told Jesus*" (Matt. xiv. 12) of the death of His great Forerunner, over whom He had pronounced so remarkable a eulogy (Luke vii. 27, 28).

30—44. RETURN OF THE TWELVE. FEEDING OF THE FIVE
THOUSAND.

30. *gathered themselves together*] Their brief tentative mission was now over, and they returned to Capernaum.

31. *there were many coming and going*] The Passover was now nigh at hand (John vi. 4) and the pilgrim companies would be on the move towards the Holy City.

32. *they departed into a desert place*] They crossed the Lake of Gennesaret (John vi. 1) and proceeded in the direction of Bethsaida-Julias, at its north-eastern corner (Luke ix. 10), just above the entrance

33 ship privately. And the people saw them departing, and many knew him, and ran afoot thither out of all cities, and outwent 34 them, and came together unto him. And Jesus, when he came out, saw much people, and was moved with compassion toward them, because they were as sheep not having a 35 shepherd, and he began to teach them many things. And when the day was now far spent, his disciples came unto him, and said, This is a desert place, and now the time 36 *is* far passed: send them away, that they may go into the country round about, and into the villages, and buy them-37 selves bread: for they have nothing to eat. He answered and said unto them, Give ye them to eat. And they say unto him, Shall we go and buy two hundred pennyworth of

of the Jordan into it. Bethsaida-Julias was originally only a village, but was rebuilt and enlarged by Herod Philip not long after the birth of Christ. He raised it to the dignity of a town, and called it *Julias* after Julia the daughter of Augustus. Philip occasionally resided there, and there died and was buried in a costly tomb (Jos. *Antiq.* XVIII. 4. 6). To the south of it was the green and narrow plain of *El-Batîhah*, "with abundant grass, and abundant space for the multitudes to have sat down" (Tristram's *Land of Israel*, p. 439).

33. *ran afoot*] The multitudes saw the vessel start from Capernaum, and quickly ran along the coast and round the northern extremity of the Lake, where they met the little company disembarking on the shore. The motive of their coming in such large numbers is stated by St John, vi. 2.

34. *he came out*] Comparing the account in the Fourth Gospel, we may conjecture that on landing the Lord and His disciples ascended the hill-side (John vi. 3) and there waited awhile till the whole multitude was assembled. Then descending, He saw them all, and moved with compassion began to "*teach them many things concerning the kingdom of God*" (Luke ix. 11), and healed them that had need of healing.

35. *a desert place*] The locality was probably part of the rich but uninhabited plain at the mouth of the Jordan.

36. *send them away*] Already earlier in the day the Lord had asked the Apostle Philip, *Whence shall we buy bread that these may eat?* and he, thinking of no other supplies save such as natural means could procure, had replied that *two hundred pence* would not suffice to provide sustenance for such a number (John vi. 5—7). Then He left this confession of inability to work in their minds, and it was now in the eventide that the Apostles came to Him with the proposition contained in this verse.

37. *Shall we go and buy*] With one mouth they seem to have reiterated what St Philip had said earlier in the day.

two hundred pennyworth] The specifying of this sum is peculiar to St Mark and St John. The word translated *penny* is the **denarius**, a

bread, and give them to eat? He saith unto them, How 38
many loaves have ye? go and see. And when they knew,
they say, Five, and two fishes. And he commanded them 39
to make all sit down by companies upon the green grass.
And they sat down in ranks, by hundreds, and by fifties. 40
And when he had taken the five loaves and the two fishes, 41
he looked up to heaven, and blessed, and brake the loaves,

silver coin of the value originally of 10 and afterwards of 16 ases. The
denarius was first coined in B.C. 269, or 4 years before the first Punic
war, and originally was of the value of 8½d. of our money, later it
= 7½d. It was the day-wages of a labourer in Palestine (Matt. xx.
2, 9, 13). "It so happens that in almost every case where the word
denarius occurs in the N. T. it is connected with the idea of a liberal
or large amount; and yet in these passages the English rendering
names a sum which is absurdly small." Prof. Lightfoot on *the Revision
of the N. T.* p. 166.

38. *go and see*] In the interval between their going and return
they learnt that a lad in their company had *five barley loaves, and two
small fishes*, which they could secure for purchase. They were only
barley loaves (John vi. 9), the food even then, for the most part, of
beasts, or of the poor and the unfortunate. Comp. 2 Kings vii. 1. The
fact has an important bearing on Judges vii. 13.

39. *by companies*] Literally, **drinking parties**. The word alludes to an
orderly social grouping, *catervatim*. The words are repeated by a
Hebraism in the original, like the "two and two" of ver. 7.

upon the green grass] St Mark alone mentions *the green grass*, "still
fresh in the spring of the year, before it had faded away in the summer
sun." It was the season of the Passover, corresponding to our March
or April, hence there was *"much grass in the place;"* comp. John vi. 10.

40. *in ranks*] Literally, **they reclined in parterres** (*areolatim*).
"As they sat in these orderly groups upon the grass, the gay red and
blue and yellow colours of the clothing, which the poorest Orientals
wear, called up in the imagination of St Peter a multitude of flower-
beds in some well-cultivated garden." Farrar's *Life of Christ*, p. 402.
"Our English '*in ranks*' does not reproduce the picture to the eye,
giving rather the notion of continuous lines. Wyclif was better, 'by
parties;' perhaps *in groups* would be as near as we could get to it in
English." Trench, *Miracles*, p. 265. St Mark here, as elsewhere,
doubtless reproduces the description of the scene by St Peter.

by hundreds, and by fifties] " Two long rows of 100, a shorter one of
50 persons. The fourth side remained, after the manner of the tables
of the ancients, empty and open." Gerlach.

41. *and blessed*] The words, though not given, were probably those of
the ordinary grace before meat in use in Israel. "He gives thanks to
God, as the father surrounded by his household was on the occasion of
the Passover wont to do, for His natural gifts and covenant blessings.
This action is made almost equally prominent in each of the four Narra-

and gave *them* to his disciples to set before them; and the
42 two fishes divided he among them all. And they did all eat,
43 and were filled. And they took up twelve baskets full of the
44 fragments, and of the fishes. And they that did eat of the
loaves were about five thousand men.

45—52. *The Walking on the Lake.*

45 And straightway he constrained his disciples to get into the
ship, and to go to the other side before unto Bethsaida, while
46 he sent away the people. And when he had sent them away,
47 he departed into a mountain to pray. And when even was
come, the ship was in the midst of the sea, and he alone on

tives, and after the thanksgiving, He distributed the food, as the father
was accustomed to do at the Paschal meal." See note on xiv. 16.

and brake the loaves, and gave them to his disciples] The first of
these words denotes an *instantaneous*, the second a *continuous* act.
The multiplication of the loaves and fishes had a beginning and went
on in the hands of Christ between the acts of breaking and distributing
the bread. Comp. 2 Kings iv. 42—44.

43. *they took up*] in obedience to our Lord's command (John vi. 12),
Who would teach them that wastefulness even of miraculous power was
wholly alien to the Divine economy.

baskets] "tuelue coffyns full," Wyclif. All the Evangelists alike
here use *cophinoi* for the small common *wicker-baskets*, in which these
fragments were collected, at the feeding of the Five Thousand, and
the word *spurides*, or large *rope-baskets*, when they describe the feeding
of the Four Thousand. These wicker baskets were the common possession of the Jews, in which to carry their food in order to avoid
pollution with heathens; "Judaeis, quorum *cophinus* foenumque supel-
lex," Juv. *Sat.* III. 14. The same distinction is made by our Lord when
He alludes to both miracles (Mark viii. 19, 20; Matt. xvi. 9, 10).

44. *five thousand men*] besides *women and children* (Matt. xiv. 21),
who would not sit down with the men, but sit or stand apart.

45—52. THE WALKING ON THE LAKE.

45. *And straightway*] The impression made upon the people by
the miracle just narrated was profound. It was the popular expectation
that the Messiah would repeat the miracles of Moses, and this "bread
of wonder," of which they had just partaken, recalled to the minds of
the multitudes the manna, which the Great Lawgiver had given to their
forefathers. They were convinced, therefore, that the Saviour was
none other than "the Prophet," of whom Moses had spoken, and in this
conviction they would have *taken Him by force and made Him a king*
(John vi. 14, 15). To defeat this intention the Saviour bade His Apostles take ship and cross over to the other side of the Lake.

unto Bethsaida] i. e. the *western* Bethsaida, the town of Philip, Andrew, and Peter, in the neighbourhood of Capernaum (John vi. 17).

the land. And he saw them toiling in rowing; for the wind 48 was contrary unto them: and about the fourth watch of the night he cometh unto them, walking upon the sea, and would have passed by them. But when they saw him walking upon 49 the sea, they supposed it had been a spirit, and cried out: for they all saw him, and were troubled. And immediately 50 he talked with them, and saith unto them, Be of good cheer: it is I; be not afraid. And he went up unto them into the 51 ship; and the wind ceased: and they were sore amazed in

47. *in the midst of the sea*] With all their efforts and the toil of the entire night they had not in consequence of contrary winds (John vi. 18) accomplished more than *five and twenty or thirty furlongs*, i. e. scarcely more than half of their way, the Lake being forty or forty-five furlongs in breadth, when one of the sudden storms, to which the Lake is subject, rushed down from the western mountains. See above, iv. 37.

48. *he saw them toiling in rowing*] The word translated "toiling," which also occurs in Matt. xiv. 24, is a very striking expression. It denotes (1) *to test metals with the touchstone*, (2) *to rack, torture*, (3) *to torment* as in Matt. viii. 29, "art Thou come to *torment* us before the time?", and Matt. viii. 6, "Lord, my servant lieth at home sick of the palsy, grievously *tormented*." Here it seems to imply that they were *tortured, baffled*, by the waves, which were boisterous by reason of the strong wind that blew (John vi. 18). Wyclif translates it "*travailing in rowing;*" Tyndale and Cranmer, "*troubled in rowing.*"

the fourth watch] The proper Jewish reckoning recognised only three watches or periods, for which sentinels or pickets remained on duty. They were entitled (1) *the first, or beginning of the watches*, from sunset to 10 p.m. (Lam. ii. 19), (2) *the middle watch*, from 10 p.m. to 2 a.m. (Judg. vii. 19), and (3) *the morning watch*, from 2 a.m. to sunrise (Ex. xiv. 24; 1 Sam. xi. 11). After the Roman supremacy the number of watches was increased to *four*, sometimes described by their numerical order, as here and in Matt. xiv. 25; sometimes by the terms (1) *even*, closing at 9 p.m.; *midnight; cock-crowing*, at 3 a.m.; *morning*, at 6 a.m.

would have passed by them] He came quite near their vessel on the storm-tost waves, and seemed to wish to lead the way before them to the western shore. Comp. Luke xxiv. 28, 29.

49. *a spirit*] An unsubstantial appearance. So they thought on the evening of the world's first Easter Day, when they saw Him after His resurrection. See Luke xxiv. 36, 37. Wyclif translates it "they gessiden him for to be a fantum;" Tyndale and Cranmer "a sprete;" the Rhemish "a ghost."

50. *be not afraid*] St Mark does not record St Peter's attempt to go to his Lord upon the Lake, which is narrated only by St Matthew, xiv. 28—30.

51. *they were sore amazed*] Observe the strong expressions here employed. Not only were they "sore amazed," but "beyond measure."

52 themselves beyond measure, and wondered. For they considered not *the miracle* of the loaves: for their heart was hardened.

53—56. *Miracles of Healing in the Land of Gennesaret.*

53 And when they had passed over, they came into the
54 land of Gennesaret, and drew to the shore. And when they were come out of the ship, straightway they knew him,
55 and ran through that whole region round about, and began to carry about in beds those that were sick, where they heard
56 he was. And whithersoever he entered, into villages, or cities, or country, they laid the sick in the streets, and besought him that they might touch if it were but the border of his garment: and as many as touched him were made whole.

Never had the disciples been so impressed by the majesty of Christ as they were now in consequence of this miracle. St Matthew, xiv. 33, tells us that the impression made extended also to those who were with them in the ship, i.e. probably the crew. Not only did they approach Him with an outward unforbidden gesture of worship, "but they avowed for the first time collectively, what one of them had long since separately declared Him to be, *the Son of God*" (Matt. xiv. 33; comp. John i. 49), Bp. Ellicott's *Lectures*, p. 211.

52. *hardened*] See note above, iii. 5.

53—56. MIRACLES OF HEALING IN THE LAND OF GENNESARET.

53. *the land of Gennesaret* is only mentioned here and in Matt. xiv. 34. It is the same as the modern *el-Ghuweir*, a fertile crescent-shaped plain, on the north-western shore of the Lake of Gennesaret, about 3 miles in length and 1 in width. From its sheltered situation, and especially from its depression of more than 500 feet below the level of the ocean, its climate is of an almost tropical character. Josephus speaks of it as if it were an earthly paradise, in which every kind of useful plant grew and flourished. Jos. *B. J.* III. 10. 8.

drew to the shore] or, as Tyndale and Cranmer translate it, "drew up into the haven."

54. *they knew him*] The dawn had now broken, and the people on shore at once recognised the Great Healer, and craved His help in behalf of their sick and afflicted.

55. *but the border of his garment*] The numbers that pressed upon Him seemed almost too large for Him to be able to heal them singly by laying His hands upon them, therefore many begged that they might be allowed to touch *if it were but the border of His garment*. Comp. above, v. 27. Soon after followed the ever memorable discourse so strikingly in accordance with the present Passover-season in the synagogue of Capernaum respecting "*the Bread of Life*" (John vi. 22—65).

1—23. *Contest with the Pharisees of Jerusalem concerning Traditions of Eating.*

Then came together unto him the Pharisees, and certain 1 of the scribes, which came from Jerusalem. And when they 2 saw some of his disciples eat bread with defiled, that is to say, with unwashen, hands, they found fault. For the 3 Pharisees, and all the Jews, except they wash *their* hands oft, eat not, holding the tradition of the elders. And *when they* 4

CH. VII. 1—23. CONTEST WITH THE PHARISEES OF JERUSALEM CONCERNING TRADITIONS OF EATING.

1. *Then came together*] A few days only were assigned to the performance of those deeds of mercy described at the close of the last chapter. But the Saviour's labours of love were soon rudely interrupted. Having kept the Feast at Jerusalem the Scribes and Pharisees returned to seek out matter for accusation against Him. The combination of the Pharisees of Galilee and the Pharisees of Judæa had already been concerted and entered upon, and they now watched His every step.

2. *with defiled, that is to say, with unwashen, hands*] Thus St Mark explains for his Roman readers, and then proceeds more fully to set forth certain Jewish usages. The Pharisees had probably crept in secretly into some of the social gatherings of the disciples.

3. *except they wash their hands oft*] *Oft*, literally, **with the fist.** "When they washed their hands, they washed *the fist unto the jointing of the arm*. The hands are polluted, and made clean *unto the jointing of the arm*." Lightfoot *Hor. Heb. upon St Mark*. When water was poured on the hands, they had to be lifted, yet so that the water should neither run up above the wrist, nor back again upon the hand; best, therefore, by doubling the fingers into a fist. The Israelites, who, like other Oriental nations, fed with their fingers, washed their hands before meals, for the sake of cleanliness. But these customary washings were distinct from the ceremonial ablutions; in the former water was *poured upon the hands;* in the latter the hands were *plunged in water*. When, therefore, some of the Pharisees remarked that our Lord's disciples ate with "*unwashen hands*," it is not to be understood literally that they did not at all wash their hands, but that they did not *wash them ceremonially* according to their own practice. And this was expected of them only as the disciples of a religious teacher; for these refinements were not practised by the class of people from which the disciples were chiefly drawn.

eat not] "The Jews of later times related with intense admiration how the Rabbi Akiba, when imprisoned and furnished with only sufficient water to maintain life, preferred to die of starvation rather than eat without the proper washings." Buxtorf, *Syn. Jud.;* quoted in Farrar's *Life of Christ*, I. p. 443; Geikie, II. 203—205.

the tradition of the elders] The Rabbinical rules about ablutions occupy a large portion of one section of the Talmud.

come from the market, except they wash, they eat not. And many other things there be, which they have received to hold, *as* the washing of cups, and pots, brasen vessels, and 5 of tables. Then the Pharisees and scribes asked him, Why walk not thy disciples according to the tradition of the elders, 6 but eat bread with unwashen hands? He answered and said unto them, Well hath Esaias prophesied of you hypocrites, as it is written, This people honoureth me with *their* lips, 7 but their heart is far from me. Howbeit in vain do they worship me, teaching *for* doctrines the commandments of 8 men. For laying aside the commandment of God, ye hold the tradition of men, *as* the washing of pots and cups: and 9 many other such like things ye do. And he said unto them, Full well ye reject the commandment of God, that ye may 10 keep your own tradition. For Moses said, Honour thy father and thy mother; and, Whoso curseth father or mo-11 ther, let him die the death: but ye say, If a man shall say to his father or mother, *It is* Corban, that is to say, a gift,

4. *except they wash*] "Wash" here implies complete immersion as contrasted with the mere washing of the hands in verse 3.

pots] The original word thus translated is one of St Mark's Latinisms. It is a corruption of the Latin *sextarius*, a Roman measure both for liquids and dry things. In Tyndale and Cranmer's Versions it is translated "*cruses.*" Earthen vessels were broken; those of metal and wood scoured and rinsed with water. See Levit. xv. 12.

tables] Rather, **banqueting-couches**, *triclinia*, the benches or couches on which the Jews reclined at meals.

6. *Well hath Esaias*] Rather, **Well**, or **full well did Esaias prophesy of you.** "*Well*" is said in irony. This expression recurs in *v.* 9, "full well ye reject" = "*finely* do ye set at naught and obliterate."

This people honoureth me] The words are found in Isaiah xxix. 13.

10. *Honour thy father*] The words are quoted partly from Ex. xx. 12, and partly from Ex. xxi. 17.

11. *If a man shall say*] Literally it runs, **If a man shall say to his father or his mother, That, from which thou mightest have been benefited by me, is Corban**, *that is to say, a gift*, or offering consecrated to God, **he shall be free, and ye suffer him no longer to do aught for his father or his mother.** A person had merely to pronounce the word *Corban* over any possession or property, and it was irrevocably dedicated to the Temple. Our Lord is quoting a regular formula, which often occurs in the Talmudic tracts *Nedarim* and *Nazir*. Others would give to the words an imperative force, **Be it Corban from which thou mightest have been benefited by me**, i.e. "If I give thee anything or do anything for thee, may it be as though I gave thee that which is devoted to God, and may I be accounted perjured and

by whatsoever thou mightest be profited by me; *he shall be free.* And ye suffer him no more to do ought for his father ₁₂ or his mother; making the word of God of none effect ₁₃ through your tradition, which ye have delivered: and many such like things do ye. And when he had called all the ₁₄ people *unto him*, he said unto them, Hearken unto me every one *of you*, and understand: there is nothing from without a ₁₅ man, that entering into him can defile him: but the things which come out of him, those are they that defile the man. If any man have ears to hear, let him hear. And when he ₁₆ was entered into the house from the people, his disciples ₁₇ asked him concerning the parable. And he saith unto them, ₁₈ Are ye so without understanding also? Do ye not perceive, that whatsoever thing from without entereth into the man, *it* cannot defile him; because it entereth not into his heart, ₁₉ but into the belly, and goeth out into the draught, purging

sacrilegious." This view certainly gives greater force to the charge made by our Lord, that the command "Whoso curseth father or mother, let him die the death" was nullified by the tradition.

13. *through your tradition*] The Jews distinguished between the "Written Law" and the traditional or "Unwritten Law." The Unwritten Law was said to have been orally delivered by God to Moses, and by him orally transmitted to the Elders. On it was founded the Talmud or "doctrine," which consists of (1) the *Mishna* or "repetition" of the Law, (2) the *Gemara* or "supplement" to it. So extravagant did the veneration for the Traditional Law become, that there was amongst many other sayings this assertion, "The Law is like salt, the Mishna like pepper, the Gemara like balmy spice." Buxtorf, *Synag. Jud.* ch. iii.

14. *all the people*] Rather, **when He had called the people again unto Him.** As Wyclif has it in his Version, "and he eftsone clepinge to þe cumpanye of peple."

17. *his disciples*] From St Matthew we learn that the questioner was St Peter (Matt. xv. 15). As in the walking on the water, so here, he modestly suppresses himself in the Gospel which was written under his eye.

the parable] They regarded the words uttered in the hearing of the mixed multitude, and which deeply offended the Pharisees (Matt. xv. 12), as a parable, or "dark saying." See note above, iv. 2.

19. *into the draught*] Comp. 2 Kings x. 27, "And they......brake down the house of Baal, and made it a *draughthouse* unto this day." Draught = *latrina*, *cloaca*, from Icel. *draf*, dregs, dirt, connected with A.S. *drabbe*, *dréfe*. Comp. Shakespeare, *Tim. of Ath.* v. 1. 105, "Hang them, or stab them, drown them in a *draught*." "There was a godde of idlenesse, a goddesse of the *draught* or jakes." Burton, *Anat. of Mel.*

20 all meats? And he said, That which cometh out of the 21 man, that defileth the man. For from within, out of the heart of men, proceed evil thoughts, adulteries, fornications, 22 murders, thefts, covetousness, wickedness, deceit, lascivious- 23 ness, an evil eye, blasphemy, pride, foolishness: all these evil things come from within, and defile the man.

21. *evil thoughts*] Thirteen forms of evil are here noticed as proceeding from the heart. The first seven in the plural number, are *predominant actions*; the latter six in the singular, *dispositions*. Comp. the blending of the singular and plural in St Paul's enumeration of the works of the flesh, Gal. v. 19—21.

adulteries] The preferable order appears to be *fornications, thefts, murders, adulteries, covetousnesses, wickednesses*.

22. *covetousness*] "avarises," Wyclif. The original word denotes more than the mere *love of money*, it is "the drawing and snatching to himself, on the sinner's part, of the creature in every form and kind, as it lies out of and beyond himself." Hence we find it joined not only with "thefts" here and with "extortion" in 1 Cor. v. 10, but also with sins of the flesh as in 1 Cor v. 11; Eph. v. 3, 5; Col. iii. 5. "Impurity and covetousness may be said to divide between them nearly the whole domain of human selfishness and vice." "Homo extra Deum quaerit pabulum in creatura materiali vel per voluptatem vel per avaritiam." See Canon Lightfoot on Col. iii. 5.

wickedness] or *wickednesses*. The word thus translated occurs in the singular in Matt. xxii. 18, "but Jesus perceived their *wickedness*," and again in Luke xi. 39; Rom. i. 29; 1 Cor. v. 8; Eph. vi. 12. In the plural it only occurs twice, here and in Acts iii. 26, where we have translated it "iniquities." It denotes the active working of evil, "the cupiditas nocendi," or as Jeremy Taylor explains it, an "aptness to do shrewd turns, to delight in mischief and trajedies; a love to trouble our neighbour and to do him ill offices; crossness, perverseness, and peevishness of action in our intercourse." Trench's *N. T. Synonyms*, p. 36.

lasciviousness] The word thus rendered is of uncertain etymology, and in our Version is translated generally "*lasciviousness*," as here and 2 Cor. xii. 21; Gal. v. 19; Eph. iv. 19; 1 Pet. iv. 3; sometimes (2) "*wantonness*," as in Rom. xiii. 13; 2 Pet. ii. 18. The Vulgate renders it now "impudicitia," now "lascivia." "Wantonness" is the better rendering. In Classical Greek it signifies "lawless insolence" or "boisterous violence" towards another; in later Greek "sensuality."

an evil eye, blasphemy] Of these the first denotes *concealed*, the second *open* enmity. The *evil eye* is notorious in the East; here it is the description of an envious look; "invidia et de malis alienis gaudium." Bengel.

pride] The substantive thus translated only occurs here in the N. T., its adjective occurs in Luke i. 51, "He hath scattered *the proud* in the imagination of their hearts;" Rom. i. 30, "*proud*, boasters;" 2 Tim. iii. 2, "*proud*, blasphemers;" James iv. 6, 1 Pet. v 5, "God

24—30. *The Syrophœnician Woman.*

And from thence he arose, and went into the borders of 24
Tyre and Sidon, and entered into an house, and would have

resisteth the *proud.*" The true seat of this sin, the German "*Hochmuth,*" is within, and consists in comparing oneself secretly *with* others, and lifting oneself *above* others, in being proud *in thought.*

foolishness] only occurs here in the Gospels, and three times in the Epistles of St Paul, 2 Cor. xi. 1, 17, 21. "Causa cur insipientia extremo loco ponatur: quae etiam reliqua omnia facit incurabiliora. Non in sola voluntate est corruptio humana." Bengel.

24—30. THE SYROPHŒNICIAN WOMAN.

24. *from thence he arose*] The malevolence of our Lord's enemies was now assuming hourly a more implacable form. The Pharisaic party in Eastern Galilee were deeply offended (Matt. xv. 12); even those who once would fain have prevented Him from leaving them (Luke iv. 42) were filled with doubts and suspicions; Herod Antipas was inquiring concerning Him (Luke ix. 9), and his inquiries boded nothing but ill. He therefore now leaves for awhile eastern Galilee and makes His way north-west through the mountains of upper Galilee into the border-land of Phœnicia. See the Analysis of the Gospel, p. 22.

the borders of Tyre and Sidon] His travelling towards these regions was the prophetic and symbolical representation of the future progress of Christianity from the Jews to the Gentiles. So in ancient times Elijah travelled out of his own land into Phœnicia (1 Kings xvii. 10—24). Our Lord, however, does not actually go into Phœnicia, but into the adjoining borders of Galilee, the district of the tribe of Asher.

Tyre] A celebrated commercial city of antiquity, situated in Phœnicia. The Hebrew name "Tzôr" signifies "a rock," and well agrees with the site of *Sû,* the modern town on a rocky peninsula, which was formerly an island, and less than 20 miles distant from Sidon. We first get glimpses of its condition in 2 Sam. v. 11 in connection with Hiram, King of Tyre, who sent cedar-wood and workmen to David and afterwards to Solomon (1 Kings ix. 11—14, x. 22). Ahab married a daughter of Ithobal, King of Tyre (1 Kings xvi. 31), and was instrumental in introducing the idolatrous worship of Baalim and Ashtaroth. The prosperity of Tyre in the time of our Lord was very great. Strabo gives an account of it at this period, and speaks of the great wealth which it derived from the dyes of the celebrated Tyrian purple. It was perhaps more populous even than Jerusalem.

Sidon] The Greek form of the Phœnician name *Zidon,* an ancient and wealthy city of Phœnicia, situated on the narrow plain between the Lebanon and the Sea. Its Hebrew name *Tsidôn* signifies "Fishing" or "Fishery." Its modern name is *Saida.* It is mentioned in the Old Testament as early as Gen. x. 19; Josh. xi. 8; Judg. i. 31, and in ancient times was more influential even than Tyre, though from the time of Solomon it appears to have been subordinate to it.

25 no man know *it;* but he could not be hid. For a *certain* woman, whose young daughter had an unclean spirit, heard 26 of him, and came and fell at his feet: the woman was a Greek, a Syrophenician by nation; and she besought him 27 that he would cast forth the devil out of her daughter. But Jesus said unto her, Let the children first be filled: for it is not meet to take the children's bread, and to cast *it* unto the 28 dogs. And she answered and said unto him, Yes, Lord: yet the dogs under the table eat of the children's crumbs.

would have no man know it] desiring seclusion and rest after His late labours.

25. *heard of him*] The fame of His miracles had already penetrated even to these old Phœnician cities, and we have seen (Mark iii. 8) "a great multitude" from Tyre and Sidon coming to Him (comp. also Matt. iv. 24).

26. *a Greek*] St Matthew describes her as a *"woman of Canaan"* (Matt. xv. 22), St Mark calls her *a Greek, a Syrophœnician.* The first term describes her religion, that she was a Gentile; the second the stock of which she came, "which was even that accursed stock once doomed of God to total excision, but of which some branches had been spared by those first generations of Israel that should have extirpated them root and branch. Everything, therefore, was against this woman, yet she was not hindered by that everything from drawing nigh, and craving the boon that her soul longed after." Trench *on the Parables,* p. 339. She is called a **Syro***phœnician,* as distinguished from the **Liby-***phœnicians,* the Phœnicians of Africa, that is, Carthage. Phœnicia belonged at this time to the province of Syria.

27. *But Jesus said unto her*] St Mark passes more briefly over the interview than St Matthew. The latter Evangelist points out three stages of this woman's trial; (i) Silence; *"He answered her not a word"* (Matt. xv. 23); (ii) Refusal; *"I am not sent but unto the lost sheep of the house of Israel"* (Matt. xv. 24); (iii) Reproach; *"It is not meet to take the children's bread and cast it to the dogs"* (Matt. xv. 26). But in spite of all she persevered and finally conquered.

the dogs] In the original the diminutive is used = *"little dogs."* "Little whelps" Wyclif; "the whelps" Tyndale, Cranmer. The Jews, *"the children of the kingdom"* (Matt. viii. 12), were wont to designate the heathen as *"dogs,"* the noble characteristics of which animal are seldom brought out in Scripture (comp. Deut. xxiii. 18; Job xxx. 1; 2 Kings viii. 13; Phil. iii. 2; Rev. xxii. 15). Here however the term is somewhat softened. The heathen are compared not to the great wild dogs infesting Eastern towns (1 Kings xiv. 11, xvi. 4; 2 Kings ix. 10), but to the small dogs attached to households. In the East now the Mahometans apply this name to the Christians.

28. *yet the dogs*] Rather, **Yea Lord, for even the little dogs under the table eat of the children's crumbs.** So it is rightly translated in

And he said unto her, For this saying go thy way; the devil 29
is gone out of thy daughter. And when she was come to her 30
house, she found the devil gone out, and her daughter laid
upon the bed.

31—37. *The Healing of one Deaf and Dumb.*

And again, departing from the coasts of Tyre and Sidon, he 31
Wyclif's and Cranmer's Versions, following the Vulgate "Etiam, Domine,
nam et catelli edunt." "*Truth it is Maister, for indeed the whelpes eat vnder
the table, of the childerns crommes.*" Geneva, 1557. Her "yea" is the
"yea" of admission not of contradiction. She accepts the declaration
of Christ, and in that very declaration she affirms is involved the granting of her petition. "Saidst Thou dogs? It is well; I accept the
title and the place; for the dogs have a portion of the meat—not the
first, not the children's portion, but a portion still—the crumbs which
fall from the table." Her words speak to us even now across the centuries, and our Church adopts her words of faith in the "Prayer of
Humble Access" at the celebration of the Holy Eucharist.

crumbs] These were probably something more than what would
accidentally fall from the table. It was the custom during the meal
for the guests after thrusting their hands into the common dish to wipe
them on the soft white part of the bread, which, having thus used, they
threw to the dogs.

30. *she found the devil gone out*] Thus the daughter was healed in
consequence of the mother's faith and in answer to her prayers. This
is an instance of a cure effected *at a distance:* other instances are, (1) the
nobleman's son at Capernaum, whom our Lord healed while Himself
at Cana (John iv. 46), (2) the centurion's servant (Luke vii. 6). The case
also of this lonely woman not suffering the Lord "to go" until He had
blessed her (comp. Gen. xxxii. 24—32) is the greatest of the three
ascending degrees of faith, "as it manifests itself in the breaking
through of hindrances which would keep from Christ. The paralytic
broke through *the outward hindrances,* the obstacles of *things merely
external* (Mark ii. 4); blind Bartimæus through *the hindrances opposed
by his fellow-men* (Mark x. 48); but this woman, more heroically than
all, through *apparent hindrances, even from Christ Himself.*" Trench
on the *Miracles,* p. 347.

31—37. THE HEALING OF ONE DEAF AND DUMB.

31. *the coasts*] A misleading archaism is this word for "border" or
"region." No allusion is made in the original word to the sea-board.
Thus we are told that Herod "slew all the children that were in Bethlehem, and in all the *coasts* thereof," though Bethlehem was not near the
sea; and again we read of "*the coasts*" (=borders) of Judæa in Matt.
xix. 1; comp. Mark x. 1, where there is no sea-coast at all; of the
coasts (=borders) of Gadara in Mark v. 17; "the *coasts* of Decapolis"
in this verse; of "the *coasts*" (=regions) of Antioch in Pisidia (Acts
xiii. 50). Comp. 1 Sam. v. 6. The word comes from the Latin *costa,*
"*a rib,*" "*side,*" through Fr. "*coste.*" Hence it = "a border" generally,

88 ST MARK, VII. [vv. 32—34.

came unto the sea of Galilee, through the midst of the coasts
32 of Decapolis. And they bring unto him one that was deaf,
and had an impediment in his speech; and they beseech him
33 to put his hand upon him. And he took him aside from the
multitude, and put his fingers into his ears, and he spit, and
34 touched his tongue; and looking up to heaven, he sighed,

though now applied to the sea-coast only. Wyclif translates it here "bitwix þe *Endis* (or *coostis*) of Tire, þe myddil *endis* of Decapoleos."

and Sidon] The preferable reading here, supported by several MSS. and found in several ancient versions, is, **And again, departing from the coasts of Tyre, He came through Sidon unto the Sea of Galilee.** This visit of the Redeemer of mankind to the city of Baal and Astarte is full of significance.

he came unto the sea of Galilee] The direction of the journey appears to have been (1) northward towards Lebanon, then (2) from the foot of Lebanon through the deep gorge of the Leontes to the sources of the Jordan, and thence (3) along its eastern bank into the regions of Decapolis, which extended as far north as Damascus, and as far south as the river Jabbok.

32. *one that was deaf*] The healing of this man, on the east side of the Jordan, is related only by St Mark.

and had an impediment] The word thus rendered does not imply that he was a mute, as some have thought, but that with his deafness was connected a disturbance of the organs of speech, so that he could make no intelligible sounds. Tyndale renders it "one that was deffe and stambred in hys speche."

they beseech him] This is one of the few instances where the friends of the sufferer brought the sick man to Christ. We have already met with another instance in the case of the paralytic borne of four (Mark ii. 3—5), and shall meet with another in the case of the blind man of Bethsaida in Mark viii. 22—26.

33. *aside from the multitude*] Comp. Mark viii. 23. Why? (1) Some think it was to avoid all show and ostentation; (2) others, to prevent a publicity which might bring together the Gentiles in crowds; (3) others, far more probably, that apart from the interruptions of the crowd the man might be more recipient of deep and lasting impressions.

and put his fingers into his ears] In this man's case there were evidently circumstances which rendered it necessary that his cure should be (1) gradual, and (2) effected by visible signs. And so our Lord (*a*) took him aside from the multitude; (*b*) put His fingers into his ears, (*c*) touched his tongue with the moisture of His mouth (comp. ch. viii. 23; John ix. 6; 2 Kings ii. 21); (*d*) looked up to heaven (comp. Matt. xiv. 19; Mark vi. 41; John xi. 41), and sighed (comp. Mark viii. 12; John xi. 33, 38), and (*e*) spake the one word *Ephphatha* (comp. Mark v. 41).

34. *looking up to heaven*] This upturned look expressive of an act of prayer and an acknowledgment of His oneness with the Father, occurs also (1) in the blessing of the five loaves and two fishes (Matt. xiv. 19;

and saith unto him, Ephphatha, that is, Be opened. And straightway his ears were opened, and the string of his tongue was loosed, and he spake plain. And he charged them that they should tell no man: but the more he charged them, so much the more a great deal they published *it;* and were beyond measure astonished, saying, He hath done all things well: he maketh both the deaf to hear, and the dumb to speak.

1—9. *The Feeding of the Four Thousand.*

In those days the multitude being very great, and having nothing to eat, Jesus called his disciples *unto him*, and saith unto them, I have compassion on the multitude, because they have now been with me three days, and have nothing to eat: and if I send them away fasting to their own houses, they will faint by the way: for divers of them came from far. And his disciples answered him, From whence can a

Mark vi. 41), (2) at the raising of Lazarus (John xi. 41), and (3) before the great high-priestly prayer for the Apostles (John xvii. 1).

he sighed] or "groaned" as in the Rhemish Version. The sigh of the "First-born among many brethren" (Rom. viii. 29), attesting that the Human sympathies of the Saviour were co-extensive with human suffering and sorrow. Comp. John xi. 33.

Ephphatha] The actual Aramaic word used by our Lord, like the "Talitha cumi" of Mark v. 41, treasured up by actual eye and ear witnesses, on whom the actions used and the word spoken made an indelible impression.

36. *he charged them*] i.e. the friends of the afflicted man, who had accompanied or followed him into the presence of his Healer.

so much the more] Observe the accumulation of comparatives, "*The more* He charged them, *so much the more a great deal* they published it, and were *beyond measure* astonished." The original word for "beyond measure" occurs nowhere else in the New Testament.

CH. VIII. 1—9. THE FEEDING OF THE FOUR THOUSAND.

1. *the multitude being very great*] The effect of these miraculous cures on the inhabitants of the half-pagan district of Decapolis was very great. So widely was the fame of them spread abroad, that great multitudes brought their sick unto the Lord (Matt. xv. 30), and upwards of four thousand, without counting women and children (Matt. xv. 38), gathered round Him and His Apostles, and continued with Him upwards of three days (Mark viii. 2).

4. *And his disciples answered him*] Though the Apostles are the writers, they do not conceal from us their own shortcomings, or the fact that they had so soon forgotten so great a miracle.

90   ST MARK, VIII.   [vv. 5—9.

man satisfy these *men* with bread here in the wilderness?
5 And he asked them, How many loaves have ye? And they
6 said, Seven. And he commanded the people to sit down
on the ground: and he took the seven loaves, and gave
thanks, and brake, and gave to his disciples to set before
7 *them;* and they did set *them* before the people. And they
had a few small fishes: and he blessed, and commanded to
8 set them also before *them.* So they did eat, and were filled:
and they took up of the broken *meat* that was left seven
9 baskets. And they that had eaten were about four thousand: and he sent them away.

From whence can a man satisfy] It has been suggested that "it is evermore thus in times of difficulty and distress. All former deliverances are in danger of being forgotten; the mighty interpositions of God's hand in former passages of men's lives fall out of their memories. Each new difficulty appears insurmountable; as one from which there is no extrication; at each recurring necessity it seems as though the wonders of God's grace are exhausted and had come to an end." Comp. (*a*) Ex. xvii. 1—7, and (*b*) Ex. xvi. 13 with Num. xi. 21, 23. Trench *on the Miracles*, p. 356. Still it has also been well observed that "many and many a time had the Apostles been with multitudes before, and yet on one occasion only had He fed them. Further, to suggest to Him a repetition of the feeding of the Five Thousand would be a presumption which their ever-deepening reverence forbade, and forbade more than ever as they recalled how persistently He had refused to work a sign, such as this was, at the bidding of others." Farrar's *Life of Christ*, I. p. 480.
6. *to sit down*] *Where* is not distinctly specified. All we can certainly gather is that it was on the eastern side of the Lake, and in a *desert spot* (Matt. xv. 33), possibly about the middle or southern end of the Lake.
8. *seven baskets*] Not the small wicker *cophinoi* of the former miracle, but large baskets of rope, such as that in which St Paul was lowered from the wall of Damascus (Acts ix. 25). We notice at once the difference between this and the Miracle of the Five Thousand:
(*a*) The people had been with the Lord upwards of three days, a point not noted on the other occasion;
(*b*) Seven loaves are now distributed and a few fishes, then five loaves and two fishes;
(*c*) Five thousand were fed then, four thousand are fed now;
(*d*) On this occasion seven large rope-baskets are filled with fragments, on the other twelve small wicker baskets.
(*e*) The more excitable inhabitants of the coast-villages of the North would have taken and made Him a king (John vi. 15); the men of Decapolis and the Eastern shores permit Him to leave them without any demonstration

10—21. *The Leaven of the Pharisees and of Herod.*

And straightway he entered into a ship with his disciples, 10 and came into the parts of Dalmanutha. And the Pharisees 11 came forth, and began to question with him, seeking of him a sign from heaven, tempting him. And he sighed deeply in 12 his spirit, and saith, Why doth this generation seek after a

10—21. THE LEAVEN OF THE PHARISEES AND OF HEROD.

10. *the parts of Dalmanutha*] or as St Matthew says, *into the coasts of Magdala* (xv. 39), or according to some MSS. *Magadan*. Nothing is known of Dalmanutha. It must clearly have been near to Magdala, which may have been the Greek name of one of the many *Migdols* (i. e. watch-towers) to be found in the Holy Land, possibly the *Migdal-el* of Josh. xix. 38, and its place may now be occupied by a miserable collection of hovels known as *el-Mejdel*, on the western side of the Lake, and at the S. E. corner of the Plain of Gennesaret. "Just before reaching Mejdel, we crossed a little open valley, the Ain-el-Barideh, with a few rich cornfields and gardens straggling among the ruins of a village, and some large and more ancient foundations by several copious fountains, and probably identical with the Dalmanutha of the New Testament." Tristram's *Land of Israel*, p. 425. If the reading *Magadan* in Matt. xv. 39 stands, we may conjecture either (*a*) that it and Dalmanutha were different names for the same place, or (*b*) that they denoted contiguous spots, either of which might give its name to the same region.

11. *And the Pharisees*] Our Lord seems purposely to have avoided sailing to Bethsaida or Capernaum, which lay a little north of Magdala, and which had become the head-quarters of the Pharisees; but they had apparently watched for His arrival, and now "*came forth*" to meet Him accompanied for the first time by the Sadducees (Matt. xvi. 1), their rivals and enemies.

began] They had made their arrangements for a decisive contest, which began with a demand for a sign.

a sign from heaven] The same request had already been twice proffered. (1) After the first cleansing of the Temple (John ii. 18); (2) after the feeding of the Five Thousand (John vi. 30); and (3) again shortly after the walking through the cornfields (Matt. xii. 38). By such a "sign" was meant an outward and visible luminous appearance in the sky or some visible manifestation of the *Shechînah*, the credentials of a prophet. They asked in effect, "Give us bread from heaven, as Moses did, or signs in the sun and moon like Joshua, or call down thunder and hail like Samuel, or fire and rain like Elijah, or make the sun turn back on the dial like Isaiah, or let us hear the *Bath-Kôl*, the 'daughter of the Voice,' that we may believe Thee."

12. *he sighed deeply in his spirit*] Not merely, we may conclude, at their hardened disbelief, but also with the feeling that the decisive crisis of the severance from the ruling powers had come. "For the

sign? verily I say unto you, There shall no sign be given
13 unto this generation. And he left them, and entering into
14 the ship again departed to the other side. Now *the
disciples* had forgotten to take bread, neither had they in
15 the ship with them more than one loaf. And he charged
them, saying, Take heed, beware of the leaven of the
16 Pharisees, and *of* the leaven of Herod. And they reasoned among themselves, saying, *It is* because we have no
17 bread. And when Jesus knew *it*, he saith unto them, Why
reason ye, because ye have no bread? perceive ye not yet,
18 neither understand? have ye your heart yet hardened? having
eyes, see ye not? and having ears, hear ye not? and do ye
19 not remember? When I brake the five loaves among five

demand for a sign from heaven was a demand that He should, as
the Messiah of their expectation, accredit Himself by a great overmastering miracle; thus it was fundamentally similar to the temptation in the wilderness, which He had repelled and overcome." Lange.

There shall no sign be given] Literally, **If a sign shall be given to
this generation,** a Hebrew form of strong abjuration. Comp. Heb. iii.
11, where see the margin; iv. 3, 5; Gen. xiv. 23; Num. xiv. 30. St
Mark does not mention the sign of "Jonah the prophet" mentioned by
St Matthew (xvi. 4).

13. *he left them*] "Justa severitas," Bengel. "It was His final
rejection on the very spot where He had laboured most, and He was
leaving it, to return, indeed, for a passing visit, but never to appear
again publicly, or to teach, or work miracles."

the other side] i.e. the eastern side of the Lake.

14. *had forgotten*] In the hurry of their unexpected re-embarkation
they had altogether omitted to make provision for their own personal
wants.

15. *the leaven of the Pharisees*] Leaven in Scripture, with the single
exception of the Parable (Matt. xiii. 33; Luke xiii. 20, 21), is always a
symbol of evil (comp. 1 Cor. v. 6, 7, 8; Gal. v. 9), especially insidious
evil, as it is for the most part also in the Rabbinical writers. See Lightfoot
on Matt. xvi. 6. The strict command to the children of Israel that they
should carefully put away every particle of leaven out of their houses
during the Passover-week, rests on this view of it as evil.

the leaven of Herod] "and," as it is in St Matthew's Gospel, "*of the
Sadducees.*" The leaven of the Pharisees was *hypocrisy* (Luke xii. 1),
of the Sadducees, *unbelief*, of Herod, *worldliness;* all which working in
secrecy and silence, and spreading with terrible certainty, cause that in
the end "the whole man is leavened," and his whole nature transformed.

17. *yet hardened*] as on the former occasion, the walking on the sea
(Mark vi. 52).

thousand, how many baskets full of fragments took ye up? They say unto him, Twelve. And when the seven among four thousand, how many baskets full of fragments took ye up? And they said, Seven. And he said unto them, How is it that ye do not understand?

22—26. *The Blind Man in Eastern Bethsaida.*

And he cometh to Bethsaida; and they bring a blind man unto him, and besought him to touch him. And he took the blind man by the hand, and led him out of the town; and when he had spit on his eyes, and put his hands upon him, he asked him if he saw ought. And he looked up, and said, I see men as trees, walking. After that he put his hands again upon his eyes, and made him look up: and he was restored, and saw every man clearly. And he sent

19. *how many baskets*] Observe how our Lord reproduces in this allusion to the putting forth of His miraculous power not only the precise number but the precise kind of baskets taken up on each occasion. See above, on vi. 43. Wyclif brings out this in his translation: "Whanne I brak fyue looues among fyve þousand, and hou many *coffyns* ful of brokene mete ye token up?...whanne also seuene looues among foure thousand, how many *leepis* of brokene mete ʒe token up?"

21. *ye do not understand*] They seem to have thought that He was warning them against buying leaven of the Pharisees and Sadducees.

22—26. THE BLIND MAN IN EASTERN BETHSAIDA.

22. *Bethsaida*] i.e. *Bethsaida Julias*, which lay upon the northeastern coast of the Sea of Tiberias.

23. *he took the blind man*] Even as He did with the other sufferer, whose case came before us in Mark vii. 33. As then, so now, the Lord was pleased to work gradually and with external signs: (i) He leads the man out of the town; (ii) anoints his eyes with the moisture of His mouth; (iii) lays His hands upon him twice (Mark viii. 23, 25); (iv) inquires of the progress of his restoration.

24. *as trees, walking*] He had not been *born* blind. He remembered the appearance of natural objects, and in the haze of his brightening vision he saw certain moving forms about him, "trees he should have accounted them from their height, but men from their motion."

25. *saw every man clearly*] or rather, *began to see all things clearly*. "So þat he syʒ clerely alle þingis," Wyclif. The word translated "clearly" literally = "far-shining," "far-beaming." The man meant that he could now see clearly *far and near*. This is one of the few instances of a strictly *progressive* cure recorded in the Gospels. "His friends asked that He would touch him. To this demand for an instant act followed by an instant cure, the Lord opposed His own slow and

him away to his house, saying, Neither go into the town, nor tell *it* to any in the town.

27—IX. 1. *Cæsarea Philippi. The Confession of St Peter.*

27 And Jesus went out, and his disciples, into the towns of Cæsarea Philippi: and by the way he asked his disciples,

circumstantial method of procedure." Lange. Comp. the cure of Naaman, 2 Kings v. 10, 11, 14.

26. *to his house*] Bethsaida, therefore, was not the place of his residence; he was to go immediately from the place to his own home—not even to the village to which he had already come, and he was not to mention it to any one dwelling in that village, or whom he might meet by the way.

27—IX. 1. CÆSAREA PHILIPPI. THE CONFESSION OF ST PETER.

27. *And Jesus went out*] The Redeemer and His Apostles now set out in a northerly direction, and travelled some 25 or 30 miles along the eastern banks of the Jordan and beyond the waters of Merom, seeking the deepest solitude among the mountains, for an important crisis in His Life was at hand. The solitude of the beautiful district, whither the Saviour now journeyed, is illustrated by the fact that it is the only district of Palestine where a recent traveller found *the pelican of the wilderness* (Ps. cii. 6). See Thomson's *Land and the Book*, pp. 260, 261; Caspari's *Introduction*, p. 163, n.

into the towns] The little company at length reached the *"villages,"* as it is literally, or the *"parts"* or *"regions"* (Matt. xvi. 13) of the remote city of Cæsarea Philippi, near which it is possible He may have passed in His circuit from Sidon a very few weeks before. See above, vii. 24, n., Bishop Ellicott's *Lectures*, p. 225.

Cæsarea Philippi] "Sezarie of Philip" (Wyclif) lay on the north-east of the reedy and marshy plain of *El Huleh*, close to Dan, the extreme north of the boundaries of ancient Israel. (i) Its earliest name according to some was Baal-Gad (Josh. xi. 17, xii. 7, xiii. 5) or Baal-Hermon (Judg. iii. 3; 1 Chron. v. 23), when it was a Phœnician or Canaanite sanctuary of Baal under the aspect of "Gad," or the god of good fortune. (ii) In later times it was known as Panium or *Paneas*, a name which it derived from a cavern near the town, "abrupt, prodigiously deep, and full of still water," adopted by the Greeks of the Macedonian kingdom of Antioch, as the nearest likeness that Syria afforded of the beautiful limestone grottoes, which in their own country were inseparably associated with the worship of the sylvan *Pan*, and dedicated to that deity. Hence its modern appellation *Baneas*. (iii) The town retained this name under Herod the Great, who built here a splendid temple, of the whitest marble, which he dedicated to Augustus Cæsar. (iv) It afterwards became part of the territory of Herod Philip, tetrarch of Trachonitis, who enlarged and embellished it, and called it *Cæsarea Philippi*, partly after his own name, and partly after that of the Emperor Tiberius. Jos. *Ant.* xv. 10. 3; *Bel. Jud.* I. 21. 3. It was called Cæsarea

saying unto them, Whom do men say that I am? And they 28
answered, John the Baptist: but some *say*, Elias; and others,
One of the prophets. And he saith unto them, But whom 29
say ye that I am? And Peter answereth and saith unto him,
Thou art the Christ. And he charged them that they should 30
tell no man of him. And he began to teach them, that the 31

Philippi to distinguish it from Cæsarea *Palestinæ*, or Cæsarea "*on the
sea.*" Dean Stanley calls it a Syrian Tivoli, and "certainly there is
much in the rocks, caverns, cascades, and the natural beauty of the
scenery to recall the Roman Tibur. Behind the village, in front of a
great natural cavern, a river bursts forth from the earth, the 'upper
source' of the Jordan. Inscriptions and niches in the face of the cliffs
tell of the old idol worship of Baal and of Pan." Tristram, *Land of
Israel*, p. 581.

he asked his disciples] It was in this desert region that the Apostles
on one occasion found Him engaged in solitary prayer (Luke ix. 18), a
significant action which had preceded several important events in His life,
as (*a*) the Baptism, (*b*) the election of the Twelve, and (*c*) the discourse
in the synagogue of Capernaum. It was now the precursor of a solemn
and momentous question. Hitherto He is not recorded to have asked
the Twelve any question respecting Himself, and He would seem to
have forborne to press His Apostles for an explicit avowal of faith in
His full Divinity. But on this occasion He wished to ascertain from
them, the special witnesses as they had been of His life and daily words,
the results of those labours, which were now drawing in one sense to a
close, before He went on to communicate to them other and more
painful truths.

28. *they answered*] In this answer we have the explanation, which
common rumour, in His own days, offered of His marvellous works.
(1) Some, like the guilty Herod, said He was John the Baptist risen
from the dead; (2) others that He was Elijah, who, like Enoch, had
never died, but was taken up bodily to heaven and had now returned
as Malachi predicted (iv. 5); (3) others that He was Jeremiah (Matt.
xvi. 14), who was expected to inaugurate the reign of the Messiah; (4)
others again that He was one of the "old prophets" (Luke ix. 19).
But they did not add that any regarded Him as the Messiah.

29. *Thou art the Christ*] To the momentous question, *But whom
say ye that I am?* St Peter, as the ready spokesman of the rest of the
Apostles, made the ever-memorable reply, *Thou art the Christ, the
Messiah* (Matt. xvi. 16; Luke ix. 20), *the Son of the living God* (Matt.
xvi. 16), but in the Gospel written under his eye the great announcement respecting his own memorable confession and the promise of
peculiar dignity in the Church the Lord was about to establish, find no
place.

31. *And he began to teach them*] The question and the answer it
called forth were alike preparatory to strange and mournful tidings,
which He now began to reveal distinctly to the Apostles respecting
Himself, for clear and full before His eyes was the whole history of

Son of man must suffer many things, and be rejected of the elders, and *of* the chief priests, and scribes, and be killed, 32 and after three days rise again. And he spake that saying openly. And Peter took him, and began to rebuke him. 33 But when he had turned about and looked on his disciples, he rebuked Peter, saying, Get thee behind me, Satan: for thou savourest not the things that be of God, but the things

His coming sufferings, the agents through whom they would be brought about, the form they would take, the place where He would undergo them, and their issue, a mysterious resurrection after three days.

32. *openly*] i.e. not publicly, but *"plainly"* (*"pleinli,"* Wyclif) and *"without disguise."* Comp. John xi. 14, "Then said Jesus unto them *plainly*, Lazarus is dead." Before this there had been intimations of the End, but then they had been dark and enigmatical. (*a*) The Baptist had twice pointed Him out as *the Lamb of God destined to take away the sin of the world* (John i. 29). (*b*) At the first Passover of His public ministry He Himself had spoken to the Jews *of a Temple to be destroyed and rebuilt in three days* (John ii. 19), and to Nicodemus of a *lifting up of the Son of Man, even as Moses had lifted up the serpent in the wilderness* (John iii. 12—16); (*c*) He had intimated moreover to the Apostles that a day would come when *the Bridegroom should be taken from them* (Matt. ix. 15), and (*d*) in the synagogue at Capernaum He had declared that He was about *to give* His *flesh for the Life of the world* (John vi. 47—51). Now for the first time He dwelt on His awful Future distinctly, and with complete freedom of speech.

And Peter] The selfsame Peter, who a moment before had witnessed so noble and outspoken a confession to his Lord's Divinity.

took him] i.e. *took Him aside* (and so Tyndale and Cranmer render it), by the hand or by the robe, and began earnestly and lovingly to remonstrate with Him. The idea of a suffering Messiah was abhorrent to him and to all the Twelve.

33. *when he had turned about and looked on his disciples*] Observe the graphic touches of St Mark. The Apostle who had restrained the Evangelist from preserving the record of that which redounded to his highest honour, suppresses the record neither of his own mistaken zeal, nor of the terrible rebuke it called forth.

Get thee behind me] The very words which He had used to the Tempter in the wilderness (Matt. iv. 10), for in truth the Apostle was adopting the very argument which the great Enemy had adopted there.

thou savourest not] Thou art **thinking of**, thy **thoughts centre on**. This rendering of the Greek word for *"to think"* is suggested by the Latin *sapere*, which is found in the Vulgate and retained from Wyclif's Version. It is derived directly from the substantive *savour*, Fr. *saveur*, Lat. *sapor*, from *sapere*. Thus Latimer quoting 1 Cor. xiii. 11 writes, "When I was a child I *savoured* as a child." "In confusion of them that so *saveren* earthely thinges." Chaucer, *Parson's Tale*. "Thy words shew," our Lord would say to the Apostle, "that in these things

that be of men. And when he had called the people *unto* 34
him with his disciples also, he said unto them, Whosoever
will come after me, let him deny himself, and take up his
cross, and follow me. For whosoever will save his life shall 35
lose it; but whosoever shall lose his life for my sake and
the gospel's, the same shall save it. For what shall it profit 36
a man, if he shall gain the whole world, and lose his own
soul? or what shall a man give in exchange for his soul? 37
Whosoever therefore shall be ashamed of me and of my 38
words in this adulterous and sinful generation; of him also
shall the Son of man be ashamed, when he cometh in the
glory of his Father with the holy angels. And he said unto 9
them, Verily I say unto you, That there be some of them
that stand here, which shall not taste of death, till they have
seen the kingdom of God come with power.

thou enterest not into the thoughts and plans of God, but considerest all
things only from the ideas of men. This attempt of thine to dissuade
Me from My 'baptism of death' is a sin against the purposes of God."

34. *he had called*] Even in these lonely regions considerable numbers would seem to have followed Him, apparently at some little distance. These He now *called to Him*, and addressed to them, as well as to His Apostles, some of His deepest teaching, making them sharers in this part of His instruction.

will] i.e. whosoever *is resolved*. "Will" here is not the will simply of the future tense, but the will of real *desire* and *resolution*. Comp. John vii. 17, *if any man will do His will* (i.e. *is resolved at all costs to do it*), *he shall know of the doctrine, whether it be of God*.

take up his cross] The first intimation of His own suffering upon the cross.

35. *shall lose it*] This solemn saying our Lord is found to have uttered on no less than *four* several occasions: (*a*) here, which corresponds with Matt. xvi. 25, Luke ix. 24; (*b*) Matt. x. 39; (*c*) Luke xvii. 33; (*d*) John xii. 25.

37. *in exchange*] i.e. to *purchase back*. By soul here is meant "life" in the higher sense. The "price" which the earthly-minded man gives for the world is his soul. But after having laid that down as the price, what has he for a "ransom-price," to purchase it again? The LXX. use the original word in Ruth iv. 7; Jer. xv. 13.

38. *adulterous*] The generation is called "adulterous," because its heart was estranged from God. Comp. Jer. xxxi. 32; Isai. liv. 5.

IX. **1.** *And he said unto them*] The opening verse of the Ninth Chapter connects closely with what goes before.

Verily I say unto you] This well-known formula occurs 13 times in St Mark, 31 times in St Matthew, 7 times in St Luke, 25 times in St John. It always introduces solemn and important announcements.

the kingdom of God] On this expression see above, ch. i. 15. Of

2—13. *The Transfiguration.*

2 And after six days Jesus taketh *with him* Peter, and James, and John, and leadeth them up into an high mountain apart by themselves: and he was transfigured before

those then standing with the Lord, three six days afterwards beheld Him transfigured; all, save one, were witnesses of His resurrection; one at least, St John, survived the capture of Jerusalem and the destruction of the Temple, and on each of these occasions "the kingdom of God" came "with power."

CH. IX. 2—13. THE TRANSFIGURATION.

2. *after six days*] St Luke's words *"about an eight days after"* (ix. 28) may be considered an inclusive reckoning.

Peter, and James, and John] the flower and crown of the Apostolic band, the privileged Three, who had already witnessed His power over death in the chamber of Jairus: St Peter who loved Him so much (John xxi. 17), St John whom He loved so much (John xxi. 20), and St James "who should first attest that death could as little as life separate from His love (Acts xii. 2)." Trench's *Studies in the Gospels*, p. 191.

leadeth them up] It is the same expression in the original, which is used in reference to His own Ascension (Luke xxiv. 51).

into an high mountain] One of the numerous mountain-ranges in the neighbourhood, probably one of the spurs of the magnificent snow-clad Hermon, the most beautiful and conspicuous mountain in Palestine or Syria. The Sidonians called it Sirion = "*breastplate*," a name suggested by its rounded glittering top, when the sun's rays are reflected by the snow that covers it (Deut. iii. 9; Cant. iv. 8). It was also called Sion = "*the elevated*," and is now known as *Jebel-esh Sheikh*, "*the chief mountain.*" "In whatever part of Palestine the Israelite turned his eye northward, Hermon was there terminating the view. From the plain along the coast, from the mountains of Samaria, from the Jordan valley, from the heights of Moab and Gilead, from the plateau of Bashan, that pale-blue, snow-capped cone forms the one feature on the northern horizon."

apart by themselves] St Luke (ix. 28) tells us that one object of His own withdrawal was that He might engage in *solitary prayer*. We may infer, therefore (comparing Luke ix. 37), that *evening* was the time of this solitary retirement. The fact that it was night must have infinitely enhanced the grandeur of the scene.

was transfigured] St Luke, writing primarily for Greek readers, avoids the word, "transfigured," or "transformed,"—"metamorphosed" would be a still closer rendering,—which St Matthew and St Mark do not shrink from employing. He avoids it, probably, because of the associations of the heathen mythology which would so easily, and almost inevitably, attach themselves to it in the imagination of a Greek. In naming this great event, the German theology, calling it "*die Verklärung,*" or "the Glorification," has seized this point, not

them. And his raiment became shining, exceeding white as 3 snow; so as no fuller on earth can white them. And there 4 appeared unto them Elias with Moses: and they were talking with Jesus. And Peter answered and said to Jesus, 5 Master, it is good for us to be here: and let us make three

exactly the same as our "Transfiguration." From the records of the three Evangelists we infer that while He was engaged in prayer (Luke ix. 29), a marvellous change came over the Person of our Lord. The Divinity within Him shone through the veiling flesh, till His raiment became *exceeding white* as *the light* (Matt. xvii. 2), or as the glittering *snow* (Mark ix. 3) on the peaks above Him, so *as no fuller on earth could white them;* moreover *the fashion of His countenance was altered* (Luke ix. 29), and His face glowed with a sunlike majesty (Matt. xvii. 2, comp. Rev. i. 16). "St Mark borrows one image from the world of nature, another from that of man's art and device; by these he struggles to set forth and reproduce for his readers the transcendant brightness of that light which now arrayed, and from head to foot, the Person of the Lord, breaking forth from within, and overflowing the very garments which He wore; until in their eyes who beheld, He seemed to clothe Himself with light as with a garment, light being indeed the proper and peculiar garment of Deity (Ps. civ. 2; Hab. iii. 4)." Trench's *Studies*, pp. 194, 195.

4. *there appeared unto them*] The three Apostles had not witnessed the beginning of this marvellous change. They *had been weighed down with sleep* (Luke ix. 32), lying wrapped like all Orientals in their *abbas* on the ground, but awakened probably by the supernatural light, they *thoroughly roused themselves* (Luke ix. 32), and *saw His glory*, and the two men standing with Him. It was clearly no waking vision or dream.

Elias with Moses] (i) Among all the prophets and saints of the Old Testament these were the two, of whom one had not died (2 Kings ii. 11), and the other had no sooner tasted of death than his body was withdrawn from under the dominion of death and of him that had the power of death (Deut. xxxiv. 6; Jude 9). Both, therefore, came from the grave, but from the grave conquered. (ii) Again, these two were the acknowledged heads and representatives, the one of the Law, the other of the Prophets (comp. Matt. vii. 12).

they were talking] St Luke tells us what was the subject of mysterious converse which the Three were privileged to hear—"*the decease, which He was about to accomplish at Jerusalem*" (Luke ix. 31). St Peter himself reproduces this remarkable word in his second Epistle i. 15. "Vocabulum valde grave, quo continetur Passio, Crux, Mors, Resurrectio, Ascensio." Bengel.

5. *And Peter*] Eager, ardent, impulsive as always. This proposal he made as the mysterious visitants were being parted from Him (Luke ix. 33). It was for him too brief a converse, too transient a glimpse and foretaste of the heavenly glory.

it is good for us to be here] "Better, as no doubt he felt, than to be

tabernacles; one for thee, and one for Moses, and one for
6 Elias. For he wist not what to say; for they were sore
7 afraid. And there was a cloud that overshadowed them:
and a voice came out of the cloud, saying, This is my be-
8 loved Son: hear him. And suddenly, when they had looked

---

rejected of the Jews, better than to suffer many things of the Elders and
Chief Priests and Scribes and be killed" (Matt. xvi. 21). Trench's
Studies, p. 202.
 three tabernacles] Three booths of wattled boughs, like those of the
Feast of Tabernacles. It seemed to him that the hour for the long-
looked-for reign had come. From the slopes of Hermon he would have
had the Laws of the New Kingdom proclaimed, so that all men might
recognise the true Messiah attended by the representatives of the Old
Dispensation.
 6. *he wist not*] "Soþli he *wiste* not what he schulde *seie.*" Wyclif.
This word also occurs Ex. xvi. 15, and =*he knew not*. *Wist* is the
past tense of A. S. *witan*=to know. Compare wit=*knowledge* (Ps.
cvii. 27), and wit=*to know* (Gen. xxiv. 21), "And the man wondering
at her held his peace, to *wit* whether the Lord had made his journey
prosperous or not;" Ex. ii. 4, "And his sister stood afar off, to *wit* what
would be done to him;" 2 Cor. viii. 1, "Moreover, brethren, we do
you to *wit* (=cause you to know) of the grace of God." Witan=to
know, Du. *weten*, G. *wissen;* the pr. t. in A. S. *ic wát*, Mœso-Goth. *ik
wait*, E. *I wot;* the pt. t. in A. S. *ic wiste*, Mœso-Goth. *ik wissa*, E. *I
wist*.
 sore afraid] The original word only occurs here and in Heb. xii.
21, "Moses said, I *exceedingly fear* and quake;" comp. Deut. ix.
19. Wyclif's rendering is very striking, "forsoþe þei weren *agast by
drede.*"
 7. *a cloud*] not dark and murky, but *bright* (Matt. xvii. 5), overshadowed the lawgiver and the prophet, and perhaps also the Lord.
"Light in its utmost intensity performs the effects of darkness, hides as
effectually as the darkness would do." Comp. 1 Tim. vi. 16, and the
words of Milton, "dark with excess of light," and of Wordsworth, "a
glorious privacy of light." Trench's *Studies*, pp. 205, 206.
 a voice came out of the cloud] The same Voice which had been heard
once before at the Baptism (Matt. iii. 17), and which was to be heard
again when He stood on the threshold of His Passion (John xii. 28),
attesting His Divinity and Sonship at the beginning, at the middle, and
at the close of His ministry. Looking back afterwards on the scene now
vouchsafed to him and to the "sons of thunder," St Peter speaks of himself and them as "eyewitnesses of His majesty" (2 Peter i. 16), i.e. literally,
as men who had been *admitted and initiated into secret and holy mysteries*,
and says that the Voice "came from the excellent glory" (2 Peter i. 17),
from Him, that is, Who dwelt in the cloud, which was the symbol and
the vehicle of the Divine Presence. St John also clearly alludes to the
scene in John i. 14 and 1 John i. 1.

round about, they saw no man any more, save Jesus only with themselves. And as they came down from the moun- 9 tain, he charged them that they should tell no man what things they had seen, till the Son of man were risen from the dead. And they kept that saying with themselves, questioning 10 one with another what the rising from the dead should mean. And they asked him, saying, Why say the scribes that 11 Elias must first come? And he answered and told them, 12 Elias verily cometh first, and restoreth all things; and how

This is my beloved Son] "In the words themselves of this majestic installation there is a remarkable honouring of the Old Testament, and of it in all its parts, which can scarcely be regarded as accidental; for the three several clauses of that salutation are drawn severally from the Psalms (Ps. ii. 7), the Prophets (Isaiah xlii. 1), and the Law (Deut. xviii. 15); and together they proclaim Him, concerning whom they are spoken, to be the King, the Priest, and the Prophet of the New Covenant." Trench, *Studies*, p. 207.

8. *when they had looked round about*] At first (1) they fell prostrate on their faces (Matt. xvii. 6; comp. Ex. iii. 6; 1 Kings xix. 13), then (2) recovering from the shock of the Voice from heaven (Matt. xvii. 6; comp. Ex. xx. 19; Hab. iii. 2, 16; Heb. xii. 19), they (3) suddenly gazed all around them, and *saw no man, save Jesus only*. "Hinc constat, hunc esse Filium, audiendum, non Mosen, non Eliam." Bengel. "Quæ ex Verbo cœperunt, in Verbo desinunt." S. Ambrose.

9. *they should tell no man*] This implies that they were forbidden to reveal the wonders of the night, and what they had seen, even to their fellow-Apostles. The seal set upon their lips was not to be removed till after the Resurrection.

10. *questioning one with another*] St Mark alone mentions the perplexity which this language of their Lord occasioned to the Apostles. It was not the question of the resurrection generally, but of *His* resurrection, and the *death*, so abhorrent to their prejudices, that rendered it possible and necessary, which troubled them.

11. *first come*] that is before the Messiah (Mal. iv. 5). The Pharisees and Scribes may have urged as a capital objection against the Messiahship of their Master that no Elias went before Him. "It would be an infinite task," says Lightfoot, "to produce all the passages out of the Jewish writings which one might concerning the expected coming of Elias." He was to restore to the Jews the pot of manna and the rod of Aaron, to cry to the mountains, "Peace and blessing come into the world, peace and blessing come into the world!" "Salvation cometh, Salvation cometh, to gather all the scattered sons of Jacob, and restore all things to Israel as in ancient times."

12. *and how*] Rather, **but how is it written of the Son of Man that He must suffer many things and be set at naught?** See Tischendorf, *Synop. Evang.* The words *that He must*, or *in order that He may*, are very striking. They set before us the design of the *It is*

it is written of the Son of man, that he must suffer many
13 things, and be set at nought. But I say unto you, That
Elias is indeed come, and they have done unto him whatsoever they listed, as it is written of him.

written. "Elias cometh first. But how or to what purpose is it written of the Son of Man that He cometh? *In order that He may suffer*, not conquer like a mighty prince."

13. *That Elias is indeed come*] that is in the person of John the Baptist, to whom men acted even as it had been written of the persecution of the real Elijah. A few remarks here will not be out of place (i) *On the three accounts of the Transfiguration;* (ii) *On the meaning and significance of the event itself.*

(i) *The three accounts.* (*a*) All three Evangelists relate the conversation which preceded, and the Miracle which succeeded it. (*b*) St Matthew alone records the prostration of the disciples through excessive fear, and the Lord's strengthening touch and cheering words uttered once before on the stormy lake (Matt. xvii. 6, 7, xiv. 27), recalling, as the Hebrew Evangelist, the scene in the Exodus when the face of Moses shone, and the children of Israel *were afraid to come nigh him* (Ex. xxxiv. 29, 30). (*c*) St Mark, in describing the effect of the Transfiguration, uses the strongest material imagery, "white as *snow*," "so as *no fuller on earth can whiten*," and he alone has the sudden vanishing of the heavenly visitors, and the inquiring look around of the disciples, and their questioning amongst themselves what "*the rising from the dead could mean.*" (*d*) St Luke alone tells us that our Lord was engaged in prayer at the moment of His glorification (Luke ix. 29), and mentions the slumbrous and wakeful condition of the three witnesses, the subject of mysterious converse between the Lord and His visitors from the other world (Luke ix. 31), and the fact that the Heavenly Voice *succeeded their departure* (Luke ix. 35). (*e*) Both St Matthew and St Mark place in immediate connection with the Event the remarkable conversation about Elias, but St Matthew alone applies the Lord's words concerning that great prophet to John the Baptist (Matt. xvii. 13).

(ii) *The meaning and significance of the Event.* This we may believe had respect (*a*) to the Apostles, and (*b*) to our Lord Himself.

(*a*) *As regards the Apostles.* This one full manifestation of His Divine glory, during the period of the Incarnation, was designed to confirm their faith, to comfort them in prospect of their Master's approaching sufferings, to prepare them to see in His Passion the fulfilment alike of the Law and the Prophets, to give them a glimpse of the celestial Majesty of Him, whom they had given up all to follow.

(*b*) *As regards our Lord.* As regards the Redeemer we may conclude that the transaction marked His consecration as the Divine Victim, Who was to accomplish the great "Decease" at Jerusalem, even as the Baptism inaugurated the commencement of His public ministry; it was the solemn attestation of His perfect oneness with

14—29. *The Healing of the Lunatic Child.*

And when he came to *his* disciples, he saw a great multitude about them, and the scribes questioning with them. And straightway all the people, when they beheld him, were greatly amazed, and running to *him* saluted him. And he asked the scribes, What question ye with them? And one of the multitude answered and said, Master, I have brought unto thee my son, which hath a dumb spirit; and wheresoever he taketh him, he teareth him: and he foameth, and

His Father in heaven at the very time when He was about to descend into the valley of the shadow of death. It was, as it has well been called, "the summit-level" of the Life Incarnate. From this time forward there is a perceptible change. (*a*) *Miracles*, which hitherto had abounded in prodigal profusion, well-nigh cease. Only five mark the period between the Transfiguration and the Passion. Those, for whom "signs" could avail, were already won. For the rest, no more could be done. They were like those, amongst whom in His earlier ministry, "He could do no mighty work because of their unbelief." (*b*) As regards His *teaching*, public addresses, before the rule, now become few and rare; His special revelations of the future to the chosen Twelve become more frequent, and they uniformly circle, unenshrouded in type or figure or dark saying, round the Cross.

14—29. THE HEALING OF THE LUNATIC CHILD.

14. *And when he came to his disciples*] The great picture of Raphael has enshrined for ever the contrast between the scene on the Mount of Glorification and that which awaited the Saviour and the three Apostles on the plain below, between the harmonies of heaven and the harsh discords of earth.

scribes] Thus far north had they penetrated in their active hostility to the Lord. Many of them would be found in the tetrarchy of Philip.

15. *were greatly amazed*] "was astonied and much afraid," Rhemish Version. His face would seem, like that of Moses (Ex. xxxiv. 30), to have retained traces of the celestial glory of the Holy Mount, which had not faded into the light of common day, and filled the beholders with awe and wonder. The word points to an extremity of terror. It is used four times in the New Testament, and only by St Mark. What is here said of the multitudes is said (Mark xiv. 34) of our Lord in Gethsemane, and (Mark xvi. 5) of the holy women at the Sepulchre on the first Easter-day at the sight of the Angel seated, "they were *affrighted.*"

17. *my son*] and his "only son" (Luke ix. 38).

a dumb spirit] dumb in respect to articulate sounds, to which he could give no utterance, though he could *suddenly cry out* (Luke ix. 39).

18. *wheresoever*] According to St Matthew these crises had a connection with changes of the moon (Matt. xvii. 15).

gnasheth with his teeth, and pineth away: and I spake to thy disciples that they should cast him out; and they could
19 not. He answereth him, and saith, O faithless generation, how long shall I be with you? how long shall I suffer you?
20 bring him unto me. And they brought him unto him: and when he saw him, straightway the spirit tare him; and he
21 fell on the ground, and wallowed foaming. And he asked his father, How long is it ago since this came unto him?
22 And he said, Of a child. And ofttimes it hath cast him into the fire, and into the waters, to destroy him: but if thou canst do any thing, have compassion on us, and help us.
23 Jesus said unto him, If thou canst believe, all things *are*
24 possible to him that believeth. And straightway the father of the child cried out, and said with tears, Lord, I believe;
25 help thou mine unbelief. When Jesus saw that the people

he teareth him] Probably this manifested itself in violent convulsions, St Vitus' dance, or the like.

pineth away] "wexiþ drye," Wyclif. The word may denote either that he pined away like one, the very springs of whose life were dried up, or that in the paroxysms of his disorder his limbs became unnaturally stiff and stark. The fundamental form of his malady was epilepsy in its worst form, accompanied by dumbness, atrophy, and suicidal mania (Mark ix. 22).

19. *O faithless generation*] These words, though primarily addressed to the father, apply also to the surrounding multitude, and indeed to the whole Jewish people of which he was a representative, and in a sense to the disciples.

20. *straightway the spirit*] The mere introduction to our Lord brings on one of the sudden and terrible paroxysms, to which he was liable.

21. *And he asked*] This conversation with the father is parallel to another conversation with an actual sufferer (Mark v. 9).

22. *if thou canst*] More literally, **if at all Thou canst**. This is a strong expression of an infirm faith, which at the beginning had been too weak, but had become more and more weak owing to the failure of the disciples to aid him.

23. *If thou canst*] According to the best reading here the translation would be, **Jesus said unto him, As for thy if thou canst, all things are possible to him that believeth**. For the use of the article compare Matt. xix. 18; Luke ix. 46. "Thou hast said," replies our Lord, "*if I* can do anything. But as for thy *if Thou canst*, the question is *if thou canst believe;* that is the hinge upon which all must turn." Then He pauses, and utters the further words, "*all things are possible to him that believeth.*" "Hoc, si potes credere, res est; hoc agitur." Bengel.

came running together, he rebuked the foul spirit, saying unto him, *Thou* dumb and deaf spirit, I charge thee, come out of him, and enter no more into him. And *the spirit* 26 cried, and rent him sore, and came out of him: and he was as one dead; insomuch that many said, He is dead. But 27 Jesus took him by the hand, and lifted him up; and he arose. And when he was come into the house, his disciples 28 asked him privately, Why could not we cast him out? And 29 he said unto them, This kind can come forth by nothing, but by prayer and fasting.

30—32. *Predictions of the Passion.*

And they departed thence, and passed through Galilee; 30

25. *I charge thee*] Notice the words of majestic command, *I* charge thee, I, whom thou darest not to disobey, and against whom it is vain for thee to struggle.

26. *and rent him sore*] Observe here the minuteness and exactness of the Evangelist in all the details of the incident. Who was more likely to treasure up every detail of the scene than that Apostle, who had been with His Master on the Mount of Glorification?

28. *Why could not we cast him out?*] He had given them "power and authority over all demons" (Luke ix. 1), and "against unclean spirits to cast them out" (Matt. x. 1); what was the reason of their failure now?

29. *This kind*] In His reply to their question our Lord impresses upon them a twofold lesson: (i) The omnipotence of a perfect faith (see Matt. xvii. 20, 21); (ii) that, as there is order and gradation in the hierarchy of blessed spirits, so is it with the spirits of evil (see Eph. vi. 12). There are degrees of spiritual and moral wickedness so intense and malignant that they can be exorcised by nothing save by prayer and fasting, and the austerest rules of rigour and self-denial. These last words *and fasting* are wanting in the Sinaitic MS. and some Versions.

30—32. PREDICTIONS OF THE PASSION.

30. *And they departed thence*] From the northern regions, into which our Lord had penetrated, He now turned His steps once more towards Galilee, probably taking the route by Dan across the slopes of Lebanon, thus escaping the publicity of the ordinary high roads, and securing secrecy and seclusion. "It was the last time He was to visit the scene of so great a part of His public life, and He felt, as He journeyed on, that He would no more pass from village to village as openly as in days gone by, for the eyes of His enemies were everywhere upon Him."

and passed] The word thus translated occurs five times in the N. T. It is applied to the disciples *passing through* the cornfields (Mark ii. 23); to their *passing by* along the road from Bethany and noticing the withered fig-tree (Mark xi. 20); to those that *passed by* and reviled our Lord upon the Cross (Matt. xxvii. 39; Mark xv. 29). Here it seems to

31 and he would not that any man should know *it*. For he taught his disciples, and said unto them, The Son of man is delivered into the hands of men, and they shall kill him; 32 and after that he is killed, he shall rise the third day. But they understood not that saying, and were afraid to ask him.

33—37. True Greatness in Christ's Kingdom.

33 And he came to Capernaum : and being in the house he asked them, What was it that ye disputed among your-34 selves by the way? But they held their peace : for by the way they had disputed among themselves, who *should be* the 35 greatest. And he sat down, and called the twelve, and saith unto them, If any man desire to be first, *the same* shall be 36 last of all, and servant of all. And he took a child, and set him in the midst of them : and when he had taken him in 37 his arms, he said unto them, Whosoever shall receive one of such children in my name, receiveth me : and whosoever shall receive me, receiveth not me, but him that sent me.

38—50. The Question of John.

38 And John answered him, saying, Master, we saw one

denote that, avoiding populous places, He and His Apostles sought byepaths among the hills, where He would meet few and be little known.

31. *For he taught*] The tense in the original implies that the *constant* subject of His teaching in private now was His approaching sufferings, death, and resurrection.

32. *were afraid*] St Matthew adds that they were "exceeding sorry." His words concerning His violent death contradicted all their expectations.

33—37. TRUE GREATNESS IN CHRIST'S KINGDOM.

33. *he came*] or rather **they came,** *to Capernaum.* Here, the next recorded event was the miraculous payment of the tribute-money (Matt. xvii. 24—27), the half-shekel for the Temple-service.

34. *who should be the greatest*] They called to mind perhaps the preference given on Hermon to Peter and the sons of Zebedee, and now disputed who should be the greatest in the Messianic kingdom, which they fondly believed was about to be speedily set up.

35. *And he sat down*] Observe the many graphic and pathetic touches in this and the following verse. (1) He *sits* down ; (2) He *calls* the Twelve to Him ; (3) He *takes a little child*, and *places it in the midst* of them ; (4) He *takes it into His arms*, and then He *speaks* to them.

38—41. THE QUESTION OF JOHN.

38. *And John answered him*] The words *in My name* of *v.* 37

casting out devils in thy name, and he followeth not us: and we forbad him, because he followeth not us. But Jesus 39 said, Forbid him not: for there is no man which shall do a miracle in my name, that can lightly speak evil of me. For 40 he that is not against us is on our part. For whosoever shall 41 give you a cup of water to drink in my name, because ye belong to Christ, verily I say unto you, he shall not lose his reward. And whosoever shall offend one of *these* little ones 42 that believe in me, it is better for him that a millstone were hanged about his neck, and he were cast into the sea. And 43 if thy hand offend thee, cut it off: it is better for thee to enter into life maimed, than having two hands to go into

seem to have reminded the Apostle of an incident in their recent journey.

because he followeth not us] Observe what the Apostle affirms to have been the ground of their rebuke, "because he followeth not *us*," not "because he followeth not *Thee*." It is the utterance of excited party feeling. "We gather from this passage," observes Meyer, "how mightily the words and influence of Christ had wrought outside the sphere of His permanent dependants, exciting in individuals a degree of spiritual energy that performed miracles on others."

39. *Forbid him not*] Compare the words of Joshua and the reply of Moses in Num. xi. 28, 29; "and Joshua the son of Nun, the servant of Moses...answered and said, My lord Moses, forbid them. And Moses said unto him, Enviest thou for my sake? Would God that all the Lord's people were prophets, and that the Lord would put His Spirit upon them."

41. *a cup of water*] which all gave readily in those sultry lands.

42. *a millstone*] Literally, **an ass-mill-stone**, a mill-stone turned by an ass. These were much larger and heavier than the stones of hand-mills. Comp. Ov. *Fast.* VI. 318,

"Et quæ pumiceas versat asella molas."

It was not a Jewish punishment, but was in use among the Greeks, Romans, Syrians, and Phœnicians. "Pædagogum ministrosque C. fili...*oneratos gravi pondere* cervicibus præcipitavit in flumen." Sueton. *Oct.* lxvii.

43. *offend thee*] or, as in margin, **cause thee to offend**, lead thee into sin. Our Lord makes special mention of the Hand, the Foot, the Eye, those members, whereby we *do* amiss, or *walk* astray, or *gaze on* what is sinful.

into hell] Literally, **the Gehenna**, or **the Gehenna of fire** (*v.* 47). The "Ravine of Hinnom," also called "*Topheth*" (2 Kings xxiii. 10; Isai. xxx. 33), is described in Josh. xviii. 16, as on the south of Mount Zion. Its total length is a mile and a half. It is a deep retired glen, shut in by rugged cliffs, with the bleak mountain sides rising over all,

44 hell, into the fire that never shall be quenched: where their
45 worm dieth not, and the fire is not quenched. And if thy
foot offend thee, cut it off: it is better for thee to enter halt
into life, than having two feet to be cast into hell, into the
46 fire that never shall be quenched: where their worm dieth not,
47 and the fire is not quenched. And if thine eye offend thee,
pluck it out: it is better for thee to enter into the kingdom
of God with one eye, than having two eyes to be cast into
48 hell fire: where their worm dieth not, and the fire is not
49 quenched. For every one shall be salted with fire, and
50 every sacrifice shall be salted with salt. Salt *is* good: but if
the salt have lost his saltness, wherewith will ye season it?
Have salt in yourselves, and have peace one with another.

It became notorious in the times of Ahaz and Manasseh as the scene of the barbarous rites of Molech and Chemosh, when the idolatrous inhabitants of Jerusalem cast their sons and daughters into the red-hot arms of a monster idol of brass placed at the opening of the ravine (2 Kings xvi. 3; 2 Chron. xxviii. 3; Jer. vii. 31). To put an end to these abominations the place was polluted by Josiah, who spread over it human bones and other corruptions (2 Kings xxiii. 10, 13, 14), from which time it seems to have become the common cesspool of the city. These inhuman rites and subsequent ceremonial defilement caused the later Jews to regard it with horror and detestation, and they applied the name given to the valley to *the place of torment*.

44. *where their worm*] These words are cited from Isai. lxvi. 24.

49. *every one shall be salted with fire*] Salt and fire have properties in common. Salt, like a subtle flame, penetrates all that is corruptible, and separates that which is decaying and foul, whilst it fixes and quickens that which is sound. Fire destroys that which is perishable, and thereby establishes the imperishable in its purest perfection, and leads to new and more beautiful forms of being. Thus both effect a kind of transformation. Now "every one," our Lord saith, "shall be salted with fire;" either (1) by his voluntary entering upon a course of self-denial and renunciation of his sins, and so submitting to the purifying fire of self-transformation; or (2) by his being involuntarily salted with the fire of condemning judgment (Heb. x. 27, xii. 29), as the victims on the altar were salted with salt (Lev. ii. 13; Ezek. xliii. 24). See Lange.

50. *Salt is good*] in its kind and its effect, as preserving from corruption.

have lost] "It was the belief of the Jews that salt would by exposure to the air lose its virtue (Matt. v. 13) and become saltless. The same fact is implied in the expressions of Pliny *sal iners*, *sal tabescere*, and Maundrell asserts that he found the surface of a salt rock in this condition."

his saltness] Observe *his* here, where we should now use *its*. This is frequently the case in the Bible, and indeed the word *its* does not occur at all in the English Version of 1611.

1—12. *Marriage Legislation of the Pharisees.*

And he arose from thence, and cometh into the coasts 10 of Judæa by the farther side of Jordan: and the people resort unto him again; and, as he was wont, he taught them

Have salt in yourselves] In the common life of Orientals, salt was a sign of sacred covenant engagements and obligations (Lev. ii. 13; 2 Chron. xiii. 5). To eat salt together, meant to make peace, and enter into covenant with each other. Hence the connection here between the disciples having salt in themselves and being at peace one with another, which our Lord further enforced during this "brief period of tranquillity and seclusion" by speaking of the duty not only of avoiding all grounds of offence, but also of cultivating a spirit of gentleness and forgiveness (Matt. xviii. 15—20), which He illustrated by the Parable of *the Lost Sheep* (Matt. xviii. 12—14), and *the Debtor who owed Ten Thousand Talents* (Matt. xviii. 21—35).

CH. X. 1—12. MARRIAGE LEGISLATION OF THE PHARISEES.

1. *And*] Between the events just recorded and those of which the Evangelist now proceeds to treat, many others had occurred, which he has passed over. The most important of these were

(α) *The visit of our Lord to Jerusalem at the Feast of Tabernacles* (John vii. 8—10), *which was marked by*
  (a) *The rebuke of the "Sons of Thunder" at the churlish conduct of the inhabitants of a Samaritan village on their way to the Holy City* (Luke ix. 51—56);
  (b) *Solemn discourses during the Feast, and an attempt of the Sanhedrim to apprehend Him* (John vii. 11—51, viii. 12—59);
  (c) *The opening of the eyes of one born blind* (John ix. 1—41), *the revelation of Himself as the Good Shepherd* (John x. 1—18);
(β) *Ministrations in Judæa and Mission of the Seventy* (Luke x.—xiii. 17);
(γ) *Visit to Jerusalem at the Feast of Dedication* (John x. 22—39);
(δ) *Tour in Peræa* (Luke xiii. 22—xvii. 10);
(ε) *The raising of Lazarus* (John xi. 1—46);
(ζ) *Resolve of the Sanhedrim to put Him to death, and His retirement to Ephraim* (John xi. 47—54).

he arose] The place, whither He now retired, has been identified with Ophrah, and was situated in the wide desert country north-east of Jerusalem, not far from Bethel, and on the confines of Samaria. Caspari would identify it with a place now called El-Faria, or El-Farah, about 2 hours N. E. of Nablous. *Chron. and Geog. Introd.* p. 185. Here in quiet and seclusion He remained till the approach of the last Passover, and then commenced a farewell journey along the border-line of Samaria and Galilee (Luke xvii. 11) and so *by the further side of Jordan* towards Judæa (Mark x. 1).

he taught them again] Portions of His teaching are recorded by St Luke, and include the Parables of (*a*) *the Unjust Judge*, and (*b*) *the*

2 again. And the Pharisees came to him, and asked him, Is it
3 lawful for a man to put away *his* wife? tempting him. And
  he answered and said unto them, What did Moses command
4 you? And they said, Moses suffered to write a bill of
5 divorcement, and to put *her* away. And Jesus answered and
  said unto them, For the hardness of your heart he wrote you
6 this precept. But from the beginning of the creation God
7 made them male and female. For this cause shall a man
8 leave his father and mother, and cleave to his wife; and
  they twain shall be one flesh: so then they are no more
9 twain, but one flesh. What therefore God hath joined to-
10 gether, let not man put asunder. And in the house his dis
11 ciples asked him again of the same *matter*. And he saith
  unto them, Whosoever shall put away his wife, and marry
12 another, committeth adultery against her. And if a woman
  shall put away her husband, and be married to another, she
  committeth adultery.

Pharisee and the Publican (Luke xviii. 1—14). On the frontier of the region now traversed occurred in all probability the Healing of the ten lepers (Luke xvii. 12—19).

2. *Is it lawful for a man to put away his wife*] "for every cause?" as St Matthew adds (Matt. xix. 3). On this point the rival schools of Hillel and Shammai were divided, the former adopting the more lax, the latter the stricter view: the one holding that *any dislike*, which he felt towards her, would justify a man in putting away his wife; the other, that only notorious unchastity could be a sufficient reason. It has also been suggested that the object of the question may have been to involve Him with the adulterous tetrarch, in whose territory He was.

7. *For this cause*] He thus shews that from the beginning God had designed that the marriage tie should be the closest and most indissoluble of all ties, and in the words added by St Matthew (xix. 9) rebukes the adultery of Herod Antipas, though without naming him, in the severest terms.

9. *What therefore God*] In Gen. ii. 24 these are the words of Adam; in St Matthew xix. 4 the words of God; in St Mark the words of Christ. They are words of Adam as uttering prophetically a Divine, fundamental, ordinance; they are words of God as being eternally valid; they are words of Christ, as rules for Christian life re-established by Him, Who "adorned and beautified" the holy estate of matrimony with His presence and first miracle at Cana of Galilee.

10. *in the house*] St Mark records several confidential household words of our Lord to His disciples, e.g. concerning (*a*) the power of casting out demons (ix. 28, 29); (*b*) the great in the kingdom of heaven (ix. 33—37); and (*c*) here, the Christian law of marriage.

13—16. *Suffer little Children to come unto Me.*

And they brought young children to him, that he should touch them: and *his* disciples rebuked those that brought *them*. But when Jesus saw *it*, he was much displeased, and said unto them, Suffer the little children to come unto me, and forbid them not: for of such is the kingdom of God. Verily I say unto you, Whosoever shall not receive the kingdom of God as a little child, he shall not enter therein. And he took them up in his arms, put *his* hands upon them, and blessed them.

17—31. *The Rich Young Ruler.*

And when he was gone forth into the way, there came

13—16. SUFFER LITTLE CHILDREN TO COME UNTO ME.

13. *they brought*] These probably were certain parents, who honoured Him and valued His benediction. The "children" in St Mark and St Matthew are "infants" in St Luke xviii. 15.

that he should touch them] or, as St Matthew adds, *that he should lay his hands upon them and pray* for them (xix. 13). Hebrew mothers were accustomed in this manner to seek a blessing for their children from the presidents of the synagogues, who were wont to lay their hands upon them. "After the father of the child," says the Talmud, "had laid his hands on his child's head, he led him to the elders one by one, and they also blessed him, and prayed that he might grow up famous in the Law, faithful in marriage, and abundant in good works."

14. *he was much displeased*] This feature is peculiar to St Mark. Only lately the Lord had expressed His love towards little children in a very remarkable manner (Mark ix. 36, 37).

of such] Rather, **to such belongs the Kingdom of God.** He says not *of these*, but *of such:* shewing that it is not children only, but the disposition of children which obtains the kingdom, and that to such as have the like innocence and simplicity the reward is promised.

16. *took them up in his arms*] He ever giveth more than men ask or think. He had been asked only to touch the children. He takes them into His arms, lays His Hands upon them, and blesses them. Twice we read of our Lord *taking into His arms*, and both times they were children whom He embraced, and both times the scenes are recorded only by St Mark (ix. 36, x. 16).

blessed them] Rather, **He blesses them**, according to some MSS. The present tense is in keeping with the graphic style of the Evangelist.

17—31. THE RICH YOUNG RULER.

17. *when he was gone forth*] Literally, **when He was going forth.** He was just starting, it would seem, on His last journey towards Bethany.

one running, and kneeled to him, and asked him, Good
18 Master, what shall I do that I may inherit eternal life? And
Jesus said unto him, Why callest thou me good? *there is*
19 *none good but one, that is,* God. Thou knowest the commandments, Do not commit adultery, Do not kill, Do not steal, Do not bear false witness, Defraud not, Honour thy
20 father and mother. And he answered and said unto him,
21 Master, all these have I observed from my youth. Then Jesus beholding him loved him, and said unto him, One

one] He was young (Matt. xix. 22), of great wealth, and a ruler of a local synagogue (Luke xviii. 18).
running] Running up to Him, apparently from behind, eager and breathless. Then he knelt before Him, as was usual before a venerated Rabbi.
what shall I do] He had probably observed our Lord's gracious reception of little children, and he desired to have part in the Kingdom promised to them. But his question betrays his fundamental error. Not by *doing*, but by *being*, was an entrance into it to be obtained.
18. *Why callest thou me good?*] The emphasis is on the "why." "Dost thou know what thou meanest, when thou givest Me this appellation?" If we combine the question and rejoinder as given by St Matthew and St Luke it would seem to have run, *Why askest thou Me about the good? and why callest thou Me good? None is good save One, God.* Our Lord does not decline the appellation "good." He repels it only in the superficial sense of the questioner, who regarded Him merely as a "good Rabbi."
19. *Thou knowest the commandments*] The young man is referred to the Commandments of the Second Table only, and they are cited generally from Ex. xx. 12—17. A striking instance of the free mode of quotation from the Old Testament even in such a case as the Ten Commandments.
Defraud not] The word thus rendered occurs in 1 Cor. vi. 7, 8, vii. 5; 1 Tim. vi. 5; James v. 4. It means *deprive none of what is theirs*, and has been thought to sum up the four Commandments which precede.
Honour thy father and mother] Rendered by Wyclif "*worschippe þi fadir and modir,*" which illustrates the meaning of the word as used in the Marriage Service, "with my body I thee *worship*"=honour. St Mark places this commandment at the end.
20. *all these have I observed*] adding, according to St Matthew, *what lack I yet?* We are told that when the Angel of Death came to fetch the R. Chanina, he said, "Go and fetch me the Book of the Law, and *see whether there is anything in it which I have not kept.*" Farrar's *Life of Christ*, II. 161, n.
21. *beholding him*] The same word, which occurs also in *v.* 27, in the original is applied (*a*) to the Baptist, when he "*looked upon Jesus,*" and said, "Behold the Lamb of God" (John i. 36), (*b*) to our Lord's

thing thou lackest: go thy way, sell whatsoever thou hast, and give to the poor, and thou shalt have treasure in heaven: and come, take up the cross, and follow me. And he was 22 sad at that saying, and went away grieved: for he had great possessions. And Jesus looked round about, and saith unto 23 his disciples, How hardly shall they that have riches enter into the kingdom of God! And the disciples were astonished at 24 his words. But Jesus answereth again, and saith unto them, Children, how hard is it for them that trust in riches to enter into the kingdom of God! It is easier for a camel to go 25

look at St Peter (i) when He named him Cephas (John i. 42), and (ii) when He turned and *looked upon* him just before the cock crew for the second time (Luke xxii. 61).

loved him] Literally, **esteemed him**, or *was pleased with him*, for His Eye penetrated his inmost being, and saw within him an honest striving after better things, and the noblest form of life. Lightfoot remarks that the Jewish Rabbis were wont to kiss the head of such pupils as answered well. Some gesture at least we may believe that our Lord used to shew that the young man pleased Him, both by his question and by his answer.

One thing thou lackest] He thus proposed to him one short crucial test of his real condition, and way to clearer self-knowledge. He had fancied himself willing to do whatever could be required: he could now see if he were really so.

take up the cross, and follow me] See ch. viii. 34. But some MSS. omit the words. "Poor, friendless, outlawed, Jesus abated no jot of His awful claims, loftier than human monarch had ever dreamed of making, on all who sought citizenship in His Kingdom."

22. *he was sad*] "*Sorrowful*," says St Matthew (xix. 22); "*very sorrowful*," says St Luke (xviii. 23); "sad," says St Mark, or rather **lowring**, with a cloud upon his brow. The original word only occurs in one other place, Matt. xvi. 3, "for the sky is red and *lowring*."

he had great possessions] and these he preferred to possessions in heaven, and made, as Dante calls it, "the great refusal!" "Yet within a few months," to quote the words of Keble, "hundreds in Jerusalem remembered and obeyed this saying of our Lord, and brought their goods, and laid them at the Apostles' feet" (Acts iv. 34—37).

23. *looked round about*] "Sæpe describitur vultus Christi, affectui conveniens, et affectibus auditorum attemperatus." Bengel. Comp. Mark iii. 5, 34, viii. 34; Luke vi. 10, xxii. 61.

24. *Children*] By this affectionate title He softens the sadness and sternness of His words.

for them that trust in riches] Some important MSS. omit these words, and then the verse would run, "Children, how hard it is to enter into the kingdom of God."

25. *It is easier for a camel*] This figure has been variously interpreted. (*a*) Some have rendered it an "anchor-rope," as though the word was

through the eye of a needle, than for a rich man to enter
26 into the kingdom of God. And they were astonished out
of measure, saying among themselves, Who then can be
27 saved? And Jesus looking upon them saith, With men *it
is* impossible, but not with God: for with God all things are
28 possible. Then Peter began to say unto him, Lo, we have left
29 all, and have followed thee. And Jesus answered and said,
Verily I say unto you, There is no man that hath left house,
or brethren, or sisters, or father, or mother, or wife, or chil-
30 dren, or lands, for my sake, and the gospel's, but he shall
receive an hundredfold now in this time, houses, and brethren, and sisters, and mothers, and children, and lands, with
31 persecutions; and in the world to come eternal life. But
many *that are* first shall be last; and the last first.

32—34. *Predictions of the Passion.*

32 And they were in the way going up to Jerusalem; and
Jesus went before them: and they were amazed; and as

"*kamilon*" and not "*kamelon;*" (*b*) others think it refers to the side
gate for foot passengers, close by the principal gate, called in the East
the "eye of a needle;" but (*c*) it is best to understand the words
literally. Similar proverbs are common in the Talmud.

28. *and have followed thee*] adding, as St Matthew relates, "what
shall *we* have therefore?" In reply to which our Lord uttered glorious
words respecting the Twelve Thrones to be occupied by the Apostles
"in the Regeneration," or "restoration of all things" (Matt. xix. 28).

30. *with persecutions*] An important limitation. See 2 Cor. xii. 10;
2 Thess. i. 4; 2 Tim. iii. 11.

31. *many that are first*] Very signally was the former part of this
verse fulfilled *temporarily* in the case of St Peter himself, *finally* in that
of Judas; while the latter part was wonderfully realised in the instance
of St Paul, so that this passage is chosen for the Gospel of the Festival
of "the Conversion of St Paul." It was now that, to impress upon His
hearers the important lesson that entrance into the kingdom of heaven
is not a matter of mercenary calculation, our Lord delivered the memorable Parable of the *Labourers in the Vineyard* (Matt. xx. 1—16).

32—34. PREDICTIONS OF THE PASSION.

32. *they were in the way*] Our Lord would seem to have now descended from Ephraim to the high road in order to join the caravans of
Galilæan pilgrims going up to Jerusalem. St Mark gives a special prominence to this critical period in His human history: He describes (*a*) the
prophetic elevation and solemnity of soul which He displayed; (*b*) His
advancing before them as the destined Sufferer, (*c*) the awe of the disciples as they followed Him.

and Jesus went before them] "After the manner of some leader who

they followed, they were afraid. And he took again the twelve, and began to tell them what things should happen unto him, *saying*, Behold, we go up to Jerusalem; and the 33 Son of man shall be delivered unto the chief priests, and unto the scribes; and they shall condemn him to death, and shall deliver him to the Gentiles: and they shall mock him, 34 and shall scourge him, and shall spit upon him, and shall kill him: and the third day he shall rise again.

35—45. *The Ambitious Apostles.*

And James and John, the sons of Zebedee, come unto 35 him, saying, Master, we would that thou shouldest do for us whatsoever we shall desire. And he said unto them, What 36 would ye that I should do for you? They said unto him, 37 Grant unto us that we may sit, one on thy right hand, and

heartens his soldiers by choosing the place of danger for himself." Trench, *Studies*, p. 216.

and as they followed] Or, according to the better reading, **and they that followed**, as though there were two bands of the Apostles, of whom one went foremost, while the others had fallen behind. "There are few pictures in the Gospel more striking than this of Jesus going forth to His death, and walking alone along the path into the deep valley, while behind Him, in awful reverence, and mingled anticipations of dread and hope—their eyes fixed on Him, as with bowed head He preceded them in all the majesty of sorrow—the disciples walked behind and dared not disturb His meditations." Farrar, *Life*, II. p. 179.

And he took again] This was for the third time. The two previous occasions are described in (*a*) Mark viii. 31, in the neighbourhood of Cæsarea Philippi, just after St Peter's confession, and (*b*) Mark ix. 30—32, shortly afterwards, during the return to Capernaum. The particulars are now more full and more clear than ever before. St Matthew (xx. 17) distinctly tells us that this mournful communication was made *privately* to the Apostles.

34. *and shall kill him*] Or, as St Matthew adds, "*crucify Him.*" Now for the first time is revealed this last, this greatest horror (see Matt. xx. 19). St Luke lays stress upon the fact that the disciples would not and could not understand His words (Luke xviii. 34). This absence of all sympathy was one of His greatest trials.

35—45. THE AMBITIOUS APOSTLES.

35. *James and John*] and with them their mother Salome, to ask the same favour on their behalf. She was one of the constant attendants of our Lord, and now falling on her knees preferred her request (Matt. xx. 20). Nothing could have been more ill-timed than this selfish petition when He was going forth to His death.

37. *that we may sit*] The mention of Thrones (Matt. xix. 28), as in

38 the other on thy left hand, in thy glory. But Jesus said unto them, Ye know not what ye ask: can ye drink of the cup that I drink of? and be baptized with the baptism that 39 I am baptized with? And they said unto him, We can. And Jesus said unto them, Ye shall indeed drink of the cup that I drink of; and with the baptism that I am baptized 40 withal shall ye be baptized: but to sit on my right hand and on my left hand is not mine to give; but *it shall be given* 41 *to them* for whom it is prepared. And when the ten heard *it*, they began to be much displeased with James and John. 42 But Jesus called them *to him*, and saith unto them, Ye know that they which are accounted to rule over the Gentiles

reversion for the Twelve at the coming of their Master in glory, may have suggested the idea to the aspiring Three. This session on the right hand and on the left was a Jewish form of expression for being next to the king in honour.

39. *And they said unto him, We can*] They knew not at the time what they said, and their words were recorded in heaven. They had yet to learn how serious their words were, and afterwards they were enabled to drink of that Cup, and to be baptized with that Baptism. To St James was given strength to be steadfast unto death, and be the first martyr of the Apostolic band (Acts xii. 2); to St John (*a*) to bear bereavement, first, of his brother, then of the other Apostles; (*b*) to bear a length of years in loneliness and exile in sea-girt Patmos (Rev. i. 9); and (*c*) then to die last of the Apostles, as St James first.

the cup] Comp. John xviii. 11, "*The cup* which my Father hath given me, shall I not drink it?" and Mark xiv. 36, "Take away *this cup* from me." Their thoughts were fastened on thrones and high places; His on a Cup of Suffering and a baptism of blood. For this use of the word "baptism" here, compare Luke xii. 50, "I have *a baptism* to be *baptized* with."

40. *but it shall be given*] This is not a very happy interpolation. The verse really runs thus: **But to sit on My right hand and on My left hand is not mine to give except to those for whom it is prepared.** To "give" here denotes to give, as of mere favour; to lavish out of caprice, as in kingdoms of the world. "The throne," says one of old, "is the prize of toils, not a grace granted to ambition."

41. *began to be much displeased*] "hadden endignacioun," Wyclif. The sons of Zebedee had been in a better social position than most of their brethren, and this attempt to secure a pre-eminence of honour kindled a storm of jealousy.

42. *which*] Commonly used at the time our translation was made for the relative "*who*," and applied to persons, from the A.-S. *hwilc*, Mœso-Goth. *hwĕleiks*, literally, *who-like*. Comp. Latimer's *Sermons*, p. 331, "Whosoever loveth God, will love his neighbour, *which* is made after the image of God." See *Bible Word-Book*, p. 528.

exercise lordship over them; and their great ones exercise authority upon them. But so shall it not be among you: 43 but whosoever will be great among you, shall be your minister: and whosoever of you will be the chiefest, shall be 44 servant of all. For even the Son of man came not to be 45 ministered unto, but to minister, and to give his life a ransom for many.

46—52. *Passing through Jericho.—Blind Bartimæus.*

And they came to Jericho: and as he went out of Jericho 46

are accounted]=those "who profess to exercise rule," those who have the reputation of being governors. "Qui censentur imperare; i.e. quos gentes habent et agnoscunt, quorum imperio pareant." Beza.

exercise lordship] The word is used in an unfavourable sense. It is applied in Acts xix. 16 to the man possessed with an evil spirit *prevailing against* and *overcoming* the seven sons of Sceva. St Peter himself uses it in his first Epistle (v. 3), recalling possibly this very incident, where he warns the elders of the Church "not to be *lords over* God's heritage," or as it is in the margin, "*to overrule.*" The preposition in the original is emphatic, and gives the force of oppressive, tyrannical rule, where the ruler uses his rights for the diminution of the ruled and the exaltation of himself. The same unfavourable sense attaches to the word rendered "*exercise authority*," which only occurs here and in the parallel in Matt. xx. 25.

45. *and to give his life*] We have here one of the early intimations of the mysterious *purport* of the Passion, that the Redeemer was about to give His life as *a ransom for many* (1 Tim. ii. 6). The word translated "ransom" only occurs here and in the parallel, Matt. xx. 28. Wyclif renders it "and ʒyue his soule, *or lyf*, redempcioun, *or aʒen-biyng*, for manye." The three great circles of images, which the Scriptures employ when they represent to us the purport of the death of Christ, are (*a*) *a sin-offering, or propitiation* (1 John ii. 2, iv. 10); (*b*) *reconciliation* (=*at-one-ment*) *with an offended friend* (Rom. v. 11, xi. 15; 2 Cor. v. 18, 19); (*c*), as here, *redemption from slavery* (Rom. iii. 24; Eph. i. 7; Col. i. 14).

46—52. PASSING THROUGH JERICHO.—BLIND BARTIMÆUS.

46. *And they came*] Leaving behind them the upland pastures of Peræa, the little company travelled along the road which led down to the sunken channel of the Jordan, and the luxuriant "district" of Jericho.

to Jericho] This ancient stronghold of the Canaanites,—taken by Joshua (ii., vi.), founded for the second time under Hiel the Bethelite (1 Kings xvi. 34), visited by Elisha and Elijah before the latter "went up by a whirlwind into heaven" (2 Kings ii. 4—15)—was still in the days of Christ surrounded by towers and castles. Two of them lay in ruins since the time of Pompeius, but "Kypros, the last fortress built

with his disciples and a great number of people, blind Bartimæus, the son of Timæus, sat by the highway side begging. 47 And when he heard that it was Jesus of Nazareth, he began to cry out, and say, Jesus, *thou* Son of David, have mercy on 48 me. And many charged him that he should hold his peace: but he cried the more a great deal, *Thou* Son of David, have 49 mercy on me. And Jesus stood still, and commanded him

by Herod the Great, who had called it after his mother, rose white in the sun on the south of the town.... The great palace of Herod, in the far-famed groves of palms, had been plundered and burnt down in the tumults that followed his death, but in its place a still grander structure, built by Archelaus, had arisen amidst still finer gardens, and more copious and delightful streams. A grand theatre and spacious circus, built by Herod, scandalized the Jews, while a great stone aqueduct of eleven arches brought a copious supply of water to the city, and the Roman military road ran through it." Geikie's *Life and Words of Christ*, II. p. 385.

as he went] It is most probable that at the entrance of Jericho He met one of the sufferers, who having learnt from the crowd that He was passing, joined the other sufferer, whom the Saviour encountered as He was *going out* of the city on the following morning. (Comp. Luke xviii. 35; Matt. xx. 29, 30.)

a great number] of pilgrims accompanied our Lord, who had come from Peræa and Galilee, and met at this central point to go up to the Passover, at Jerusalem.

Bartimæus] The patronymic is made into a proper name after the analogy of Bartholomew and others. The true reading seems to be **the son of Timæus, Bartimæus, a blind man.** "This account of him hints that he was a personage well known to Christians in St Mark's time as a monument of the Lord's miracle, as was probably also Simon the Leper; and the designation 'son of Timæus' would distinguish him, not merely from the father but also from other sons." Lange. As in the case of the Gadarene demoniacs, he was probably better known, and hence his case is more particularly recorded. "All the roads leading to Jerusalem, like the Temple itself, were much frequented at the time of the feasts, by beggars, who reaped a special harvest from the charity of the pilgrims."

47. *Son of David*] This was the popular designation of the Messiah. He may have heard of the recent resurrection of Lazarus, which took place in his own neighbourhood.

48. *charged him*] "þretnyden hym, þat he schulde be stille." Wyclif. They rebuked him and his companion, deeming their clamours ill-mannered and unworthy of Him, who was passing onward to Jerusalem.

49. *stood still*] in the fulness of His compassionate heart.

commanded him to be called] Or, more graphically, according to some MSS., **said, Call him.**

vv. 50—52; 1.]   ST MARK, X. XI.   119

to be called. And they call the blind man, saying unto him, Be of good comfort, rise; he calleth thee. And he, casting 50 away his garment, rose, and came to Jesus. And Jesus 51 answered and said unto him, What wilt thou that I should do unto thee? The blind man said unto him, Lord, that I might receive my sight. And Jesus said unto him, Go thy 52 way; thy faith hath made thee whole. And immediately he received his sight, and followed Jesus in the way.

1—11. *The Triumphal Entry.*

And when they came nigh to Jerusalem, unto Beth- 11

50. *casting away his garment*] i.e. his *abba*, or upper garment, *he rose*, or, according to a better reading, **leaped up.** "Sturtinge cam to him," Wyclif.

51. *Lord*] The original word is "Rabboni"=*my Master*. The blind man gives Him the title of greatest reverence that he knew. The title occurs only here and in John xx. 16, where it is used by Mary Magdalene to her risen Lord. The gradations of honour were *Rab*, *Rabbi*, *Rabban*, *Rabboni*.

52. *and followed Jesus*] or *followed him* along the road, *glorifying God*, as St Luke adds (xviii. 43), and joining the festal company of his Healer, who all likewise gave praise unto God for the miracle, which they had witnessed. Comp. Acts iii. 8—10. In the account of this Miracle the graphic power of St Mark is signally displayed. He describes (*a*) the great crowds that accompanied the Saviour, records (*b*) the full name of the blind man, (*c*) the words of the people to him, (*d*) how he cast away his garment, (*e*) started up, and (*f*) came to his Healer, (*g*) how he immediately recovered his sight, and (*h*) followed in the pilgrim train. After this signal proof of His miraculous power the Lord accepted the hospitality of Zacchæus, a superintendent of customs or tribute at Jericho (Luke xix. 1—10); uttered the Parable of *"the Pounds"* in order to correct the idea that the kingdom of heaven was about to appear immediately (Luke xix. 11—27); and at length, six days before the Passover, reached the safe seclusion of the mountain hamlet of Bethany (John xii. 1).

CH. XI. 1—11. THE TRIUMPHAL ENTRY.

1. *And when*] The order of events at this point needs explanation. (1) The Saviour apparently reached Bethany on the evening of Friday, Nisan 8. There (2) in quiet retirement He spent His last earthly Sabbath; and (3) in the evening, sat down to a festal meal provided by the sisters of Lazarus at the house of one Simon, who had been a leper (Matt. xxvi. 6; John xii. 1). (4) At this feast He was anointed by Mary (John xii. 3); and (5) during the night a council of the Jews was convened to consider the propriety of putting not Him only but Lazarus also to death (John xii. 10).

they came] Rather, **when they draw near.** The Evangelist, pass-

phage and Bethany, at the mount of Olives, he sendeth forth
2 two of his disciples, and saith unto them, Go your way into
the village over against you: and as soon as ye be entered
into it, ye shall find a colt tied, whereon never man sat;
3 loose him, and bring *him*. And if any man say unto you,
Why do ye this? say ye that the Lord hath need of him;
4 and straightway he will send him hither. And they went
their way, and found the colt tied by the door without in a

ing over for the present the peaceful scene at the festal meal (Mark xiv.
3—11), translates us at once to Palm Sunday, as to time; and, as to
place, to the region between Bethany and the mount of Olives. Observe
how he writes in the present tense.

unto Bethphage] On the first day of the Holy Week th Saviour left
Bethany and proceeded towards Bethphage = *the house of unripe figs*, a
little hamlet on the road between Jericho and Jerusalem. As in a
journey towards Jerusalem it is always mentioned before Bethany, it
seems to have been to the east of that village.

he sendeth] Note again the present tense.

two of his disciples] The minuteness of the description that follows
suggests that St Peter may have been one of these. If so, he was not
improbably accompanied by St John.

2. *into the village over against you*] Either Bethphage or an adjoining hamlet.

a colt tied] "In the East the ass is in high esteem. Statelier, livelier,
swifter than with us, it vies with the horse in favour. Among the Jews
it was equally valued as a beast of burden, for work in the field or at
the mill, and for riding. In contrast to the horse, which had been introduced by Solomon from Egypt, and was used especially for war, it
was the symbol of peace. To the Jew it was peculiarly national, for
had not Moses led his wife, seated on an ass, to Egypt; had not the
Judges ridden on white asses; and was not the ass of Abraham, the
friend of God, noted in Scripture? Every Jew, moreover, expected,
from the words of one of the prophets (Zech. ix. 9), that the Messiah would
enter Jerusalem riding on an ass. No act could be more perfectly in
keeping with the conception of a king of Israel, and no word could
express more plainly that the king proclaimed Himself the Messiah."
Geikie, II. p. 395.

whereon never man sat] This agrees with St Matthew's account of
the she-ass (Matt. xxi. 2) and her colt with her. The colt would not
have been used, so long as it was running with the mother. Unused
animals were put to sacred purposes. See Num. xix. 2; Deut. xxi. 3;
1 Sam. vi. 7.

3. *the Lord hath need of him*] The words suggest that the man may
have been a secret disciple. "Secret disciples, such as the five hundred
who afterwards gathered to one spot in Galilee, and the hundred and
twenty who met after the resurrection (1 Cor. xv. 6; Acts i. 15), were
scattered in many places,"

place where two ways met; and they loose him. And cer- 5
tain of them that stood there said unto them, What do ye,
loosing the colt? And they said unto them even as Jesus 6
had commanded: and they let them go. And they brought 7
the colt to Jesus, and cast their garments on him; and he
sat upon him. And many spread their garments in the way: 8
and others cut down branches off the trees, and strawed *them*

4. *in a place where two ways met*] So Wyclif, "in þe meeting of
tweye weyes," following the Vulgate *bivium*. The word in the original
thus rendered denotes (1) *any road that leads round a place, a street, or
a crooked lane;* (2) *a block of houses surrounded by streets;* (3) *the
quarter of a town*=Lat. *vicus*. Here it means **the passage round the
house**. They went and found the ass tied at the door, and the colt
with her, not in the highway, but in a back way or alley, which went
round the house. Observe the minuteness of the circumstances specified. The Apostles would find the colt tied; it had never been ridden;
it would be found not in the courtyard, but outside, at the door of the
house; not in the highway, but in a back lane or alley skirting the
house; and persons would be near it, and the words which they would
speak are predicted, and the answer is suggested which the Apostles
were to make. The colt, untamed, and tied at the back gate, as if
ready for a rider, has been interpreted as a symbol of the Gentile world
to be brought to Christ from the lanes and alleys of Heathendom (Luke
xiv. 21); the she-ass as symbolizing God's ancient people who were
familiar with the yoke of the Law.

7. *and cast their garments on him*] over both indeed (Matt. xxi. 7),
to do Him regal honour, just as the captains "*took every man his garment,
and put it under Jehu on the top of the stairs, and blew with trumpets,
saying, Jehu is king*" (2 Kings ix. 13).

he sat upon] the unused colt, while probably some of the Apostles led
it by the bridle.

8. *spread their garments in the way*] i.e. their "abbas" or "hykes,"
the loose blanket or cloak worn over the tunic or shirt. So myrtle-
twigs and robes had been strewn by their ancestors before Mordecai,
when he came forth from the palace of Ahasuerus (*Targ.* Esther viii. 15),
so the Persian army had honoured Xerxes when about to cross the
Hellespont (Herod. VII. 54), and so Robinson tells us the inhabitants
of Bethlehem threw their garments under the feet of the horses of the
English consul at Damascus, whose aid they were imploring (*Biblical
Researches*, II. 162).

branches] "soþeli oþere men kittiden bowis, *or branches*, fro
trees," Wyclif. These were not the "*branches*" (*kladoi*) cut from the
trees as they went along, mentioned in Matt. xxi. 8, but "*mattings*"
(*stoibades*) which they twisted out of the palm-branches as they passed.
The original word denotes (1) *a bed of straw, rushes*, or *leaves*, whether
strawed loose or stuffed into a mattress; (2) *a mattress*, especially of
soldiers; (3) the *nest* or *lair* of mice or fish.

9 in the way. And they that went before, and they that followed, cried, saying, Hosanna; Blessed *is* he that cometh in
10 the name of the Lord: blessed *be* the kingdom of our father David, that cometh in the name of the Lord: Hosanna in
11 the highest. And Jesus entered into Jerusalem, and into the temple: and when he had looked round about upon all things, and now the eventide was come, he went out unto Bethany with the twelve.

off the trees] The reading of some MSS. here is **from the gardens**, and the verse would run, And many strewed their garments in the way, and others twisted branches, cutting them from the gardens. Eastern gardens are not flower gardens, nor private gardens, but the orchards, vineyards and fig-enclosures round a town. The road from Bethany to Jerusalem wound through rich plantations of palm trees, and fruit- and olive-gardens.

9. *they that went before*] From St John xii. 12 we gather that a second stream of people issuing from the Holy City came forth to meet the Saviour, and these joining the others coming from Bethany, turned round and swelled the long procession towards Jerusalem. See Stanley's *Sinai and Palestine*, p. 191.

10. *blessed be the kingdom*] The feelings of the multitudes found expression in the prophetic language of the Psalms, and they heralded the coming of the "Son of David" to establish His Messianic kingdom. See Ps. cxviii. 26.

11. *And Jesus entered*] At a particular turn in the road the whole of the magnificent city, as if rising from an abyss, burst into view. Then it was that the procession paused, and our Lord wept over the devoted capital (Luke xix. 41—44), and afterwards resumed His route towards Jerusalem, crossing the bridge over the Kedron, and passing through the gate now St Stephen's into Bezetha, the new town, through narrow streets, "hung with flags and banners for the feast, and crowded on the raised sides, and on every roof, and at every window, with eager faces."

the temple] Jerusalem was stirred to its very centre (Matt. xxi. 10). Who is this? inquired many, and were told by His exultant northern followers and disciples that it was "*the prophet of Nazareth of Galilee.*" They doubtless expected that He would, as He passed on towards the Temple, display some unmistakable "sign," and claim the sceptre, and ascend the throne. But they were doomed to disappointment.

when he had looked round about upon all things] "The actual procession would not proceed farther than the foot of Mount Moriah, beyond which they might not advance in travelling array, or with dusty feet." Before they reached the Shushan gate they dispersed, and Jesus entered the courts of the Temple, surveyed the scene of disorder and desecration which they presented, with prolonged and calm and searching glance, and when

the eventide was come] or rather, **it being now late**, returned with the

12—19. *The Second Cleansing of the Temple.*

And on the morrow, when they were come from Bethany, 12
he was hungry: and seeing a fig tree afar off having leaves, 13
he came, if haply he might find any thing thereon: and
when he came to it, he found nothing but leaves; for the
time of figs was not *yet*. And Jesus answered and said unto it, 14
No man eat fruit of thee hereafter for ever. And his disciples
heard *it*. And they come to Jerusalem: and Jesus went into 15
the temple, and began to cast out them that sold and bought

Twelve to the seclusion of Bethany, and the great Palm Sunday was over.

12—19. THE SECOND CLEANSING OF THE TEMPLE.

12. *he was hungry*] Probably, after a night of fasting; "shewing His Humanity, as usual, when about to give a proof of His Deity, that we may believe Him to be both God and Man." Bp Wordsworth.

13. *seeing a fig tree*] The very name Bethany means *"the place for dates,"* while Bethphage is *"the place for the green or winter fig,"* a variety which remains on the trees through the winter, having ripened only after the leaves had fallen.

having leaves] It stood alone, a single fig-tree, *by the wayside* (Matt. xxi. 19), and presented an unusual show of leaves for the season.

if haply] Rather, **if therefore,** if, *as was reasonable to expect under such circumstances,* fruit was to be found.

for the time of figs was not yet] that is, the *ordinary* fig-season had not yet arrived. The rich verdure of this tree seemed to shew that it was fruitful, and there was "every probability of finding upon it either the late violet-coloured autumn figs, which often hung upon the trees all through the winter, and even until the new spring leaves had come, or the first-ripe figs (Isai. xxviii. 4; Jer. xxiv. 2; Hos. ix. 10; Nah. iii. 12), of which Orientals are particularly fond." Farrar, *Life*, II. 213. But this tree had nothing but leaves. It was the very type of a fair profession without performance; a very parable of the nation, which, with all its professions, brought forth no "fruit to perfection." Comp. Luke xix. 42.

14. *answered and said unto it*] "arbori fructum neganti." Bengel.

No man eat fruit] "*And presently,*" i.e. *immediately,* writes St Matthew (xxi. 19), "the fig tree withered away," though the disciples did not notice it till the following morning. Thus our blessed Lord exhibited at once a Parable and a Prophecy *in action*.

15. *and Jesus went into the temple*] The best MSS. omit the word *Jesus* here. The nefarious scene, which He had sternly rebuked on the occasion of His first Passover, and which is recorded only by St John (ii. 13—17), was still being enacted.

them that sold and bought] For the convenience of Jews and proselytes residing at a distance from the Holy City, a kind of market had been established in the outer court, and here sacrificial victims, incense, oil,

in the temple, and overthrew the tables of the moneychangers,
16 and the seats of them that sold doves; and would not suffer
that any man should carry *any* vessel through the temple.
17 And he taught, saying unto them, Is it not written, My
house shall be called of all nations the house of prayer? but
18 ye have made it a den of thieves. And the scribes and
chief priests heard *it*, and sought how they might destroy
him: for they feared him, because all the people was asto-
19 nished at his doctrine. And when even was come, he went
out of the city.

wine, and other things necessary for the service and the sacrifices, were to be obtained.

the tables of the moneychangers] Money would be required (1) to purchase materials for offerings, (2) to present as free offerings to the Temple treasury (Mark xii. 41; Luke xxi. 1), (3) to pay the yearly Temple-tax of half a shekel due from every Jew, however poor. All this could not be received except in a native coin called the Temple Shekel, which was not generally current. Strangers therefore had to change their Roman, Greek, or Eastern money, at the stalls of the money-changers, to obtain the coin required. This trade gave ready means for fraud, which was only too common.

that sold doves] Required for poor women coming for purification (Lev. xii. 6, 8; Luke ii. 24) from all parts of the country, and for other offerings. The sale of doves appears to have been in a great measure in the hands of the priests themselves, and one of the high priests especially is said to have gained great profits from his dovecots on Mount Olivet.

16. *any vessel*] i.e. a pail or basket. He would not allow laden porters and others to desecrate the honour due to His Father's house by crossing the Temple courts as though they were public streets, "quasi per plateam." Bengel. This particular is peculiar to St Mark.

17. *of all nations*] Rather, **for all nations**. See margin. The words are cited from Isaiah lvi. 7.

a den of thieves] Literally, **a cave of robbers** or **bandits**. See Jer. vii. 11. The distinction is to be borne in mind between "the robber," brigand or violent spoiler (Matt. xxi. 13, xxvi. 55; Luke xxii. 52; John xviii. 40; 2 Cor. xi. 26), and the "thief" or secret purloiner (Matt. vi. 19; John xii. 6; 1 Thess. v. 2; Rev. iii. 3, xvi. 15). Trench's *Synonyms*, § 44. What our Lord alludes to is one of "those foul caves which He had so often seen, where brigands wrangled over their ill-gotten gains." Farrar, *Life*, II. 205.

18. *chief priests*] This title was applied to (i) the high-priest properly so called; (ii) to all who had held the high-priesthood (the office under Roman sway no longer lasting for life, and becoming little more than annual); (iii) the heads of the twenty-four courses (1 Chron. xxiv., Luke i. 9).

was astonished at his doctrine] and hung upon His lips eager to

20—26. *The Withered Fig-Tree.*

20 And in the morning, as they passed by, they saw the fig tree dried up from the roots. 21 And Peter calling to remembrance saith unto him, Master, behold, the fig tree which thou cursedst is withered away. 22 And Jesus answering saith unto them, Have faith in God. 23 For verily I say unto you, That whosoever shall say unto this mountain, Be thou removed, and be thou cast into the sea; and shall not doubt in his heart, but shall believe that those things which he

hear Him (Luke xix. 48), and while He was thus high in favour, no one knew how far they might not be disposed to rise on His behalf, if an open effort was made to seize Him. Caution was therefore essential.

19. *he went out*] or rather, **they went out**, of the city, crossed the ridges of Olivet, and sought once more the retirement of Bethany.

20—26. THE WITHERED FIG-TREE.

20. *And in the morning*] The early morning of Tuesday in Holy Week.
as they passed by] On their return to the Holy City.
dried up from the roots] From St Matthew (xxi. 19) it would appear that "some beginnings of the threatened withering began to shew themselves, almost as soon as the word of the Lord was spoken; a shuddering fear may have run through all the leaves of the tree, which was thus stricken at its heart." Trench.

21. *And Peter*] who doubtless related the incident with all its attendant circumstances to St Mark.

22. *Have faith in God*] as the personal source of miraculous power. (Comp. Matt. xvii. 20; Luke xvii. 6.)

23. *verily I say unto you*] With great solemnity He seeks to impress upon them a truth which would be of the greatest import to them, when they went forth, as His Apostles, to establish and spread His kingdom—that an unfaltering faith in God would overcome all difficulties, even the most insuperable to the eye of sense.
shall say unto this mountain] Language like this was familiar in the schools of the Jews. They used to set out those teachers among them, that were more eminent for the profoundness of their learning, or the splendour of their virtues, by such expressions as these, "He is a *rooter up* or *remover of mountains*." "They called Rabbah Bar Nachmani, *A rooter up of mountains*, because he had a piercing judgment." Lightfoot, *Hor. Heb.*
shall not doubt in his heart] The word here translated "doubt" (*a*) in the active voice means *to discriminate, distinguish, discern*, as Matt. xvi. 3, "ye can *discern* the face of the heaven;" Acts xv. 9, "He put *no difference* between us and them;" 1 Cor. xi. 29, "not

saith shall come to pass; he shall have whatsoever he saith. 24 Therefore I say unto you, What things soever ye desire, when ye pray, believe that ye receive *them*, and ye shall have 25 *them*. And when ye stand praying, forgive, if ye have ought against any: that your Father also which is in heaven may 26 forgive you your trespasses. But if ye do not forgive, neither will your Father which is in heaven forgive your trespasses.

27—33. *Question respecting John the Baptist.*

27 And they come again to Jerusalem: and as he was walking in the temple, there come to him the chief priests, and 28 the scribes, and the elders, and say unto him, By what au-

discerning the Lord's Body." (*b*) In the passive and middle voice, it means (i) *to get a decision, to go to law, to dispute*, as Acts xi. 2, "they of the circumcision *contended* with him;" Jas. ii. 4, "are ye not *partial* (become *litigants* or *partisans*) in yourselves?" (ii) *to dispute with oneself, to doubt, waver*, as Acts x. 20, "go with them, *doubting nothing;*" Rom. iv. 20, "*he staggered not* at (i. e. *with regard to*) the promise through unbelief;" Jas. i. 6, "but let him ask in faith, nothing *wavering*; for he that *wavereth* is like a wave of the sea."

24. *What things soever ye desire, when ye pray*] Because *Prayer* is the very language of *Faith*, He passes on to speak concerning Prayer.

25. *when ye stand praying*] The posture of prayer among the Jews seems to have been most often *standing;* comp. the instance of Hannah (1 Sam. i. 26), and of the Pharisee (Luke xviii. 11). When the prayer was offered with especial solemnity and humiliation, this was naturally expressed by (*a*) *kneeling;* comp. the instance of Solomon (1 Kings viii. 54), and Daniel (vi. 10); or (*b*) *prostration*, as Joshua (vii. 6), and Elijah (1 Kings xviii. 42).

forgive] In this place, where our Lord connects the strong assurance of the marvellous power of faith with the cursing of the fig-tree, He passes on most naturally to declare how such a faith could not be sundered from forgiving love, that it should never be used in the service of hate or fanaticism.

26. *your trespasses*] The original word thus translated denotes (1) *a falling beside, a falling from the right way*. It is rendered in our Version (1) *fault* in Gal. vi. 1; Jas. v. 16; (2) *offence* in Rom. iv. 25, v. 15, 17, 18, 20; (3) *fall* in Rom. xi. 11, 12; (4) *trespass*, here, and in Matt. vi. 14, 15; 2 Cor. v. 19; Eph. ii. 1; Col. ii. 13; (5) *sins* in Eph. ii. 5; Col. ii. 13.

27—33. QUESTION RESPECTING JOHN THE BAPTIST.

27. *as he was walking*] This is in keeping with St Mark's vivid style of delineation.

thority doest thou these things? and who gave thee this authority to do these things? And Jesus answered and said 29 unto them, I will also ask of you one question, and answer me, and I will tell you by what authority I do these things. The baptism of John, was *it* from heaven, or of men? an- 30 swer me. And they reasoned with themselves, saying, If we 31 shall say, ·From heaven; he will say, Why then did ye not believe him? But if we shall say, Of men; they feared the 32 people: for all *men* counted John, that he was a prophet indeed. And they answered and said unto Jesus, We cannot 33 tell. And Jesus answering saith unto them, Neither do I tell you by what authority I do these things.

elders] "eldere men," Wyclif. The ancient senators or representatives of the people. With the chief priests and scribes they constituted on this occasion a formal deputation from the Sanhedrim. We find the earliest notice of *the elders* acting in concert as a political body in the time of the Exodus (Ex. xix. 7; Deut. xxxi. 9). Their authority, which extended to all matters of the common weal, they exercised under (*a*) the Judges (Judg. ii. 7; 1 Sam. iv. 3); under (*b*) the Kings (1 Sam. xxx. 26; 1 Chron. xxi. 16; 2 Sam. xvii. 4); during (*c*) the Captivity (Jer. xxix. 1; Ezek. viii. 1); after (*d*) the Return (Ezra v. 5, vi. 7, 14, x. 8, 14); under (*e*) the Maccabees (1 Macc. xii. 6; 2 Macc. i. 10); in (*f*) the time of our Lord, when they denoted a distinct body in the Sanhedrim, amongst whom they obtained their seat by election, or nomination from the executive authority.

28. *By what authority doest thou these things?*] They evidently wished to bring Him to account for His act of the day before, and for His assumption to teach as a Rabbi, without any license from the Schools, which was contrary to the established rule. The same question had been put to Him three years before and by the same persons (John ii. 18).

29. *And Jesus answered*] They doubtless hoped that He would have claimed Divine authority, and then they would have had matter for accusation against Him, but He answered their question by another.

30. *The baptism of John*] John was the most recent upholder of the validity of the prophetic order in Israel, and he had distinctly testified to the Messianic authority of our Lord (John i. 29—34, 36); from whom did *he* receive *his* commission to baptize? Was it from heaven, or a mere human assumption of his own?

32. *if we shall say, Of men*] Observe the impressive abruptness here, which is more significant than the full expression of St Matthew (xxi. 26) and St Luke (xx. 6). They dared not face the alternative, and were driven to a feeble evasion.

33. *Neither do I tell you*] The counter-question of Jesus was the consequence of the question of these men. "Him that inquires," saith

128   ST MARK, XII.   [v. 1.

1—12. *Parable of the Wicked Husbandmen.*

12 And he began to speak unto them by parables. A *certain* man planted a vineyard, and set an hedge about *it*, and digged *a place for* the winefat, and built a tower, and let

one of old, "we are bound to instruct; but him that tempts, we may defeat with a stroke of reasoning."

CH. XII. 1—12. PARABLE OF THE WICKED HUSBANDMEN.

1. *by parables*] Another Parable spoken at this time was that of "*the Two Sons*" (Matt. xxi. 28—32), and "*the Marriage of the King's Son*" (Matt. xxii. 1—14). St Mark relates only the second of these three Parables.

A certain man planted a vineyard] Our Lord seems to take up the words of the prophet Isaiah (v. 1—7) and to build His teaching the more willingly on the old foundations, as He was accused of destroying the Law. Comp. Deut. xxxii. 32; Ps. lxxx. 8—16; Ezek. xv. 1—6; Hos. x. 1. By the Vineyard we are to understand the Kingdom of God, as successively realized in its idea (1) by the Jew, and (2) by the Gentile. Trench's *Parables*, p. 193.

planted] The householder not merely possessed, he "*planted*" the vineyard. So God *planted* His spiritual vineyard (*a*) under Moses (Deut. xxxii. 12—14; Ex. xv. 17), (*b*) under Joshua, when the Jews were established in the land of Canaan.

an hedge about it] Not a hedge of thorns, but a stone wall to keep out wild boars (Ps. lxxx. 13), jackals, and foxes (Num. xxii. 24; Cant. ii. 15; Neh. iv. 3). The word only occurs (*a*) here, (*b*) in the parallel Matt. xxi. 33, (*c*) in Luke xiv. 23, "go ye into the highways and *hedges*," and (*d*) Eph. ii. 14, "the middle *wall* of *partition*." "Enclosures of loose stone, like the walls of fields in Derbyshire or Westmoreland, everywhere catch the eye on the bare slopes of Hebron, of Bethlehem, and of Olivet." Stanley, *Sinai and Palestine*, p. 421.

a place for the winefat] "dalf a lake," Wyclif; "digged a pit to receauve the lycour of the wynepresse," Geneva; "digged a trough," Rhemish Version. The original word only occurs here in the N.T., and = the Latin *lacus*. The winepress, = *torcular* (Matt. xxi. 33), consisted of two parts; (1) the press (*gath*) or trough above, in which the grapes were placed, and there trodden by the feet of several persons amidst singing and other expressions of joy (Judg. ix. 27; Isaiah xvi. 10; Jer. xxv. 30); (2) a smaller trough (*yekeb*), into which the expressed juice flowed through a hole or spout (Neh. xiii. 15; Isaiah lxiii. 2; Lam. i. 15). Here the smaller trough, which was often hollowed ("digged") out of the earth or native rock and then lined with masonry, is put for the whole apparatus, and is called a *wine*-FAT. This word occurs also in Isaiah lxiii. 2; Hos. ix. 2, marg.; compare press-*fat*, Hag. ii. 16; and *fat*, Joel ii. 24, iii. 13. *Fat* from A.S. fæt = a vessel, vat, according to the modern spelling. Comp. Shakespeare, *Ant. and Cleop.* II. 7. 120:—

it out to husbandmen, and went into a far country. And at 2
the season he sent to the husbandmen a servant, that he
might receive from the husbandmen of the fruit of the vineyard. And they caught *him*, and beat him, and sent *him* 3
away empty. And again he sent unto them another servant; 4
and at him they cast stones, and wounded *him* in the head,

"Come thou monarch of the vine,
Plumpie Bacchus, with pinke eyne:
In thy *fattes* our cares be drown'd."

and built a tower] i.e. a "tower of the watchman," rendered *"cottage"* in Isaiah i. 8, xxiv. 20. Here the watchers and vinedressers lived (Isaiah v. 2), and frequently, with slings, scared away wild animals and robbers. At the corner of each enclosure "rises its square grey towers, at first sight hardly distinguishable from the ruins of ancient churches or fortresses, which lie equally scattered over the hills of Judæa." Stanley, p. 421.

to husbandmen] By these the spiritual leaders and teachers of the Jewish nation (Mal. ii. 7; Ezek. xxxiv. 2) are intended. Their land, secluded and yet central, was hedged round on the east by the river Jordan, on the south by the desert of Idumæa, on the west by the sea, on the north by Libanus and Anti-Libanus, while they themselves were separated by the Law, *"the middle wall of partition"* (Eph. ii. 14), from the Gentiles and idolatrous nations around.

went into a far country] *"for a long while,"* adds St Luke, or *"many times."* "At Sinai, when the theocratic constitution was founded, and in the miracles which accompanied the deliverance from Egypt, the Lord may be said to have openly manifested Himself to Israel; but then to have withdrawn Himself again for awhile, not speaking to the people again face to face (Deut. xxxiv. 10—12), but waiting in patience to see what the Law would effect, and what manner of works the people, under the teaching of their spiritual guides, would bring forth." Trench, *Parables*, p. 197.

2. *at the season*] i.e. when the fruit season drew near.

a servant] So Luke xx. 10; *his servants*, Matt. xxi. 34; the prophets and other eminent messengers of God raised up at particular periods for particular purposes. "Servi sunt ministri extraordinarii, majores; agricolæ, ordinarii." Bengel.

of the fruit] The householder's share. The rent not being paid in money, but in a stipulated portion of the produce, according to the well-known *metayer* system once prevalent over great part of Europe. The prophets were sent to the people from time to time to require of them "the repentance and the inward longing after true inward righteousness, which the Law was unable to bring about."

3. *they caught him*] The gradual growth of the outrage is clearly traced: (i) The first servant they *"caught, beat, and sent away empty;"* (ii) at the second they *"cast stones, and wounded him in the head, and sent him away shamefully handled;"* (iii) the third *"they killed."*

4. *wounded him in the head*] The original word, which generally

5 and sent *him* away shamefully handled. And again he sent another; and him they killed, and many others; beating
6 some, and killing some. Having yet therefore one son, his well-beloved, he sent him also last unto them, saying, They
7 will reverence my son. But those husbandmen said among themselves, This is the heir; come, let us kill him, and the
8 inheritance shall be ours. And they took him, and killed
9 *him*, and cast *him* out of the vineyard. What shall therefore the lord of the vineyard do? he will come and destroy the

denotes to *comprehend in one sum, or under one head*, is nowhere else used in this sense. Some MSS. omit the words *they cast stones*, and instead of "*sent him away shamefully handled*," read simply, "*used him shamefully*" (comp. 2 Sam. x. 4). Thus Jezebel "*slew the prophets of the Lord*" (1 Kings xviii. 13); Micaiah was thrown into a dungeon by Ahab (1 Kings xxii. 24—27); Elijah was threatened with death by Jezebel (1 Kings xix. 2); Elisha by Jehoram (2 Kings vi. 31); Zechariah was stoned at the commandment of Joash (2 Chron. xxiv. 21; comp. xxxvi. 16); Jeremiah was stoned by the exiles in Egypt; Isaiah, according to Jewish tradition, was sawn asunder (Heb. xi. 37, 38; 2 Chron. xxxvi. 15, 16).

6. *Having yet therefore*] Note here the description of this last of the ambassadors of the householder. Not only was he his son, but his *only one*, his *well-beloved*, "a sone most dereworþ," Wyclif. This marks as strongly as possible the difference of rank between Christ and the prophets, by whom "*at sundry times and in divers manners God spake in times past unto the fathers*" (Heb. i. 1), the distinction between them and the dignity of Him, Who only was in the highest sense His Son, and Whom He hath "*appointed heir of all things*" (Heb. i. 2, iii. 5, 6).

7. *This is the heir*] "he for whom the inheritance is meant, and to whom it will in due course rightfully arrive—not as in earthly relations, by the death, but by the free appointment, of the actual possessor." Christ is "heir of all things," not as He is the Son of God, but as He is the Son of Man.

come, let us kill him] Comp. Gen. xxxvii. 20; and especially John xi. 47—53, where "the servants" conspiring against "the Heir of all things" actually assign as their motive that "if they let Him alone," they "will lose both their place and nation."

8. *and killed him, and cast him out of the vineyard*] The order is reversed in the first and third Gospels, which remind us of Naboth, whom they "carried forth *out of the city*, and stoned him with stones that he died" (1 Kings xxi. 13), and of Him, Who *suffered without the gate* (Heb. xiii. 12, 13; John xix. 17). The second Evangelist represents them as first killing the son, and then flinging forth the body and denying it the ordinary rites of sepulture.

9. *he will come*] According to St Matthew, this was the answer of

husbandmen, and will give the vineyard unto others. And 10 have ye not read this scripture; The stone which the builders rejected is become the head of the corner: this was the 11 Lord's doing, and it is marvellous in our eyes? And they 12 sought to lay hold on him, but feared the people: for they

the Pharisees themselves, either, before they were aware, pronouncing sentence against themselves, or pretending in the hardness of their hearts not to see the drift of the Parable. The answer was followed by "a deep God forbid" from several voices (Luke xx. 16).

10. *And have ye*] Rather, **And did ye never read this Scripture?** referring them to Psalm cxviii. 22, 23, a Psalm which the Jews applied to the Messiah, and which is actually twice applied to Him by St Peter, in Acts iv. 11; 1 Pet. ii. 7. St Luke (xx. 17) tells us that our Lord fastened His eyes upon His wondering hearers, while He directed their attention to this ancient prophecy respecting Himself in the very Psalm, whence had been taken the loud Hosannas of Palm Sunday (Mark xi. 9).

the head of the corner] The image of the vineyard is for a moment abandoned for that of a building. The "head of the corner" was a large and massive stone so formed as when placed at a corner to bind together the two outer walls of an edifice. Comp. for the application of the expression to Christ, Eph. ii. 20, and consult Isaiah xxviii. 16; Dan. ii. 44. The penalties of rejecting Him are more fully brought out in Matt. xxi. 43, 44; Luke xx. 18.

12. *they sought*] All three Evangelists take note of the exasperation of our Lord's hearers at words which they now clearly perceived were directed against themselves. The chief priests and Pharisees sought to arrest Him on the spot at once (Luke xx. 19), but they were afraid of the multitudes, who regarded Him if not with the same deep feelings as on Palm Sunday, yet still as *a prophet* (Matt. xxi. 46), so they *left Him and went their way* (Mark xii. 12). One more Parable followed, that of the "*Marriage of the King's Son*" (Matt. xxii. 1—14), and once more the rulers of the nation were solemnly warned of the danger they were incurring. "Thus within a few hours of crucifixion, and conscious of the fact; in the intervals of mortal contest with the whole forces of the past and present, the wandering Galilæan Teacher, meek and lowly in spirit, so that the poorest and the youngest instinctively sought Him; full of Divine pity, so that the most sunken and hopeless penitent felt He was their friend; indifferent to the supports of influence, wealth, or numbers; alone and poor, the very embodiment of weakness, as regarded all visible help, still bore Himself with a serene dignity more than human. In the name of God He transfers the spiritual glory of Israel to His own followers; throws down the barriers of caste and nationality; extends the new dominion, of which He is Head, to all races, and through all ages, here and hereafter; predicts the Divine wrath on His enemies in this world, as the enemies of God, and announces the decision of the final judgment as turning on the attitude of men *towards Himself and His message.*" Geikie's *Life*

knew that he had spoken the parable against them: and they left him, and went their way.

13—17. *The Question of the Tribute Money.*

13 And they send unto him certain of the Pharisees and of 14 the Herodians, to catch him in *his* words. And when they were come, they say unto him, Master, we know that thou art true, and carest for no man: for thou regardest not the person of men, but teachest the way of God in truth: Is it 15 lawful to give tribute to Cæsar, or not? Shall we give, or shall we not give? But he, knowing their hypocrisy, said unto them, Why tempt ye me? bring me a penny, that I

and *Words of Christ*, II. pp. 414, 415; Liddon's *Bampton Lectures*, pp. 113—118, Sixth Edition.

13—17. THE QUESTION OF THE TRIBUTE MONEY.

13. *And they send*] Having failed themselves, the Jewish authorities resolved to send some of the Pharisees in company with the Herodians, to try to force Him to commit Himself by the answers He might give to their treacherous questions. A series of distinct attacks was now made upon our Lord. (*a*) The Pharisees took the lead with theirs, which was, indeed, the most cunningly devised; (*b*) the Sadducees followed; and then (*c*) came the Scribes of the Pharisees' party.

the Herodians] See note on ch. iii. 6. As before, so now, the Jewish royalists united themselves with the ultra-orthodox Pharisaic party. The Herodians came *in person*. The Pharisees sent *some of their younger scholars* (Matt. xxii. 16) to approach Him with the pretended simplicity of a guileless spirit, and a desire to solve a perplexing question (Luke xx. 20).

14. *Master, we know*] This was said in a spirit of hypocritical flattery, as though they were ready to pay Him honour as the Messiah. We find Nicodemus saying the same thing in a spirit of sincerity (John iii. 2).

and carest for no man] This was a cunning temptation to lift Himself above all respect for the Roman authorities.

Is it lawful to give tribute...?] The snare was no longer laid in the sphere of ecclesiastical questions, but in the more dangerous area of political duty. The tribute-money alluded to was a capitation tax levied by the Roman government, and keenly resented by Judas the Gaulonite (Acts v. 37) and his followers. If our Lord held the payment unlawful, He would compromise Himself with the Romans; if He sanctioned it, He would embroil Himself with the national party.

15. *knowing their hypocrisy*] "verum se eis ostendit, ut dixerant." Bengel.

bring me] "They would not be likely to carry with them the hated Roman coinage with its heathen symbols, though they might have been at once able to produce from their girdles the Temple shekel.

may see *it.* And they brought *it.* And he saith unto them, 16
Whose *is* this image and superscription? And they said
unto him, Cæsar's. And Jesus answering said unto them, 17
Render to Cæsar the things that are Cæsar's, and to God the
things that are God's. And they marvelled at him.

18—27. *The Question of the Sadducees respecting the Resurrection.*

Then come unto him the Sadducees, which say there is 18

But they would only have to step outside the Court of the Gentiles, and obtain from the money-changers' tables a current Roman coin." Farrar, *Life*, II. p. 231.

a penny] Literally, **a denarius**, for the value of which see vi. 37.

16. *Whose is this image*] "The little silver coin, bearing on its surface the head encircled with a wreath of laurel, and bound round with the sacred fillet—the well-known features, the most beautiful and the most wicked, even in outward expression, of all the Roman Emperors, with the superscription running round, in the stately language of imperial Rome, *Tiberius Cæsar, Divi Augusti filius Augustus, Imperator.*" The image of the Emperor would be regarded by the stricter Jews as idolatrous, and to spare their feelings, the Romans had allowed a special coinage to be struck for Judæa, without any likeness upon it, and only the name of the Emperor, and such Jewish emblems as palms, lilies, grapes, and censers.

17. *Render*] Literally, **Give back, pay as being due.** "þerefore ȝelde ȝe to Cæsar," Wyclif. It was not a question of a *voluntary gift*, but of a *legal due*. The head of the Emperor on the coin, the legend round it, and its circulation in the country, were undeniable proofs of the right of the actually existing government to levy the tax. "Ubicunque numisma alicujus regis obtinet, illic incolæ regem istum pro domino agnoscunt;" Maimonides. Remembrance of this precept "would have spared the Jewish war, the destruction of Jerusalem, and the downfall of their nation." Lange.

and to God] He would remind them that besides the claims of the ruling powers, they had also the claim upon them of their Spiritual King, and obedience to Cæsar must ever be conditioned by obedience to God. "Render unto Cæsar all that he can lawfully demand, but render also to God, what He requires of you as His spiritual subjects." "Give to God that which has the image and superscription of God, the soul" Erasmus.

they marvelled at him] Neither the orthodox Pharisee nor the aristocratic royalist had expected such an answer from the Galilæan Teacher.

18—27. THE QUESTION OF THE SADDUCEES RESPECTING THE RESURRECTION.

18. *the Sadducees*] Hitherto the Sadducees, "few, rich, and

19 no resurrection; and they asked him, saying, Master, Moses wrote unto us, If a man's brother die, and leave *his* wife *behind him*, and leave no children, that his brother should 20 take his wife, and raise up seed unto his brother. Now there were seven brethren: and the first took a wife, and 21 dying left no seed. And the second took her, and died, 22 neither left he any seed: and the third likewise. And the seven had her, and left no seed: last of all the woman died 23 also. In the resurrection therefore, when they shall rise, whose wife shall she be of them? for the seven had her 24 to wife. And Jesus answering said unto them, Do ye not therefore err, because ye know not the scriptures, neither 25 the power of God? For when they shall rise from the dead, they neither marry, nor are given in marriage; but are as 26 the angels which are in heaven. And as touching the dead,

dignified," had stood aloof, and affected to ignore the disciples of the despised "Prophet of Nazareth."

19. *Moses wrote*] The Law concerning the Levirate marriage is found in Deuteronomy xxv. 5. It was ordained for the preservation of families, that if a man died without male issue, his brother should marry his widow, and that the firstborn son should be held in the registers to be the son of the dead brother.

20. *there were seven brethren*] It was probably a fictitious case, for the Jews were averse to the fulfilling of the enactment at all.

23. *In the resurrection therefore*] Their difficulty originated entirely in a carnal notion that the connections of this life must be continued in another.

24. *because ye know not*] Our Lord traces their error to ignorance (i) of the Scriptures, and (ii) of the power of God. He deals with the latter phase of ignorance first.

25. *when they shall rise*] Had they known the power of God they could not have imagined that it was limited by death, or that the life of "the children of the resurrection" was a mere repetition of man's present mortal existence. Compare the argument of St Paul in 1 Cor. xv. 39—44, based on the endless variety of the creative power of God.

as the angels] The Sadducees denied not only the Resurrection, but the existence also of angels and spirits (Acts xxiii. 8). In His reply, therefore, our Lord embraces the whole area of their unbelief. He refers to the angels in heaven as persons, whose personal existence was a fact. Moreover in these words we have one of the few revelations which He was pleased to make as to the state after death. They imply that, as St Paul teaches, at the Resurrection "*we shall be changed*" (1 Cor. xv. 44), and the "*spiritual body*" will not be liable to the passions of the "*natural body*."

that they rise: have ye not read in the book of Moses, how in the bush God spake unto him, saying, I *am* the God of Abraham, and the God of Isaac, and the God of Jacob? He is not the God of the dead, but the God of the living: 27 ye therefore do greatly err.

28—34. *The Question of the Scribe.*

And one of the scribes came, and having heard them 28 reasoning together, and perceiving that he had answered them well, asked him, Which is the first commandment of

26. *in the book of Moses*] They had brought forward the name of *Moses* to perplex *Him*, He now appeals to the same great name in order to confute *them*. He does not reprove them for attaching a higher importance to the Pentateuch than to the Prophets, but for not tracing the Divine Mind on the important subject of the Resurrection even *there*.

in the bush] i.e. in the section of the Book of Exodus (iii. 6) called "*the Bush.*" Similarly "*the lament of David over Saul and Jonathan*" in 2 Sam. i. 17—27 was called "*the Bow*;" and Ezekiel i. 15—28 "*the Chariot.*" Compare also Rom. xi. 2; "in Elias"=*the section concerning Elias*. In the Koran the chapters are named after the matter they contain, and so also the Homeric poems. Wyclif alone of our English translators gives the right meaning, "Han 3e not rad in þe book of Moyses *on þe bousche*, how God seide to him."

God spake unto him, saying] On that momentous occasion, which marked an epoch in the national history, God had revealed Himself to Moses *as a personal God*, by the august and touching title of "*the God of Abraham, and the God of Isaac, and the God of Jacob*," and therefore as bearing *a personal relation* to these patriarchs, upon whom He had set His seal of Circumcision, and so admitted them into covenant union with Himself. How unworthy would such a title be, if He, the Eternal and Unchangeable, had revealed Himself only as the God of men who had long since crumbled to dust and passed away into annihilation! How meaningless such a Name, if the souls of men at death perished with the body, "as the cloud faileth and passeth away"! Was it possible to believe He would have deigned to call Himself the God "of dust and ashes"?

27. *He is not the God of the dead*] Our Lord thus taught them that the words implied far more than that God was the God, in Whom Abraham and the patriarchs trusted and worshipped.

but the God of the living] Jehovah could not have called Himself the God of persons who do not exist, and over whom death had completely triumphed. The patriarchs, therefore, though their bodies were dead, must themselves have been still living in the separate state, and awaiting the resurrection.

28—34. THE QUESTION OF THE SCRIBE.

28. *one of the scribes*] From Matt. xxii. 34, 35, it appears that he was a Pharisee, and a Master of the Law.

Which is the first commandment of all?] This question, on which

29 **all?** And Jesus answered him, The first of all the commandments *is*, Hear, O Israel; The Lord our God is one 30 Lord; and thou shalt love the Lord thy God with all thy heart, and with all thy soul, and with all thy mind, and with 31 all thy strength: this *is* the first commandment. And the second *is* like, *namely* this, Thou shalt love thy neighbour as thyself. There is none other commandment greater than 32 these. And the scribe said unto him, Well, Master, thou hast said the truth: for there is one God; and there is none 33 other but he: and to love him with all the heart, and with all the understanding, and with all the soul, and with all the strength, and to love *his* neighbour as himself, is more than 34 all whole burnt offerings and sacrifices. And when Jesus

the schools of Hillel and Shammai were disagreed, the Lawyer put, tempting our Lord (Matt. xxii. 35), hoping that He would commit Himself as an enemy of the Traditions. The Rabbinical schools taught that there were important distinctions between the Commandments, some being great and others small, some hard and weighty, others easy and of less importance. Great commands were the observance of the Sabbath, circumcision, minute rites of sacrifice and offering, the rules respecting fringes and phylacteries. Indeed, all the separate commandments of the ceremonial and moral Law had been carefully weighed and classified, and it had been concluded that there were "248 affirmative precepts, being as many as the members in the human body, and 365 negative precepts, being as many as the arteries and veins, or the days of the year; the total being 613, which was also the number of the letters in the Decalogue."

29. *And Jesus answered him*] Pointing, it may be, to the Scribe's *tephillah*, תפלה, the little leather box containing in one of its four divisions the *Shema* (Deut. vi. 4), which every pious Israelite repeated twice a day.

The first of all the commandments] The Saviour quotes the introduction to the ten Commandments (Deut. vi. 4, 5) as the first command, not as forming one of the commandments, but as containing *the principle* of all.

31. *the second is like, namely this*] According to the best MSS. the reading is, **the second is this.** The Lord had named only one commandment as great to the rich young ruler (Luke x. 27). To the Scribe He names two, as forming together "the great and first commandment." Besides quoting Deut. vi. 4, 5, He refers him to Lev. xix. 18.

33. *burnt offerings and sacrifices*] The Scribe gathers up in his reply some of the great utterances of the Prophets, which prove the superiority of love to God and man over all mere ceremonial observances. See 1 Sam. xv. 22; Psalm li.; Hosea vi. 6; Micah vi. 6—8.

saw that he answered discreetly, he said unto him, Thou art not far from the kingdom of God. And no man after that durst ask him *any question*.

35—37. *Our Lord's Counter-question*.

And Jesus answered and said, while he taught in the 35 temple, How say the scribes that Christ is the Son of David? For David himself said by the Holy Ghost, The LORD said 36 to my Lord, Sit thou on my right hand, till I make thine enemies thy footstool. David therefore himself calleth him 37 Lord; and whence is he *then* his son? And the common people heard him gladly.

34. *discreetly*] "wysely," Wyclif. The word only occurs here in the N. T., and denotes "with knowledge and understanding."

Thou art not far] The perception of Divine truth which his answer had shewed, revealed that he wanted but little to become a disciple of Christ. "Si non procul es, intra; alias præstiterit, procul fuisse."

no man...durst] No other attempt was henceforth made to entangle the Redeemer by replies to subtle questions; "all alike kept aloof from one, from Whom chief priests and Rabbis equally went away humbled." Some, however, would refer to this occasion the question respecting the woman taken in adultery (John viii. 1—11).

35—37. OUR LORD'S COUNTER-QUESTION.

35. *And Jesus answered and said*] He seemed to have turned to a number of the Pharisees (Matt. xxii. 41) who had collected together, to converse probably over the day's discomfiture. The great counter-question is brought forward by St Matthew in all its historic importance as the decisive concluding interrogation addressed to the Pharisees. St Mark points out by the words "*Jesus answered*" that the statement contained a reply to some question already put.

36. *David himself said*] The Pharisees are referred to the cxth Psalm, which the Rabbis regarded as distinctly Messianic. "*The Lord (Jehovah) said unto my Lord (Adonai), Sit thou on My right hand till I make thy foes a footstool for thy feet.*" In this lofty and mysterious Psalm, David, speaking by the Holy Ghost, was carried out of and beyond himself, and saw in prophetic vision that his Son would also be his Lord. The Psalm is more frequently cited by the New Testament writers than any other single portion of the ancient Scriptures (Acts ii. 34, 35; 1 Cor. xv. 25; Heb. i. 13, v. 6, vii. 17, 21). "In later Jewish writings nearly every verse of it is quoted as referring to the Messiah." Perowne *on the Psalms*, II. 291.

37. *whence is he then his son?*] Abraham had never called Isaac or Jacob or any of his descendants *his lord*. Why then had David done so? There could be but one answer: "Because that Son would be David's Son as regarded human birth, his Lord as regarded His Divine

38—40. *Admonition to beware of the Scribes.*

38 And he said unto them in his doctrine, Beware of the scribes, which love to go in long clothing, and *love* salu-
39 tations in the marketplaces, and the chief seats in the
40 synagogues, and the uppermost rooms at feasts: which devour widows' houses, and for a pretence make long prayers: these shall receive greater damnation.

Nature." This answer, however, the Pharisees declined to make, not through ignorance, but through unbelief in our Lord's Messianic claims.

the common people] Rather, **the great multitude.** "And *moche cumpany* gladli herde him." Wyclif. This fact is peculiar to St Mark, and implies that they listened to Him gladly, not merely in the general sense, but with special reference to His Divine dignity as the Messiah.

38—40. ADMONITION TO BEWARE OF THE SCRIBES.

38. *And he said*] The terrible denunciations of the moral and religious shortcomings of the leaders of the nation, which now fall from our Lord's lips, are given far more fully by St Matthew, xxiii. 1—39. It was only the Jewish Christians, for whom that Evangelist wrote, who could at once, and at that time, understand and enter into the terrible declension of Pharisaic Judaism. To the Gentile Christians of Rome, for whom St Mark wrote, "the great woe-speech" would be to a certain extent unintelligible. Hence the picture of the Scribes is here shortly given in their three principal features; (1) ambition, (2) avarice, and (3) hypocritical external piety.

in long clothing] "þat wolen wandre in stoolis," Wyclif. *Stoolis* from Latin *stola* = a robe. They came out to pray in long sweeping robes, wearing phylacteries of extra size, and exaggerated tassels, hung at the corners of their *talliths.* Many such were doubtless to be seen at Jerusalem at this very time, who had come up to celebrate the Feast of the Passover. See note on p. 64.

love salutations] The sounding title of "Rabbi," "Rabbi."

39. *the chief seats*] The seats of honour for the elders of the synagogue were placed in front of the ark containing the Law, in the uppermost part, where they sat with their faces to the people. In the synagogue at Alexandria there were seventy-one golden chairs, according to the number of the members of the Great Sanhedrim.

the uppermost rooms] Rather, **the chief seats,** "þe first sitting places in soperis," Wyclif. The highest place on the divan, as amongst the Greeks. Amongst the Romans, when a party consisted of more than three persons, it was the custom to arrange three of the couches on which they reclined round a table, so that the whole formed three sides of a square, leaving the bottom of it open for the approach of the attendants. These couches were then respectively designated *lectus medius, summus,* and *imus.* The middle place in the *triclinium* was considered the most dignified. At a large feast there would be many such *triclinia.*

41—44. *The Widow's Mite.*

And Jesus sat over against the treasury, and beheld how 41 the people cast money into the treasury: and many that were rich cast in much. And there came a certain poor 42 widow, and she threw in two mites, which make a farthing.

40. *devour widows' houses*] as guardians and administrators of their property.

greater damnation] "þei taken longe dom," Wyclif. The word denotes "judgment," "punishment." The verb from which it comes denotes "to judge," pass sentence, condemn. In 1 Cor. xi. 29, the words rendered *damnation, discerning, judged,* and *condemnation,* are all, in the original, parts or derivations of one and the same word; and so Wyclif admirably rendered them into the language of his day by words connected with one and the same English verb; "He that etith and drinkith vnworthili, etith and drinkith *doom* to him, not wisely *demyng* the bodi of the Lord...and if we *demyden* wiseli us silf we schulden not be *demyd,* but while we be *demyd* of the lord we ben chastised, that we be not *dampnyd* with this world." Compare also Chaucer, *Monk's Tale,* 15091,
"*Dampnyd* was he to deye in that prison."
Bible Word-Book, pp. 142, 143.

41—44. THE WIDOW'S MITE.

41. *And Jesus sat*] In perfect calm and quiet of spirit after all the fierce opposition of this "day of Questions."

the treasury] This treasury, according to the Rabbis, consisted of thirteen brazen chests, called "trumpets," because the mouths through which the money was cast into the chest were wide at the top and narrow below. They stood in the outer "Court of the Women." "Nine chests were for the appointed temple-tribute, and for the sacrifice-tribute, that is, money-gifts instead of the sacrifices; four chests for freewill-offerings, for wood, incense, temple-decoration, and burnt-offerings." Lightfoot, *Hor. Heb.*

beheld] The imperfect tense in the original implies that He **continued watching and observing** the scene. "Christus in hodierno quoque cultu spectat omnes." Bengel.

how the people] "Before the Passover, freewill offerings in addition to the temple-tax were generally presented." Lange.

42. *a certain poor widow*] One of the helpless class which He had just described as *devoured* by the extortion of the Scribes and Pharisees. In three words St Mark presents to us a picture of her desolation: she was alone, she was a widow, and she was poor.

two mites] "Sche sente tweye mynutis, þat is, a ferþing," Wyclif. Mite is a contraction of *minute,* from Lat. *minutum,* though Fr. *mite.* Thus Becon says, "let us with the poor widow of the gospel at the least give *two minutes,* and God will surely approve and accept our good will." The *Lepton,* here mentioned, was the very smallest copper coin. Two made one Roman *quadrans,* which was ¼th of an *as.* The

140   ST MARK, XII. XIII.   [vv. 43, 44; 1.

43 And he called *unto him* his disciples, and saith unto them, Verily I say unto you, That this poor widow hath cast more
44 in, than all they which have cast into the treasury: for all *they* did cast in of their abundance; but she of her want did cast in all that she had, *even* all her living.

1—13. *Prophecies of the Destruction of Jerusalem.*

13 And as he went out of the temple, one of his disciples saith

as in Cicero's time=nearly a halfpenny, and the *quadrans*=one-eighth of a penny. This poor widow gave two, though, as Bengel remarks, she might have kept back one. She gave her "all." "If we have regard to the origin of the expression, it argues more of presumption than humility to call any gift, as many do, however liberal, unless it were our all, a 'mite,' while the frequent use of the term to excuse some shabby offering which costs the donor nothing, is a remarkable example of the serene unconsciousness with which persons will sometimes pass the most bitter sarcasms upon themselves." Davies, *Bible English*, p. 251.

43. *he called unto him*] "De re magna. Specimen judicii olim exercendi, pro statu cordium." Bengel.

more in, than all they] It is not said that the gifts of the others were worthless. Many possessed, no doubt, no worth (Matt. vi. 1); others, a greater or a less. The greatest value, however, attached itself to her gift, because of the self-denial which it implied.

44. *of their abundance*] i.e. of their *superfluity*, "of þat þing þat was plenteuous to hem." Wyclif.

she of her want] "of hir myseste sente alle þingis þat she hadde, al hir lyflode," Wyclif. Observe all the graphic touches in the account of the widow's mite. (i) Our Lord was *sitting* over against the Treasury; (ii) He was *watching* the people casting in their contributions; (iii) He *called* to Him His disciples; and (iv) He points out to them the full meaning of her act of self-denial. After this incident in the "court of the women," and apparently while the Saviour was still there, it came to pass, that two of the Apostles, Andrew and Philip, brought to Him the "inquiring Greeks," who had desired to see Him (John xii. 20—22). No sooner did He behold these "inquirers from the West," than He broke forth into words of mysterious joy (John xii. 24—26), and presentiments of His coming Passion (John xii. 27, 28); after which was heard the last of the Three Heavenly Voices, attesting the true dignity of His mission (John xii. 28). And so with the clear prevision that He was about to be "*lifted up*" upon His Cross, and, if "*lifted up*," would "*draw all men unto Him*" (John xii. 32), He prepared to leave the Temple, which He was never to enter again. His public work was over. His last counsels, His final warnings, had been delivered.

CH. XIII. 1—13. PROPHECIES OF THE DESTRUCTION OF JERUSALEM.

1. *And as he went*] Leaving the Temple, He passed with His

unto him, Master, see what manner of stones and what buildings *are here!* And Jesus answering said unto him, Seest thou 2 these great buildings? there shall not be left one stone upon another, that shall not be thrown down. And as he sat upon 3 the mount of Olives over against the temple, Peter and James and John and Andrew asked him privately, Tell us, when 4 shall these things be? and what *shall be* the sign when all these things shall be fulfilled? And Jesus answering them 5 began to say, Take heed lest any *man* deceive you: for 6

Apostles down the eastern steps toward the valley of the Kidron. As they were passing on,
 one of his disciples] invited His attention to the marvellous structure they were quitting, to the enormous size of its marble blocks, the grandeur of its buildings, and the gorgeous gifts with which, though still unfinished, it had been endowed (Luke xxi. 5). Josephus tells us that while some of the stones were forty-five feet, most were thirty-seven and a half feet long, twelve feet high, and eighteen broad. Jos. *Bell. Jud.* v. 6. 6; *Ant.* xv. 11. 3.
 2. *there shall not be left*] Though now they seem fixed in their places for eternity. And even as He said, less than forty years afterwards, "Zion was *ploughed as a field*, and Jerusalem became heaps, and the mountain of the House as the high places of the forest" (Micah iii. 12). Titus himself was amazed at the massive buildings of Jerusalem, and traced in his triumph the hand of God (Jos. *Bell. Jud.* vi. 9. 1). At his departure after the capture of the city, he left the tenth legion under the command of Terentius Rufus to carry out the work of demolition, and Josephus tells us (*Bell. Jud.* vii. 1. 1) that the whole inclosing walls and precincts of the Temple were "so thoroughly levelled and dug up that no one visiting the city would believe it had ever been inhabited."
 3. *the mount of Olives*] Nothing more appears to have been said now, and crossing the valley of the Kidron, the little company ascended the steep footpath that leads over the mount of Olives in the direction of Bethany. When they had reached the summit, He sat down (Matt. xxiv. 3; Mark xiii. 3)
 over against the temple] Notice this minuteness as regards details of *place* peculiar to the second Evangelist, and see Introduction, p. 19.
 Peter and James and John and Andrew] Observe again these minute particulars as to *persons*, and see Introd. p. 18. These Apostles probably now sat nearest to their Master, and were the most favoured of the apostolic band.
 4. *what shall be the sign*] The question is given more fully by St Matthew, xxiv. 3. It embraced three points: (i) the time of the destruction of the Temple; the sign (ii) of His Coming, and (iii) of the end of the world.
 5. *Take heed*] "The four moral key-notes of the Discourse on the Last Things are "*Beware,*" "*Watch,*" "*Endure,*" "*Pray.*" Farrar, *Life*, II. p. 258.

many shall come in my name, saying, I am *Christ;* and
7 shall deceive many. And when ye shall hear of wars and
rumours of wars, be ye not troubled: for *such things* must
8 needs be; but the end *shall* not *be* yet. For nation shall
rise against nation, and kingdom against kingdom: and
there shall be earthquakes in divers places, and there shall be
famines and troubles: these *are* the beginnings of sorrows.
9 But take heed to yourselves: for they shall deliver you up
to councils; and in the synagogues ye shall be beaten:
and ye shall be brought before rulers and kings for my
10 sake, for a testimony against them. And the gospel must

6. *many shall come*] Five tokens are here given, to which the Lord directs the attention of His disciples: (i) the rise of false prophets; (ii) wars and rumours of wars; (iii) the rising of nation against nation; (iv) earthquakes; (v) famines (some MSS. omit *troubles*); but the Apostles were not to be terrified, these things were

8. *the beginnings of sorrows*] rather, of **birth-pangs**. The word only occurs in four places in the N.T. Here; in the parallel, Matt. xxiv. 8; in Acts ii. 24, "having loosed *the pains* (rather **the pangs**) of death;" and 1 Thess. v. 3, "then sudden destruction cometh upon them, as *travail* (or **birth-pangs**) upon a woman with child." The occurrence of the expression here is remarkable, and recals other places of Scripture, where Creation is said to be "groaning and *travailing*" (Rom. viii. 22), waiting for its *regeneration* (Matt. xix. 28) or New Birth. For the fulfilment of these prophecies comp. Jos. *Ant.* XIX. 1; Tac. *Ann.* XII. 38, XV. 22, XVI. 13; Sen. *Ep.* XCI. Tacitus describing the epoch (*Hist.* I. 2) calls it "opimum casibus, atrox præliis, discors seditionibus, ipsâ etiam pace sævum." These "signs" then ushered in the epoch of the destruction of Jerusalem, but realized on a larger scale they are to herald the End of all things; comp. 1 Thess. v. 3; 2 Thess. ii. 2.

9. *to councils*] Of the actual hearers of the Lord some were destined to find this true within little more than fifty days. Thus, in Acts iv. 3, we find all the Apostles brought before the Sanhedrim, and again in Acts v. 18, 27. Similarly, St Paul was brought before the same Council, Acts xxiii. 1.

in the synagogues ye shall be beaten] "Of the Jews," says St Paul (2 Cor. xi. 24), "five times received I forty *stripes* save one;" "thrice was I *beaten with rods*." It was part of the duties of the Chazzan, or minister in each synagogue, to maintain order, and scourge the condemned.

before rulers and kings] Thus St Paul stood before *Felix* (Acts xxiv. 10—22), before *Festus* (Acts xxv. 1—11), before *Agrippa* (Acts xxvi. 1—23), before *Nero* (2 Tim. iv. 16). Our Lord also, we may believe, alluded to the general persecutions of the Christians in later times, and especially to that of the emperor Nero, in which St Peter and St Paul suffered martyrdom.

first be published among all nations. But when they shall 11 lead *you*, and deliver you up, take no thought beforehand what ye shall speak, neither do ye premeditate: but whatsoever shall be given you in that hour, that speak ye: for it is not ye that speak, but the Holy Ghost. Now the bro- 12 ther shall betray the brother to death, and the father the son; and children shall rise up against *their* parents, and shall cause them to be put to death. And ye shall be hated 13 of all *men* for my name's sake: but he that shall endure unto the end, the same shall be saved.

10. *the gospel must first be published*] And even so while many of His hearers were yet alive, the Gospel was proclaimed throughout the Roman Empire, from Arabia to Damascus, from Jerusalem to Illyricum, in Italy and in Spain. Comp. Rom. xv. 19, 24, 28; Col. i. 6, 23.

11. *take no thought beforehand*] Rather, **be not anxious beforehand, or distracted beforehand with anxiety.** "Nyle þe þenke what ȝe schulen speke," Wyclif. "*Thought*," when our translation was made, signified *undue care* or *anxiety*. Thus Bishop Ridley in the *Account of the Disputation at Oxford*, 1544, says, "No person of any honesty, without *thinking*, could abide to hear the like spoken by a most vile varlet;" and Shakespeare, *Jul. Cæs.* II. I. 186, says,

"If he love Cæsar, all that he can do
Is to himself, *take thought* and die for Cæsar,"

and *Hamlet* III. 1. 84,

"And thus the native hue of resolution
Is sicklied o'er with the pale cast of *thought*,"

and *Ant. and Cleop.* III. 13. 1,

"*Cleo.* What shall we do, Enobarbus?
Eno. *Think*, and die."

See the *Bible Word-Book*, sub loc.; and Davies, *Bible English*, pp. 99, 100.

but whatsoever shall be given you] Comp. Matt. x. 19, 20, where the words occur as a portion of our Lord's charge to His Twelve Apostles. "These were very weighty words for the Roman Christians, at a time when the martyrdom of the Apostles Peter and Paul, in Rome, was about to take place." Lange.

13. *he that shall endure*] "he þat schol *susteyne in* to þe ende," Wyclif. The endurance here spoken of is the *brave and persistent endurance* of the Christian in faith and love. In this noble word, the "queen of virtues," as Chrysostom does not fear to call it, "there always appears in the New Testament a background of *manliness;* it does not mark merely the *endurance*, the 'sustinentiam,' or even the 'patientiam,' but the '*perseverantiam*,' the 'brave

14—23. *Immediate Tokens of the Downfall of Jerusalem.*

14 **But when ye shall see the abomination of desolation, spoken of by Daniel the prophet, standing where it ought**

patience' with which the Christian contends against the various hindrances, persecutions, and temptations, that befall him in his conflict with the inward and outward world." Bp Ellicott on 1 Thess. i. 3. The verb occurs twice in St Matthew, once in St Mark, eight times in St Paul's Epistles, twice in St James, and is twice used by St Peter in the striking passage 1 Pet. ii. 20, "if when ye be buffeted for your faults, *ye shall take it patiently;*"..."if when ye do well, and suffer, ye *take it patiently.*"

14—23. IMMEDIATE TOKENS OF THE DOWNFALL OF JERUSALEM.

14. *But when ye shall see*] Hitherto He had distinctly foretold the destruction of the Holy City, now He gives them tokens which should forewarn them of its approach, and tells them how they may secure their own safety.

the abomination of desolation] The reference here is to Dan. ix. 27, "and for the *overspreading of abominations* he shall make it *desolate,*" or, as it is rendered in the margin, "and upon the battlements shall be the *idols of the desolator.*" The LXX. render it, "and upon the temple the abomination of desolations;" comp. 1 Macc. i. 54; 2 Macc. vi. 2. Hengstenberg would translate it, "and over the top of abomination comes the desolation."

   i. The verb from which the Greek word rendered "abomination" comes means *to cause disgust by bad smell or otherwise.* Hence it is translated by Tertullian "abominamentum."

   ii. In the Septuagint it is specially applied to (*a*) idols, and (*b*) things pertaining to idols. Thus in 1 Kings xi. 5 "Milcom" (=Molech) is called "*the abomination* of the Ammonites," and in 1 Kings xi. 7 "Chemosh" is called "*the abomination* of Moab." Again Ahab is said (1 Kings xxi. 26) "to have done *very abominably* in following idols," and Ahaz (2 Kings xvi. 3) to have made "his son to pass through the fire according to *the abominations* of the heathen." Comp. also 2 Kings xxi. 2.

   iii. Thus the word passes into the New Testament, where it occurs 6 times. (*a*) Here; (*b*) in the parallel, Matt. xxiv. 15; (*c*) Luke xvi. 15, "that which is highly esteemed among men is *abomination* in the sight of God;" and (*d*) Rev. xvii. 4, "having a golden cup in her hand full *of abominations.*" Comp. also Rev. xvii. 5, xxi. 27.

   iv. The key to the interpretation seems to be supplied by St Luke, who says (xxi. 20), "And when ye shall see Jerusalem *compassed with armies,* then know that *the desolation* thereof is nigh," and thus shews that it is to be explained in some connection with the Roman legions.

   v. Hence (*a*) Some would understand it to denote the vile abominations practised by the Romans on the place where the Temple stood. (*b*) Others, the Eagles, the standards of the Roman army,

not, (let him that readeth understand,) then let them that
be in Judæa flee to the mountains: and let him that is 15
on the housetop not go down into the house, neither enter
therein, to take any thing out of his house: and let him that 16
is in the field not turn back again for to take up his garment.
But woe to them that are with child, and to them that give 17
suck in those days! And pray ye that your flight be not in 18

which were held in abomination by the Jews, both on account of the
representations of the Emperor which they bore, and because the
soldiers were known to offer sacrifice to them. The Roman Eagles,
therefore, rising over the site of the Temple, "*where they ought
not,*" and "*compassing*" the city (Luke xxi. 20), was the sign that
the Holy Place had fallen under the dominion of the idolaters. (*c*)
Others again would refer the words not only to the Roman Eagles,
but to the outrages of lust and murder perpetrated by the "Zealots,"
which drove every worshipper in horror from the sacred Courts.
See Jos. *Bell. Jud.* IV. 3. 7. But even this was in consequence of
the compassing of the city by the Imperial Legions.

let him that readeth] This of course is said parenthetically.

flee to the mountains] Compare the flight of Lot from the doomed
"cities of the plain" to "the mountains," Gen. xix. 17. In accordance with these warnings the Christian Jews fled from Jerusalem to
the Peræan town of Pella, a distance of about 100 miles. "Somewhere
on the slopes of Gilead, near the scene of Jacob's first view of the land
of his descendants, and of the capital of the exiled David, was Pella
(identified with *Tabathat Fakkil*), so called by the Macedonian Greeks
from the springing fountain, which likened it to the birthplace of their
own Alexander.......From these heights Abner in his flight from the
Philistines, and David in his flight from Absalom, and the Israelites on
their way to Babylon, and the Christian Jews of Pella, caught the last
glimpse of their familiar mountains." Stanley's *Sinai and Palestine*,
p. 330.

15. *neither enter therein*] The houses of Palestine, as we have seen
in the case of the "paralytic borne of four," ch. ii. 3—12, were
furnished with a flight of steps outside, by which the housetop could
be reached without actually entering the house. The Christians were
thus warned by our Lord to flee along the flat roofs to the city wall,
and so make their escape.

16. *his garment*] i.e. his "outer garment."

18. *be not in the winter*] with its rains and storms and swollen
torrents, "*neither*," as St Matthew adds (xxiv. 20), "*on the Sabbath
day.*" We may well believe that the Christians made both these
petitions theirs. At any rate we know what did take place. (*a*) The
compassing of the city by the Roman armies spoken of by St Luke
(xxi. 20) took place at the commencement of October, A.D. 66, when
the weather was yet mild and favourable for travelling. (*b*) The final
siege, if any Christian Jews lingered on till then, took place in the still
more open months of April or May. See Lewin's *Fasti Sacri*, p. 344

19 the winter. For *in* those days shall be affliction, such as was not from the beginning of the creation which God 20 created unto this time, neither shall be. And except that the Lord had shortened those days, no flesh should be saved: but for the elect's sake, whom he hath chosen, he 21 hath shortened the days. And then if any man shall say to

and p. 358. The Jewish custom, which forbade travelling on the Sabbath beyond a distance of 2000 ells, would make the Christian Jews' travelling on that day infinitely more difficult, even though they might themselves be possibly free from any scruple. "They would in addition to other embarrassments, expose themselves to the severest persecutions of fanaticism." Lange.

19. *in those days*] There is no "in" here properly. **Those days shall be affliction,** "þe ilke dayes of tribulacioun schulen be suche," Wyclif.

such as was not from the beginning of the creation] The unexampled atrocities of the siege of Jerusalem are fully described by Josephus. He declares that "the misfortunes of all men, *from the beginning of the world*, if they be compared to those of the Jews, are not so terrible as theirs were," "nor did any age ever produce a generation more fruitful in wickedness *from the beginning of the world.*" The horrors of war and sedition, of famine and pestilence, were such as exceeded all example or conception. The city was densely crowded by the multitudes which had come up to the Passover. Pestilence ensued, and famine followed. The commonest instincts of humanity were forgotten. Acts of violence and cruelty were perpetrated without compunction or remorse, and barbarities enacted which cannot be described. Mothers snatched the food from the mouths of their husbands and children, and one actually killed, roasted, and devoured her infant son. (Comp. Lev. xxvi. 29; Deut. xxviii. 56, 57). Dead bodies filled the houses and streets of the city, while cruel assassins rifled and mangled with the exultation of fiends. The besieged devoured even the filth of the streets, and so excessive was the stench that it was necessary to hurl 600,000 corpses over the wall, while 97,000 captives were taken during the war, and more than 1,100,000 perished in the siege. See Josephus, *Bell. Jud.* VI. 9. 3; Tacitus, *Hist.* V. 13; Milman's *History of the Jews* II. 16; Merivale's *History of the Romans*, VI. 59.

20. *except that the Lord had shortened*] The word rendered "*shortened*" only occurs here and in the parallel, Matt. xxiv. 22. It denotes *to dock* or *curtail*. It occurs in the LXX. version of 2 Sam. iv. 12, where we read that David "commanded his young men, and they *cut off* the hands and the feet" of the murderers of Ishbosheth. If in God's pitying mercy the number of those awful days had not been shortened, no flesh could have been saved.

for the elect's sake] i.e. for the sake of the Christians.

he hath shortened] Had the horrors within and without which accompanied the siege of Jerusalem been prolonged, the utter desola-

you, Lo, here *is* Christ ; or, lo, *he is* there ; believe *him* not:
for false Christs and false prophets shall rise, and shall shew 22
signs and wonders, to seduce, if *it were* possible, even the
elect. But take ye heed: behold, I have foretold you all 23
things.

24—31. *The Second Advent of the Lord.*

But in those days, after that tribulation, the sun shall be 24
darkened, and the moon shall not give her light, and the 25
stars of heaven shall fall, and the powers that are in heaven

---

tion of the country would have been the result. But in mercy they were shortened, (1) by the swift and energetic measures of the invading armies, and (2) by the infatuation of the besieged. On his part Titus encircled the city with a wall five miles in extent, and fortified it with thirteen strong garrisons in the almost incredibly short space of three days, and Josephus makes special mention of his eagerness to bring the siege to an end. On the other hand, the leaders of the factions within slew the men who would have taught them how the siege might be prolonged, burnt the corn which would have enabled them to hold out against the enemy, and abandoned the towers, which were in reality impregnable. Thus the city, which in the time of Zedekiah (2 Kings xxv. 1—6; Jer. xxxix. 1, 2) had resisted the forces of Nebuchadnezzar for sixteen months, was taken by the Romans in less than five.

22. *for false Christs and false prophets*] Josephus tells us that false prophets and impostors prevailed on multitudes to follow them into the desert, promising there to display signs and wonders (comp. Acts xxi. 38); and even at the last, when the Temple was in flames, numbers of all ages flocked thither from the city upon the proclamation of a false prophet, and of six thousand assembled there on this occasion, not one escaped the fire or the sword. But such imposture is to be still more signally realized with *"signs and lying wonders"* before the final coming of Christ (2 Thess. ii. 1—10).

23. *But take ye heed*] Repeated and emphatic exhortation to watchfulness.

24—31. THE SECOND ADVENT OF THE LORD.

24. *in those days*] He, to Whom *"a thousand years are as one day, and one day as a thousand years"* (2 Pet. iii. 8), to Whom there is no past or future but one eternal Present, passes from one chapter to another in the history of the world with the ease of One, Who seeth all things clearly revealed.

the sun shall be darkened] Two of those then listening to the Lord, have themselves described the signs in the physical world which are to usher in the End; (*a*) St Peter, in his second Epistle, iii. 1—13, and (*b*) St John, in Rev. xx. xxi.

26 shall be shaken. And then shall they see the Son of man
27 coming in the clouds with great power and glory. And then
shall he send his angels, and shall gather together his elect
from the four winds, from the uttermost part of the earth to
28 the uttermost part of heaven. Now learn a parable of the
fig tree; When her branch is yet tender, and putteth forth
29 leaves, ye know that summer is near: so ye in like manner,
when ye shall see these things come to pass, know that it is
30 nigh, *even* at the doors. Verily I say unto you, that this
generation shall not pass, till all these things be done.

26. *shall they see the Son of man*] Even when speaking of the
"glorious majesty" of His Second Advent, He calls Himself by the
name which links Him to the Humanity He came to save. For the
title see note on ch. ii. 10, and compare John v. 22, 27, "the Father
judgeth no man, but hath committed all judgment unto the Son, and
hath given him authority to execute judgment also, because *he is
the Son of man*."

in the clouds] And so the Angels distinctly stated to the Apostles at
the Ascension (Acts i. 11); and Daniel foresaw Him *coming with the
clouds of heaven* (Dan. vii. 13, 14).

27. *then shall he send his angels*] As *the only begotten Son,
who is in the bosom of the Father* (John i. 18), alone ever declared or
manifested Him to His creatures, so to Him God hath delegated the
universal and ultimate judgment of mankind, that "as in our nature He
performed all that was requisite to save us, as in our nature He was
exalted to God's right hand to rule and bless us, so He shall in our
nature appear to judge us." Barrow's *Sermons;* comp. also Pearson *On
the Creed*, Art. vii.

28. *a parable*] Rather, **its parable**, the lesson which in similitude it
was meant to teach.

of the fig tree] They had already been taught one lesson from the
withered fig-tree, they are now bidden to learn another from the tree
when her branch is yet tender.

29. *it is nigh*] Rather, **He is nigh**, i.e. the Judge spoken of in verse 26.

even at the doors] There is no "*even*" in the original. So St James
says, "Behold, the Judge standeth *before the door*" (James v. 9).
"There is something solemn in the brevity of the phrase, without the
nominative expressed." Bp Wordsworth.

30. *this generation shall not pass*] The word thus rendered denotes
(1) *birth, age*, as in the phrases "younger," "older in *age;*" (2) *descent;*
(3) *a generation* of men living at the same time; (4) in a wider sense, *a
race.* He, Who surveys all things as an Eternal Present, "turns the
thoughts of His disciples to two horizons, one near and one far off:"—

(i) *In reference to the destruction of Jerusalem*, He declares that the
generation of the literal Israel then living would not pass away before
the judgments here predicted would fall upon Jerusalem, just as
God had made their forefathers wander in the wilderness "until *all*

Heaven and earth shall pass away: but my words shall not 31
pass away.

32—37. *Final Exhortation to Watchfulness.*

But of that day and *that* hour knoweth no man, no, not 32
the angels which are in heaven, neither the Son, but the
Father. Take ye heed, watch and pray: for ye know not 33
when the time is. *For the Son of man is* as a man taking a 34
far journey, who left his house, and gave authority to his

> *the generation* was consumed" that had come out of Egypt "and
> done evil in the sight of the Lord" (Num. xxxii. 13);
> (ii) *In reference to His own Second Coming,* and the world at large,
> He affirms that the race of men, and especially *the generation* of
> them *that sought the Lord* (Ps. xxiv. 6), the faithful seed of Abra-
> ham, should not pass away until all these things should be fulfilled.
> 31. *but my words shall not pass away*] Never did the Speaker seem
> to stand more utterly alone than when He uttered this majestic utter-
> ance. Never did it seem more improbable that it should be fulfilled.
> But as we look across the centuries we see how it has been realised.
> His words have passed into laws, they have passed into doctrines, they
> have passed into proverbs, they have passed into consolations, but they
> have never "passed away." What human teacher ever dared to claim
> an eternity for his words?

32—37. FINAL EXHORTATION TO WATCHFULNESS.

32. *neither the Son*] As our Lord is said to have "increased *in
wisdom*" as well as "in stature" (Luke ii. 52), to have *prayed* to the
Father (Matt. xiv. 23, xxvi. 39, 42—44, &c.); to have *received commandment* from the Father (John xiv. 31), even so it is here said by
Himself that His knowledge is limited. But we may believe (1) that it
is only as the *Son of Man,* that anything could be unknown to Him, Who
said "*I and my Father are one;*" and (ii) that as the Eternal Word, the
one Messenger of Divine Revelation, He did not know of that day and
that hour *so as to reveal them to man.* "*In* Patre Filius *scit,* though it
is no part of His office to reveal it *a* Patre." St Augustine, quoted by
Bp Wordsworth.

33. *Take ye heed, watch and pray*] "Se 3e, wake 3e, and preie
3e," Wyclif. The word rendered "watch" only occurs 4 times in the
New Testament: (1) here; (2) in the parallel, Luke xxi. 36; (3) Eph.
vi. 18, "Praying always...and *watching thereunto* with all perseve-
rance;" (4) Heb. xiii. 17, "Obey them that have the rule over you,...for
they *watch for* your souls." It denotes (1) *to be sleepless,* (2) *to be
vigilant.*

34. *For the Son of man is*] These words do not occur in the original.
taking a far journey] Literally, one **who is absent from his people,
who goes on foreign travel.** "Which gon fer in pilgrimage," Wyclif.
The verb formed from it occurs in chap. xii. 1, "A certain man planted
a vineyard...and *went into a far* country." Even so our Lord left His

servants, and to every man his work, and commanded the
35 porter to watch. Watch ye therefore: for ye know not when
the master of the house cometh, at even, or at midnight, or
36 at the cockcrowing, or in the morning: lest coming suddenly
37 he find you sleeping. And what I say unto you I say unto
all, Watch.

1, 2. *The Sanhedrim in Council.*

14 After two days was *the feast of* the passover, and of

Church, gave authority to His servants the Apostles, and to those who should come after them, and to every man his work, and is now waiting for the consummation of all things.

35. *at even, or at midnight*] On the night watches see above, ch. vi. 48. In the Temple the priest, whose duty it was to superintend the night sentinels of the Levitical guard, might at any moment knock at the door and demand entrance. "He came suddenly and unexpectedly, no one knew when. The Rabbis use almost the very words in which Scripture describes the unexpected coming of the Master, when they say, Sometimes he came at the cockcrowing, sometimes a little earlier, sometimes a little later. He came and knocked, and they opened to him." Mishnah, *Tamid*, I. 1, 2, quoted in Edersheim's *The Temple and its Services*, p. 120.

36. *lest coming suddenly he find you sleeping*] "During the night the 'captain of the Temple' made his rounds. On his approach the guards had to rise and salute him in a particular manner. Any guard found asleep when on duty was beaten, or his garments were set on fire —a punishment, as we know, actually awarded." Edersheim, p. 120.

37. *Watch*] Observe in this chapter the emphasis given to Christ's exhortation, "*Watch!*" The Apostle, under whose eye St Mark wrote his Gospel, would seem to wish us to notice in spite of what frequent warnings he himself failed to watch and fell. St Matthew tells us how the Lord sought to impress these lessons of watchfulness and faithfulness still more deeply by the Parables of the "*Ten Virgins*" (Matt. xxv. 1—13), and the "*Talents*" (Matt. xxv. 14—30), and closed all with a picture of the Awful Day, when the Son of Man should separate all nations one from another as the shepherd divideth his sheep from the goats (Matt. xxv. 31—46). So ended the great discourse on the Mount of Olives, and the sun set, and the Wednesday of Holy Week had already begun before the little company entered the hamlet of Bethany.

CH. XIV. 1, 2. THE SANHEDRIM IN COUNCIL.

1. *After two days*] From St Matthew's account we gather that it was as they entered Bethany that our Lord Himself reminded the Apostles (Matt. xxvi. 1, 2) that after two days the Passover would be celebrated, and *the Son of Man be delivered up to be crucified*. He thus indicated the precise time when "the Hour" so often spoken of before

unleavened bread: and the chief priests and the scribes sought how they might take him by craft, and put *him* to death. But they said, Not on the feast *day*, lest there be an ² uproar of the people.

3—9. *The Feast in Simon's House. The Anointing by Mary.*

And being in Bethany in the house of Simon the leper, 3

should come, and again speaks of its accompanying circumstances of unutterable degradation and infamy—**death by Crucifixion**.

and of unleavened bread] The Passover took place on the 14th of Nisan, and the "Feast of unleavened bread" commenced on the 15th and lasted for seven days, deriving its name from the *Mazzoth*, or unleavened cakes, which was the only bread allowed during that week (Exod. xii. 34, 39; Deut. xvi. 3). From their close connection they are generally treated as one, both in the Old and in the New Testament, and Josephus, on one occasion, even describes it as "a feast for eight days." Jos. *Antiq.* II. 15. 1; Edersheim, p. 177.

and the chief priests] While our Lord was in quiet retirement at Bethany the rulers of the nation were holding a formal consultation in the court of the palace of Caiaphas (Matt. xxvi. 3) how they could put Him to death. Disappointed as they had been in ensnaring Him into matter for a capital charge, they saw that their influence was lost unless they were willing to take extreme measures, and the events of the Triumphal Entry had convinced them of the hold He had gained over many of the nation, especially the bold and hardy mountaineers of Galilee. The only place where He appeared in public after the nights had been spent at Bethany was the Temple, but to seize Him there would in the present excited state of popular feeling certainly lead to a tumult, and a tumult to the interposition of Pilate, who during the Passover kept a double garrison in the tower of Antonia, and himself had come up to Jerusalem.

by craft] It was formally resolved therefore to take Him *by craft*, and for this purpose to wait and take advantage of the course of events and of any favourable opportunity which might present itself.

3—9. THE FEAST IN SIMON'S HOUSE. THE ANOINTING BY MARY.

3. *And being in Bethany*] Meanwhile circumstances had occurred which in their result presented to the Jewish authorities a mode of apprehending Him which they had never anticipated. To relate these the Evangelist goes back to the evening before the Triumphal Entry, and places us in the house of

Simon the leper] He had, we may believe, been a leper, and possibly had been restored by our Lord Himself. He was probably a near friend or relation of Lazarus. Some suppose he was his brother, others that he was the husband of Mary.

as he sat at meat, there came a woman having an alabaster box of ointment of spikenard very precious; and she brake 4 the box, and poured *it* on his head. And there were some that had indignation within themselves, and said, Why was 5 this waste of the ointment made? for it might have been

as he sat at meat] We learn from St John that the sisters had made Him a feast, at which Martha served, while Lazarus reclined at the table as one of the guests (John xii..2).

there came a woman] This was Mary the sister of Lazarus, full of grateful love to Him, who had poured back joy into her once desolated home.

having an alabaster box] "hauynge a box of precious oynement spikanard," Wyclif. At Alabastron in Egypt there was a manufactory of small vases for holding perfumes, which were made from a stone found in the neighbouring mountains. The Greeks gave to these vases the name of the city from which they came, calling them *alabastrons*. This name was eventually extended to the stone of which they were formed; and at length the term *alabaster* was applied without distinction to all perfume vessels, of whatever materials they consisted.

of ointment of spikenard] Or, as in margin, **of pure** (=*genuine*) **nard** or **liquid nard. Pure** or **genuine** seems to yield the best meaning, as opposed to the *pseudo-nardus*, for the spikenard was often adulterated. Pliny, *Nat. Hist.* XII. 26. It was drawn from an Indian plant, brought down in considerable quantities into the plains of India from such mountains as Shalma, Kedar Kanta, and others, at the foot of which flow the Ganges and Jumna rivers.

very precious] It was the costliest anointing oil of antiquity, and was sold throughout the Roman Empire, where it fetched a price that put it beyond any but the wealthy. Mary had bought a vase or flask of it containing 12 ounces (John xii. 3). Of the costliness of the ointment we may form some idea by remembering that it was among the gifts sent by Cambyses to the Ethiopians (Herod. III. 20), and that Horace promises Virgil a whole *cadus* (= 36 quarts nearly) of wine, for a small onyx box of spikenard (*Carm.* IV. xii. 16, 17),

"Nardo vina merebere;
"Nardi parvus onyx eliciet cadum."

brake the box] i.e. she broke the narrow neck of the small flask, and poured the perfume first on the head, and then on the feet of Jesus, drying them with the hair of her head. She did not wish to keep or hold back anything. She offered up all, gave away all, and her "all" was a tribute worthy of a king. "To anoint the feet of the greatest monarch was long unknown; and in all the pomps and greatnesses of the Roman prodigality, it was not used till Otho taught it to Nero." Jeremy Taylor's *Life of Christ*, III. 13.

4. *And there were some*] The murmuring began with Judas Iscariot (John xii. 4), and his spirit of murmuring infected some of the others, simple Galileans, little accustomed to such luxury.

sold for more than three hundred pence, and have been
given to the poor. And they murmured against her. And
Jesus said, Let her alone; why trouble ye her? she hath
wrought a good work on me. For ye have the poor with
you always, and whensoever ye will ye may do them good:
but me ye have not always. She hath done what she could:
she is come aforehand to anoint my body to the burying.
Verily I say unto you, Wheresoever this gospel shall be
preached throughout the whole world, *this* also that she hath
done shall be spoken of for a memorial of her.

10, 11. *The Compact of Judas with the Chief Priests.*

And Judas Iscariot, one of the twelve, went unto the chief

5. *for more than three hundred pence*] i.e. for more than 300 denarii,
=300 × 7½*d.* = about £10. To Judas it was intolerable there should be
such an utter waste of good money.

they murmured] This word has already been explained in the note on
chap. i. 43. Wyclif renders it here "þei groyneden in to hir." De
Wette, "they scolded her." The word "expresses a passionate feeling,
which we strive to keep back in the utterance." "St Mark, without a
doubt, presents here the most accurate historic picture; St John defines
most sharply the motive; St Matthew gives the especially practical historic form." Lange.

8. *she is come aforehand*] The word thus rendered only occurs three
times in the New Testament. (1) Here; (2) 1 Cor. xi. 21, "for in eating
every one *taketh before other* his own supper;" (3) Gal. vi. 1, "if a man
be *overtaken* in a fault," = "be *surprised* or *detected* in the act of com-
mitting any sin." It denotes (1) *to take beforehand;* (2) *to take before
another;* (3) *to outstrip, get the start of, anticipate.*

9. *this gospel shall be preached*] A memorable prophecy, and to this
day memorably fulfilled. The story of her devoted adoration has gone
forth into all lands.

10, 11. THE COMPACT OF JUDAS WITH THE CHIEF PRIESTS.

10. *And Judas Iscariot*] The words "*to the burying*" must have fallen
like the death knell of all his Messianic hopes on the ears of Judas Iscariot,
"the only southern Jew among the Twelve," and this, added to the consciousness that his Master had read the secret of his life (John xii. 6),
filled his soul with feelings of bitterest mortification and hostility.
Three causes, if we may conjecture anything on a subject so full of
mystery, would seem to have brought about his present state of mind, and
precipitated the course which he now took: (1) *avarice;* (2) *disappointment of his carnal hopes;* (3) *a withering of internal religion.*

(i) *Avarice.* We may believe that his practical and administrative
    talents caused him to be made the almoner of the Apostles. This
    constituted at once his opportunity and his trial. He proved unfaithful

11 priests, to betray him unto them. And when they heard *it*, they were glad, and promised to give him money. And he sought how he might conveniently betray him.

to his trust, and used the common purse of the brotherhood for his own ends (John xii. 6). The germs of avarice probably unfolded themselves very gradually, and in spite of many warnings from his Lord (Matt. vi. 19—34, xiii. 22, 23; Mark x. 25; Luke xvi. 11; John vi. 70), but they gathered strength, and as he became entrusted with larger sums, he fell more deeply.

(ii) *Disappointment of his carnal hopes*] Like all his brother Apostles, he had cherished gross and carnal views of the Messianic glory, his heart was set on the realization of a visible kingdom, with high places, pomp, and power. If some of the brotherhood were to sit on thrones (Matt. xix. 28), might he not obtain some post, profitable if not splendid? But the issue of the Triumphal Entry, and the repeated allusions of his Master to His death and His burying, sounded the knell of all these temporal and earthly aspirations.

(iii) *A withering of internal religion*] He had been for three years close to Goodness Incarnate, but the good seed within him had become choked with the thorns of greed and carnal longings. "The mildew of his soul had spread apace," and the discovery of his secret sin, and its rebuke by our Lord at Bethany, turned his attachment to his Master more and more into *aversion*. The presence of Goodness so close to him ceasing to *attract* had begun to *repel*, and now in his hour of temptation, while he was angry at being suspected and rebuked, and possibly jealous of the favour shewn to others of the brotherhood, arose the question, prompted by none other than the Evil One (Luke xxii. 3), *Why should he lose everything? Might he not see what was to be gained by taking the other side?* (Matt. xxvi. 15).

went unto the chief priests] Full of such thoughts, in the darkness of the night he repaired from Bethany to Jerusalem, and being admitted into the council of the chief priests asked what they would give him for betraying his Master into their hands.

11. *they were glad*] They shuddered not at the suggested deed of darkness. His proposal filled them with joy.

and promised] How much he expected when he went over to them we cannot tell. But by going at all he had placed himself in their hands. He had made his venture, and was obliged to take what they offered. *Thirty pieces of silver* (Matt. xxvi. 15), the price of a slave (Exod. xxi. 32), were equivalent to 120 denarii $= 120 \times 7\frac{1}{2}d. =$ about £3. 13s. of our money. At this time the ordinary wages for a day's labour was one denarius; so that the whole sum amounted to about four months' wages of a day labourer. It is possible, however, the sum, which seems to us so small, may have been earnest-money.

conveniently] That is without raising the hostility of the populace, and possibly after the conclusion of the Passover and the dispersion of the Galilean pilgrims to their own homes.

12—16. *Preparations for the Last Supper.*

And the first day of unleavened bread, when they killed 12
the passover, his disciples said unto him, Where wilt thou
that we go and prepare that thou mayest eat the passover?
And he sendeth forth two of his disciples, and saith unto 13
them, Go ye into the city, and there shall meet you a man
bearing a pitcher of water: follow him. And wheresoever 14
he shall go in, say ye to the goodman of the house, The

12—16. PREPARATIONS FOR THE LAST SUPPER.

12. *the first day of unleavened bread*] Wednesday in Passion week would seem to have been spent by our Lord in deep seclusion at Bethany preparing Himself for the awfulness of the coming struggle, and is hidden by a veil of holy silence. That night He slept at Bethany for the last time on earth. "On the Thursday morning He awoke never to sleep again." Farrar, *Life*, II. p. 275.

when they killed the passover] i.e. the Paschal victim. Comp. Luke xxii. 7, "when the *Passover* must be *killed;*" 1 Cor. v. 7, "Christ *our Passover* (=*Paschal Lamb*) is sacrificed for us." The name of the Passover, in Hebrew *Pesach*, and in Aramæan and Greek *Pascha*, is derived from a root which means to "step over," or to "*overleap*," and thus points back to the historical origin of the Festival. "And when I see the blood, I will *pass over* you, and the plague shall not be upon you to destroy you, when I smite the land of Egypt" (Exod. xii. 13).

Where wilt thou] On this Thursday morning the disciples came to our Lord for instructions as to the Passover. They may have expected, considering the complete seclusion of Wednesday, that He would eat it at Bethany, for "the village was reckoned as regards religious purposes part of Jerusalem by the Rabbis, and the Lamb might be eaten there, though it must be killed at the Temple." Lightfoot, *Hor. Heb.*

that we go and prepare] The lamb had, we may believe, already been bought on the tenth of Nisan, according to the rule of the Law (Exod. xii. 3), the very day on which He, the true Paschal Lamb, entered Jerusalem in meek triumph.

13. *he sendeth forth two of his disciples*] The Apostles Peter and John (Luke xxii. 8).

and there shall meet you] Observe the minuteness of the directions and of the predictions as to the events which would happen. It is the same mysterious minuteness which distinguishes the preparations for the Triumphal Entry.

a man] It was generally the task of women to carry water. Amongst the thousands at Jerusalem they would notice this *man* carrying an earthen jar of water drawn from one of the fountains. We need not conclude, because it was a slave's employment to do this (Deut. xxix. 11; Josh. ix. 21), that he was a slave. The Apostles were to follow him to whatever house he entered.

14. *say ye to the goodman of the house*] The words addressed to him, and the confidential nature of the communication, make it probable that

Master saith, Where is the guestchamber, where I shall eat
15 the passover with my disciples? And he will shew you
a large upper room furnished *and* prepared: there make
16 ready for us. And his disciples went forth, and came into
the city, and found as he had said unto them: and they
made ready the passover.

the owner of the house was a believing follower. "Discipulus, sed non ex duodecim," Bengel. Some have conjectured it was Joseph of Arimathæa, others John Mark; but the Gospels and tradition alike are silent. "Universal hospitality prevailed in this matter, and the only recompence that could be given was the skin of the paschal lamb, and the earthen dishes used at the meal." Geikie, II. 462.

the guestchamber] Curiously translated by Wyclif, "my fulfilling, *or etyng place.*" The original word only occurs here, in the parallel Luke xxii. 11, and Luke ii. 7, "and she brought forth her firstborn son, and laid him in a manger, because there was no room for them *in the inn.*"

15. *a large upper room furnished*] "a greet souping place strewid," Wyclif. The guest-chamber was on the upper floor, ready, and provided with couches, as the custom of reclining at meals required. We may conclude also from the word *prepared* that the searching for and putting away of every particle of leaven (1 Cor. v. 7), so important a preliminary to the Passover, and performed in perfect silence and with a lighted candle, had been already carried out.

16. *they made ready the passover*] This preparation would include the provision of the unleavened cakes, of the bitter herbs, the four or five cups of red wine mixed with water, of everything, in short, necessary for the meal. At this point it may be well to try to realise the manner in which the Passover was celebrated amongst the Jews in the time of our Lord. (i) With the Passover, by Divine ordinance, there had always been eaten two or three flat cakes of unleavened bread (Exod. xii. 18), and the rites of the feast by immemorial usage had been regulated according to the succession of four cups of red wine always mixed with water (Ps. xvi. 5, xxiii. 5, cxvi. 13). These were placed before the master of the house where the Paschal Feast was celebrated, or the most eminent guest, who was called the Celebrant, the President, or Proclaimer of the Feast. (ii) After those assembled had reclined, he took one of the Four Cups, known as the "Cup of Consecration," in his right hand, and pronounced the benediction over the wine and the feast, saying, "*Blessed be Thou, Jehovah, our God, Thou King of the universe, Who hast created the fruit of the vine.*" He then tasted the Cup and passed it round. (iii) Water was then brought in, and he washed, followed by the rest, the hands being dipped in water. (iv) The table was then set out with the bitter herbs, such as lettuce, endive, succory, and horehound, the sauce called *Charoseth,* and the Passover lamb. (v) The Celebrant then once more blessed God for the fruits of the earth, and taking a portion of the

17—21. *Commencement of the Supper. Revelation of the Traitor.*

And in the evening he cometh with the twelve. And as 17/18

bitter herbs, dipped it in the *charoseth*, and ate a piece of it of "the size of an olive," and his example was followed by the rest. (vi) The *Haggadah* or "shewing forth" (1 Cor. xi. 26) now commenced, and the Celebrant declared the circumstances of the delivery from Egypt, as commanded by the Law (Exod. xii. 27, xiii. 8). (vii) Then the second Cup of wine was filled, and a child or proselyte inquired, "*What mean ye by this service?*" (Exod. xii. 26), to which reply was made according to a prescribed formula or liturgy. The first part of the "Hallel," Psalms cxiii., cxiv., was then sung, and the second Cup was solemnly drunk. (viii) The Celebrant now washed his hands again, and taking two of the unleavened cakes, broke one of them, and pronounced the thanksgiving in these words, "*Blessed be Thou, O Lord our God, Thou King of the universe, Who bringest forth fruit out of the earth.*" Then he distributed a portion to each, and all wrapping some bitter herbs round their portion dipped it in the *charoseth* and ate it. (ix) The flesh of the lamb was now eaten, and the Master of the house, lifting up his hands, gave thanks over the third Cup of wine, known as the "Cup of Blessing," and handed it round to each person. (x) After thanking for the food of which they had partaken and for their redemption from Egypt, a fourth Cup, known as the "Cup of Joy," was filled and drunk, and the remainder of the Hallel (Pss. cxv.—cxviii.) was sung. See Buxtorf, *de Cœna Domini;* Lightfoot, *Temple Service;* Edersheim, pp. 206—209.

17—21. COMMENCEMENT OF THE SUPPER. REVELATION OF THE TRAITOR.

17. *in the evening*] "It was probably while the sun was beginning to decline in the horizon that Jesus and the disciples descended once more over the Mount of Olives into the Holy City. Before them lay Jerusalem in her festive attire. White tents dotted the sward, gay with the bright flowers of early spring, or peered out from the gardens and the darker foliage of the olive-plantations. From the gorgeous Temple buildings, dazzling in their snow-white marble and gold, on which the slanting rays of the sun were reflected, rose the smoke of the altar of burnt offering....The streets must have been thronged with strangers, and the flat roofs covered with eager gazers, who either feasted their eyes with a first sight of the Sacred City for which they had so often longed, or else once more rejoiced in view of the well-remembered localities. It was the last day-view which the Lord had of the Holy City—till His resurrection!" Edersheim's *The Temple and its Services*, pp. 194, 195.

he cometh with the twelve] Judas must have stolen back to Bethany before daylight, and another day of hypocrisy had been spent under the penetrating glance of Him Who could read the hearts of men.

they sat and did eat, Jesus said, Verily I say unto you, One
19 of you which eateth with me shall betray me. And they
began to be sorrowful, and to say unto him one by one, *Is*
20 *it I?* And others said, *Is* it I? And he answered and said
unto them, *It is* one of the twelve, that dippeth with me in
21 the dish. The Son of man indeed goeth, as it is written of

18. *And as they sat*] Grouping together the four narratives, which, as they approach the Passion, expand into the fulness of a diary, we infer that (i) when the little company had taken their places on the *triclinia*, the Saviour as Celebrant or Proclaimer of the Feast, remarking that with desire He had desired to eat this Passover before He suffered, took the first cup and divided it amongst them (Luke xxii. 15—18). (ii) Then followed the unseemly dispute touching priority (Luke xxii. 24—30), to correct which and to teach them in the most striking manner possible a lesson of humility, He washed His disciples' feet, covered with dust from their walk along the road from Bethany (John xiii. 1—11). Then the meal was resumed and He reclined once more at the table (John xiii. 12), the beloved disciple lying on His right, with his head close to the Redeemer's breast.

One of you which eateth with me shall betray me] He had already said, after washing their feet, "now ye are clean, but *not all*" (John xiii. 10), but at this moment the consciousness of the traitor's presence so wrought upon Him (John xiii. 21) that He broke forth into words of yet plainer prediction.

19. *they began to be sorrowful*] The very thought of treason was to their honest and faithful hearts insupportable, and excited great surprise and deepest sorrow.

one by one] Observe the pictorial and minute details of St Mark.

Is it I?] None of them said "Is it *he?*" So utterly unconscious were they of the treachery that lurked in their midst.

20. *he answered and said unto them*] "*Answered*" is omitted in the best MSS. The intimation was made privately to St John, to whom St Peter had made a sign that he should ask who could be so base (John xiii. 23—26).

one of the twelve] One of His own "familiar friends" (Ps. xli. 9).

that dippeth with me] "He who is just about to dip with Me a piece of the unleavened cakes into the *charoseth*"—a sauce consisting of a mixture of vinegar, figs, dates, almonds, and spice, provided at the Passover—"and to whom I shall give some of it presently" (John xiii. 26). To this day at the summit of Gerizim the Samaritans on the occasion of the Passover hand to the stranger a little olive-shaped morsel of unleavened bread enclosing a green fragment of wild endive or some other bitter herb, which may resemble, except that it is not dipped in the dish, the very 'sop' which Judas received at the hands of Christ." Farrar, *Life*, II. p. 290.

21. *Woe to that man*] The intimation just given was uttered privately for the ear of St John alone, and through him was possibly made known to St Peter; but the incident was of so ordinary a character, that

him: but woe to that man by whom the Son of man is betrayed! good were it for that man if he had never been born.

22—25. *Institution of the Holy Eucharist.*

And as they did eat, Jesus took bread, and blessed, and 22 brake *it*, and gave to them, and said, Take, eat: this is my body. And he took the cup, and when he had given thanks, 23 he gave *it* to them: and they all drank of it. And he said 24 unto them, This is my blood of the new testament, which is

it would fail to attract any notice whatever, and could only be a sign to the Apostle of Love. Then aloud, as we may believe, the Holy One uttered His final warning to the Traitor, and pronounced words of immeasurable woe on him by whom He was about to be betrayed, "*It were good for that man if he had never been born.*" But the last appeal had no effect upon him. "*Rabbi, is it I?*" he inquired, steeling himself to utter the shameless question. "*Thou hast said,*" replied the Saviour, in words probably heard only by those close by, and gave him "the sop," and Satan entered into him, as St John tells us (xiii. 27) with awful impressiveness. "*That thou doest, do quickly,*" the Saviour continued; and the traitor arose and went forth, and it *was night* (John xiii. 27—30), but the night was not darker than the darkness of his soul.

22—25. INSTITUTION OF THE HOLY EUCHARIST.

22. *And as they did eat*] On the departure of the Traitor the Saviour, as though relieved of a heavy load, broke forth into words of mysterious triumph (John xiii. 31—35), and then, as the meal went on, proceeded to institute the Holy Eucharist.

Jesus took bread] that is one of the unleavened cakes that had been placed before Him as the Celebrant or Proclaimer of the Feast.

and blessed] giving thanks and pronouncing the consecration, probably in the usual words, see above, verse 16.

Take, eat] "Eat" is omitted here in the best editions.

this is my body] St Luke adds, "*which is being* (or *on the point of being*) *given for you;*" St Paul (1 Cor. xi. 24), "*which is being* (or *on the point of being*) *broken for you,*" while both add, "*do this in remembrance of Me.*"

23. *he took the cup*] probably the third Cup, and known as the "Cup of Blessing." See above, verse 16.

24. *This is my blood of the new testament*] or rather, **Covenant.** Some of the best MSS. here omit "new." He reminds them of the old Covenant also made in blood with their fathers in the wilderness (Exod. xxiv. 8).

which is shed for many] i.e. *which is being* (or *on the point of being*) *shed for many.* St Matthew (xxvi. 28) adds, "*unto the remission of sins;*" St Paul adds (1 Cor. xi. 25), "*Do this, as oft as ye shall drink it, in remembrance of Me.*" Thus did our Lord ordain Bread and Wine to be the "outward part" or "sign" of the Sacrament of our Redemption by His

25 shed for many. Verily I say unto you, I will drink no more of the fruit of the vine, until that day that I drink it new in the kingdom of God.

26—31. *The Flight of the Apostles foretold and the Denials of St Peter.*

26 And when they had sung an hymn, they went out into the 27 mount of Olives. And Jesus saith unto them, All ye shall be offended because of me this night: for it is written, I will smite the shepherd, and the sheep shall be scattered. 28 But after that I am risen, I will go before you into Galilee. 29 But Peter said unto him, Although all shall be offended, yet 30 *will* not I. And Jesus saith unto him, Verily I say unto thee, That this day, *even* in this night, before the cock crow

death. In the ordinary Paschal Feast these elements had been subordinate. He now gives to them the first importance. In the ordinary Paschal Feast the Lamb occupied the chief place. Now the type was succeeded by the Antitype; now the "very Paschal Lamb" was come, and was about to offer Himself from the altar of His Cross for the sins of the whole world. Of the Jewish Paschal Lamb, therefore, no word is said, but in its place our Lord puts the Bread and Wine, the Sacramental Symbols of His Body and Blood. Gradually and progressively He had prepared the minds of His disciples to realise the idea of His death as a sacrifice. He now gathers up all previous announcements in the institution of this Sacrament.

26—31. THE FLIGHT OF THE APOSTLES FORETOLD AND THE DENIALS OF ST PETER.

26. *when they had sung an hymn*] In all probability the concluding portion of the Hallel. See above, note on verse 16.

27. *And Jesus saith unto them*] These words really were uttered as they sat at the table just after the institution of the Holy Eucharist.

for it is written] The words are taken from Zech. xiii. 7. The Good Shepherd quotes the allusion to Himself in His truest character (John x. 4).

28. *after that I am risen*] The Angel afterwards referred to these very words at the open Sepulchre on the world's first Easter-Day (Mark xvi. 6, 7).

29. *But Peter said unto him*] Ardent and impulsive as ever, the Apostle could not endure the thought of such desertion. His protestations of fidelity are more fully given in Matt. xxvi. 33 and John xiii. 37.

30. *in this night*] Before the dawn of the morrow should streak the eastern sky, and in the darkness the cock should twice have crowed, he who had declared he would *never* be offended, would *thrice* deny that

twice, thou shalt deny me thrice. But he spake the more 31 vehemently, If I should die with thee, I will not deny thee in any wise. Likewise also said they all.

32—42. *The Agony in the Garden of Gethsemane.*

And they came to a place which was named Gethsemane: 32 and he saith to his disciples, Sit ye here, while I shall pray. And he taketh with him Peter and James and John, and 33 began to be sore amazed, and to be very heavy; and saith 34

he had ever known his Lord. St Mark, as usual, records two points which enhance the force of the warning and the guilt of Peter, viz. (*a*) that the cock should crow *twice*, and (*b*) that after such warning he repeated his protestation with greater vehemence.

81. *If I should*] Literally, **If it be necessary for me to die with Thee**; as Wyclif renders it, "*if it bihoue* me to dye to gidere wiþ þee." After this the Lord engaged in earnest conversation with His Apostles, not as at the ordinary Passover on the great events of the Exodus, but on His own approaching departure to the Father and the coming of the Comforter (John xiv. 1—31); of Himself as the true Vine and His disciples as the branches (John xv. 1—6); of the trials which the Apostles must expect and the assured aid of the Comforter (John xvi.); and at the close lifting up His eyes to heaven solemnly committed them to the care of the Eternal Father, and dedicated to Him His completed work (John xvii.). Then the concluding part of the Hallel (Pss. cxv.—cxviii.) was sung, i.e. chanted, and the little company went forth into the darkness towards the Mount of Olives. A perusal of these Psalms will reveal their appropriateness to this solemn occasion.

32—42. THE AGONY IN THE GARDEN OF GETHSEMANE.

32. *And they came*] They would pass through one of the city gates, "open that night as it was Passover," down the steep side of the Kidron (John xviii. 1), and coming by the bridge, they went onwards towards *a place which was named Gethsemane*] The word Gethsemane means "the Oil-Press." It was a *garden* (John xviii. 1) or an olive orchard on the slope of Olivet, and doubtless contained a press to crush the olives, which grew in profusion all around. Thither St John tells us our Lord was often wont to resort (xviii. 2), and Judas "knew the place." Though at a sufficient distance from public thoroughfares to secure privacy, it was yet apparently easy of access. For a description of the traditional site see Stanley's *Sinai and Palestine*, p. 455.

33. *he taketh with him*] the three most trusted and long-tried of the Apostolic body, who had been before the privileged witnesses of the raising of the daughter of Jairus and of the Transfiguration.

began to be sore amazed] "To drede," Wyclif. We have already met this word in ch. ix. 15, where it was applied to the *amazement* of

unto them, My soul is exceeding sorrowful unto death: 35 tarry ye here, and watch. And he went forward a little, and fell on the ground, and prayed that, if it were possible, 36 the hour might pass from him. And he said, Abba, Father,

the people when they saw the Lord after the Transfiguration, and we shall meet with it again in ch. xvi. 5, 6, where it is applied to the holy women at the Sepulchre. St Mark alone applies the word to our Lord's sensations at this crisis of His life.

to be very heavy] "to heuye," Wyclif. The original word thus translated only occurs (1) here, (2) in the parallel, Matt. xxvi. 37, and (3) in Phil. ii. 26, "for he (Epaphroditus) longed after you all, and was *full of heaviness*." Buttmann suggests that the root idea is that of being "*away from home*," and so "confused," "beside oneself." Others consider the primary idea to be that of "loathing" and "discontent." Truly in respect to His human nature our Lord was *far from home*, far from His native skies, and the word may be taken to describe the awfulness of His isolation, unsupported by a particle of human sympathy,—a troubled, restless state, accompanied by the keenest mental distress.

34. *My soul is exceeding sorrowful*] Here again we have a remarkable word. We met with it before (ch. vi. 26), where Herod is said to have been "*exceeding sorry*" at the request for the Baptist's head; St Luke also uses the word (xviii. 23, 24) to describe how the rich young ruler was "*very sorrowful*," when he was bidden to sacrifice his wealth. It points here to a depth of anguish and sorrow, and we may believe that he, who at the first temptation had left the Saviour "*for a season*" (Luke iv. 13), had now returned, and whereas before he had brought "to bear against the Lord all things pleasant and flattering, if so he might by aid of these entice or seduce Him from His obedience, so now he thought with other engines to overcome His constancy, and tried Him with all painful things, as before with all pleasurable, hoping to terrify, if it might be, from His allegiance to the truth, Him whom manifestly He could not allure." Trench's *Studies*, pp. 55, 56, and above, i. 12.

and watch] "*with Me*" adds St Matthew (xxvi. 38). Perfect man, "of a reasonable soul and human flesh subsisting," He yearned, in this awful hour, for human sympathy. It is almost the only personal request He is ever recorded to have made. It was but "a cup of cold water" that He craved. But it was denied Him! Very Man, He leaned upon the men He loved, and they failed Him! He *trod the winepress alone;* and of the people *there was none with him* (Isaiah lxiii. 3).

35. *forward a little*] "*about a stone's throw*" (Luke xxii. 41), perhaps out of the moonlight into the shadow of the garden.

36. *Abba*] St Mark alone has preserved for us this word. St Peter could not fail to have treasured up the words of murmured anguish, which, "*about a stone's throw*" apart, he may have caught before he was overpowered with slumber. It is used only twice more in the New Testament, and both times by St Paul, Rom. viii. 15,

all things *are* possible unto thee; take away this cup from me: nevertheless not what I will, but what thou wilt. And he cometh, and findeth them sleeping, and saith unto Peter, Simon, sleepest thou? couldest not thou watch one hour? Watch ye and pray, lest ye enter into temptation. The spirit truly *is* ready, but the flesh *is* weak. And again he went away, and prayed, and spake the same words. And when he returned, he found them asleep again, (for their eyes were heavy,) neither wist they what to answer him. And he cometh the third time, and saith unto them, Sleep on now, and take *your* rest: it is enough, the hour is come; behold, the Son of man is betrayed into the hands of sinners. Rise up, let us go; lo, he that betrayeth me is at hand.

"we have received the spirit of adoption, whereby we cry *Abba, Father*," and Gal. iv. 6, "God hath sent forth the Spirit of his Son into your hearts, crying *Abba, Father*." In Syriac it is said to have been pronounced with a double *b* when applied to a spiritual father, with a single *b* when used in its natural sense. With the double letter at all events it has passed into the European languages, as an ecclesiastical term, 'abbas,' 'abbot.' See Canon Lightfoot on Gal. iv. 6.

Father] St Mark adds this probably to explain the Aramaic word, after his wont.

37. *and saith unto Peter*] who had made so many impetuous promises.

38. *the flesh is weak*] It is not of course implied that His own "will" was at variance with that of His Father; but, very Man, He had a *human will*, and knew the mystery of the opposition of the strongest, and at the same time the most innocent, instincts of humanity. The fuller account of the "Agony" is found in St Luke xxii. 43, 44.

40. *their eyes were heavy*] "soþli her yȝen were greuyd," Wyclif. Even as had been the case on the Mount of Transfiguration. The original word supported by the best MSS. only occurs here, and denotes that the Apostles were utterly tired, and their eyes "weighed *down.*"

neither wist they what to answer him] A graphic touch peculiar to the second Evangelist, just as the imperfect tense equally graphically implies that the eyes of the Apostles were **constantly becoming weighed down** in spite of any efforts they might make to keep awake. Comp. the scene at the Transfiguration, Mark ix. 6.

41. *the third time*] The Temptation of the Garden divides itself, like that of the Wilderness, into three acts, following close on one another.

Sleep on now] for ever if ye will. The words are spoken in a kind of gentle irony and sorrowful expostulation. The Golden Hour for watching and prayer was over.

it is enough] Their wakefulness was no longer needed.

43—52. *The Betrayal.*

43 And immediately, while he yet spake, cometh Judas, one of the twelve, and with him a great multitude with swords and staves, from the chief priests and the scribes and the elders. 44 And he that betrayed him had given them a token, saying, Whomsoever I shall kiss, that same is he; take him, and lead 45 *him* away safely. And as soon as he was come, he goeth straightway to him, and saith, Master, master; and kissed him. 46 47 And they laid their hands on him, and took him. And one

43—52. THE BETRAYAL.

43. *And immediately*] while He yet spake, the garden was filled with armed men, and flashed with the light of numerous lanterns and torches, though the Paschal moon was at the full, for "in the rocky ravine of the Kidron there would fall great deep shadows from the declivity of the mountains and projecting rocks, and there were caverns and grottoes in which a fugitive might retreat." Lange, *Life of Christ*, IV. 292.

cometh Judas] During the two hours that had elapsed since he had gone forth from the Upper Room he had not been idle. He had reported to the ruling powers that the favourable moment had come, and had doubtless mentioned "the Garden" whither his Master was wont to resort. He now returned, but not alone, for

with him a great multitude with swords and staves] These consisted partly (*a*) of the regular Levitical guards of the Temple, the apparitors of the Sanhedrim, and partly (*b*) of the detachment from the Roman cohort quartered in the Tower of Antonia under the "chiliarch" or tribune in command of the garrison (John xviii. 3, 12). The highpriest, we may believe, had communicated with Pilate, and represented that the force was needed for the arrest of a false Messiah, dangerous to the Roman power.

44. *a token*] Judas had never imagined that our Lord would Himself come forth to meet His enemies (John xviii. 2—5). He had anticipated the necessity of giving a signal whereby they might know Him. He had pressed forward and was in front of the rest (Luke xxii. 47). The word translated "a tokene," Wyclif, only occurs here.

take him] Or rather, **seize Him at once.**

45. *and kissed him*] Rather, **kissed Him tenderly or fervently.** The customary kiss of a disciple to his teacher. The same word in the original with its intensifying preposition is used to express (i) the kissing of our Lord by the woman who was a sinner (Luke vii. 38, 45); (ii) the kissing of the prodigal son by his father (Luke xv. 20); and (iii) the kissing of St Paul by the Christians on the sea-shore of Miletus (Acts xx. 37). The Latin compound, having the same force, is "*de*osculari," or "*ex*osculari."

47. *And one of them that stood by*] This we know from St John was Simon Peter (John xviii. 10), displaying his characteristic impetuosity to

of them that stood by drew a sword, and smote a servant of the high priest, and cut off his ear. And Jesus an- 48 swered and said unto them, Are ye come out, as against a thief, with swords and *with* staves to take me? I was daily 49 with you in the temple teaching, and ye took me not: but the scriptures must be fulfilled. And they all forsook him, 50 and fled. And there followed him a certain young man, 51 having a linen cloth cast about *his* naked *body;* and the

the end. Some think the Apostle's name was omitted by the Synoptists lest the publication of it in his lifetime should expose him to the revenge of the unbelieving Jews.

a servant of the high priest] In none of the Synoptic Gospels do we find mention of his name either. This we are told by St John was Malchus. St John was an acquaintance of the high-priest's, and probably a frequenter of his house; hence he knew the name of his servant.

his ear] Both St Mark and St John use a diminutive = *little ear.* St Luke alone (xxii. 50) tells us it was his *right* ear. Perhaps it was not completely severed, for St Luke, who alone also records the healing, says that our Lord simply touched it and healed him.

48. *answered and said unto them*] Those to whom He now spoke were, as we learn from St Luke xxii. 52, some chief priests and elders and officers of the Temple guard, who had been apparently watching His capture.

a thief] Rather, a **robber** or bandit. See above, note on ch. xi. 17.

49. *the scriptures must be fulfilled*] Rather, **but that the Scriptures may be fulfilled** all this has come to pass.

50. *they all forsook him, and fled*] Even the impetuous Peter who had made so many promises; even the disciple whom He loved.

51. *a certain young man*] This forms an episode as characteristic of St Mark as that of the two disciples journeying to Emmaus is of St Luke. Some have conjectured he was the owner of the garden of Gethsemane; others Lazarus (see Professor Plumptre's Article on "Lazarus" in Smith's *Bible Dict.*); others Joses, the brother of the Lord; others, a youth of the family where Jesus had eaten the Passover. It is far more probable that it was St Mark himself, the son of Mary, the friend of St Peter. The minuteness of the details given points to him. Only one well acquainted with the scene from personal knowledge, probably as an eyewitness, would have introduced into his account of it so slight and seemingly so trivial an incident as this.

having a linen cloth] He had probably been roused from sleep, or just preparing to retire to rest in a house somewhere in the valley of Kidron, and he had nothing to cover him except the *sindôn* or upper garment, but in spite of this he ventured in his excitement to press on amongst the crowd. The word *sindôn* in Matt. xxvii. 59, Mark xv. 46 and Luke xxiii. 53 is applied to the *fine linen,* which Joseph of Arimathæa

52 young men laid hold on him: and he left the linen cloth, and fled from them naked.

53—65. *The Jewish Trial.*

53 And they led Jesus away to the high priest: and with him were assembled all the chief priests and the elders and 54 the scribes. And Peter followed him afar off, even into the palace of the high priest: and he sat with the servants, and 55 warmed himself at the fire. And the chief priests and all the council sought for witness against Jesus to put him to

bought for the Body of Jesus. The LXX. use the word in Judg. xiv. 12 and in Prov. xxxi. 24 for "*fine under garments.*"

the young men] This is omitted by Lachmann, Tischendorf, and Tregelles. The crowd was probably astonished at the strange apparition.

52. *naked*] This need not imply that he was absolutely naked. It may mean, like the Latin *nudus,* "with only the *under* robe on." Comp. 1 Sam. xix. 24; John xxi. 7; Virg. *Georg.* I. 299.

53—65. THE JEWISH TRIAL.

53. *And they led Jesus away*] They bound Him first (John xviii. 12), and then conducted Him across the Kidron and up the road leading into the city.

to the high priest] This we know from St John was Caiaphas. But our Lord was first brought to the palace of Annas his father-in-law (John xviii. 13). This was either at the suggestion of some of the ruling powers, or in accordance with previous arrangement, that his "snake-like" astuteness as president of the Sanhedrim might help his less crafty son-in-law. The palace seems to have been jointly occupied by both as a common official residence, and thither, though it was deep midnight, the chief priests, elders, and scribes repaired.

54. *And Peter*] Before the palace or within its outer porch appears to have been a large open square court, in which public business was transacted. Into it Peter and John ventured to follow (John xviii. 15). The latter, as being acquainted with the high-priest, easily obtained admittance; Peter, at first rejected by the porteress, was suffered to enter at the request of his brother Apostle.

and warmed himself] The night was chilly, and in the centre of the court the servants of the high-priest had made a fire of charcoal, and there Peter, now admitted, was warming himself at the open hearth.

55. *And the chief priests*] St Mark passes over the details of the examination before Annas and the first commencement of insult and violence, recorded only by St John (xviii. 19—24). He places us in the mansion of Caiaphas, whither our Lord was conducted across the courtyard, and where a more formal assembly of the council of the nation had met together.

sought for witness] By the Law they were bound to secure the agreement of two witnesses on some specific charge. Before Annas an

death; and found none. For many bare false witness 56
against him, but their witness agreed not together. And 57
there arose certain, and bare false witness against him, saying, We heard him say, I will destroy this temple that 58
is made with hands, and within three days I will build
another made without hands. But neither so did their wit- 59
ness agree together. And the high priest stood up in the 60
midst, and asked Jesus, saying, Answerest thou nothing?
what *is it which* these witness against thee? But he held 61
his peace, and answered nothing. Again the high priest

attempt had been made to entangle the Accused with insidious questions. A more formal character must now be given to the proceedings.

56. *but their witness agreed not together*] "þe witnessingis weren
not *couenable,*" Wyclif. The Law required that at least two witnesses
must agree. See Deut. xvii. 6, xix. 15. But now some who came
forward had nothing relevant to say, and others contradicted themselves.

57. *And there arose certain*] Two at last came forward, whose
evidence appeared likely to be more satisfactory.

58. *We heard him say*] The statements now made are given with
more detail by St Mark than any other of the Evangelists. He alone tells
us they said that they had heard our Lord declare, "He would destroy
the Temple *made with hands* and in three days build another *made
without hands.*" In the opposition *made with hands* and *made without
hands* we have proof of the falseness of the accusation.

59. *neither so*] The utterance of words tending to bring the Temple
into contempt was regarded as so grave an offence that it afterwards
formed a capital charge against the first martyr, Stephen (Acts vi. 13).
But dangerous as was the charge, it broke down. The statements
of the witnesses did not tally, and their testimony was therefore
worthless. Their memories had travelled over three years to the
occasion of the first Passover at Jerusalem and the first cleansing of
the Temple. But they perverted the real facts of the case (John ii.
18—22). St Mark alone notices the disagreement of their testimony.
"The differences between the recorded words of our Lord and the
reports of the witnesses are striking: '*I can destroy*' (Matt. xxvi. 61);
'*I will destroy*' (Mark xiv. 58); as compared with '*Destroy...and I will
raise*' (John ii. 19)." Westcott's *Introduction*, p. 326 n.

60. *And the high priest stood up*] The impressive silence, which our
Lord preserved, while false witnesses were being sought against Him
(Matt. xxvi. 62), was galling to the pride of Caiaphas, who saw that
nothing remained but to force Him, if possible, to criminate Himself.
Standing up, therefore, *in the midst* (a graphic touch which we owe
to St Mark alone), he adjured Him in the most solemn manner possible
(Matt. xxvi. 63) to declare whether He was "the Malcha Meschicha"—
the King Messiah, the Son of the Blessed.

asked him, and said unto him, Art thou the Christ, the Son
62 of the Blessed? And Jesus said, I am: and ye shall see
the Son of man sitting on the right hand of power, and
63 coming in the clouds of heaven. Then the high priest rent
his clothes, and saith, What need we any further witnesses?
64 Ye have heard the blasphemy: what think ye? And they
65 all condemned him to be guilty of death. And some began
to spit on him, and to cover his face, and to buffet him, and

62. *And Jesus said. I am*] Thus adjured, the Lord broke the silence He had hitherto maintained. His answer to such a question must be liable to no misinterpretation. Peter in an ecstatic moment had declared He was the King Messiah, *"the Son of the living God"* (Matt. xvi. 16), and He had not refused the awful Name. Thousands also of Galilean pilgrims had saluted Him with Hosannas in this character through the streets of Jerusalem. But as yet He had not openly declared Himself. The supreme moment, however, had at length arrived, and He now replied, "I AM—*the Messiah, the Son of God, the Son of Man—and hereafter ye shall see Me sitting on the right hand of power, and coming in the clouds of heaven.*" Comp. Dan. vii. 13; Ps. viii. 4, cx. 1.

63. *Then the high priest*] Caiaphas had now gained his end. The Accused had spoken. He had criminated Himself. All was uproar and confusion. The high-priest rent his linen robes. This was not lawful for him to do in cases of mourning (Lev. x. 6, xxi. 10), but was allowable in cases of blasphemy (see 2 Kings xviii. 37). It was to be performed standing, and so that the rent was to be from the neck straight downwards. The use of the plural "his clothes," by St Mark, seems to intimate that he tore all his clothes, except that which was next his body.

64. *they all condemned him*] Worse than false prophet, worse than false Messiah, He had declared Himself to be the *"Son of God,"* and that in the presence of the high-priest and the great Council. He had incurred the capital penalty. But though they thus passed sentence, they could not execute it. The right had been taken from them ever since Judæa became a Roman province. The sentence, therefore, needed confirmation, and the matter must be referred to the Roman governor.

65. *And some began*] It was now about three o'clock in the morning, and till further steps could be taken our Lord was left in charge of soldiers of the guard and the servants and apparitors of the high-priest.

to spit on him] In those rough ages a prisoner under sentence of death was ever delivered over to the mockery of his guards. It was so now with the Holy One of God. Spitting was regarded by the Jews as an expression of the greatest contempt (Num. xii. 14; Deut. xxv. 9). Seneca records that it was inflicted at Athens on Aristides the Just, but it was only with the utmost difficulty any one could be found willing to do it. But those who were excommunicated were specially liable to this expression of contempt (Isaiah l. 6).

to say unto him, Prophesy: and the servants did strike him with the palms of their hands.

66—72. *The Denial of our Lord by St Peter.*

And as Peter was beneath in the palace, there cometh 66 one of the maids of the high priest: and when she saw Peter 67 warming himself, she looked upon him, and said, And thou also wast with Jesus of Nazareth. But he denied, saying, I 68 know not, neither understand I what thou sayest. And he went out into the porch; and the cock crew. And a maid 69 saw him again, and began to say to them that stood by, This is *one* of them. And he denied it again. And a little 70

did strike him with the palms of their hands] "The hands they bound had healed the sick, and raised the dead; the lips they smote had calmed the winds and waves. One word and His smiters might have been laid low in death. But as He had begun and continued, He would end—as self-restrained in the use of His awful powers on His own behalf as if He had been the most helpless of men—Divine patience and infinite love knew no wearying."

66—72. THE DENIAL OF OUR LORD BY ST PETER.

66. *And as Peter*] During the sad scene enacted in the hall of trial above, an almost sadder moral tragedy had been enacted in the court below.

67. *warming himself*] This seems to have been shortly after his entrance, as related above. The maid who approached probably was the porteress who had admitted him.

she looked upon him] with fixed and earnest gaze, as the original word used by St Luke (xxii. 56) implies.

68. *but he denied*] Thrown off his guard and perhaps disconcerted by the searching glances of the bystanders, Peter replied at first evasively, that he neither knew nor understood what she meant. See Lange, *Life*, IV. p. 316. Others think it means, "*I know Him not, neither understand I what thou sayest.*"

into the porch] Anxious probably for a favourable opportunity of retiring altogether, the Apostle now moved towards the darkness of the porch. Here the second denial took place (Matt. xxvi. 71, 72), and for the first time *a cock crew.*

69. *a maid saw him again*] Recognised at the porch, Peter seems to have returned once more towards the fire, and was conversing in his rough Galilean dialect with the soldiers and servants when, after the lapse of an hour, another maid approached.

to them that stood by] On this occasion she addressed herself to the bystanders, amongst whom was a kinsman of Malchus (John xviii. 26).

70. *And he denied it again*] This denial was probably addressed to those round the fire. But escape was hopeless. "Surely," said one,

after, they that stood by said again to Peter, Surely thou art *one* of them: for thou art a Galilæan, and thy speech agreeth
71 thereto. But he began to curse and to swear, *saying*, I know
72 not this man of whom ye speak. And the second time the cock crew. And Peter called to mind the word that Jesus said unto him, Before the cock crow twice, thou shalt deny me thrice. And when he thought thereon, he wept.

1—15. *The Examination before Pilate.*

15 And straightway in the morning the chief priests held a

"*this fellow is one of them;*" "*Thou art a Galilæan,*" said another, "and *thy speech agreeth thereto.*" These last words are omitted by Lachmann, Tischendorf, and Tregelles. "*Thy speech bewrayeth thee*" are the words used by St Matthew (xxvi. 73). The Galilean burr was rough and indistinct. Hence the Galileans were not allowed to read aloud in the Jewish synagogues.

71. *he began to curse and to swear*] Assailed by the bystanders just mentioned and by the kinsman of Malchus (John xviii. 26), the Apostle now fell deeper still. With oaths and curses he denied that he had ever known the Man of whom they spoke, and at that moment, for the second time, the cock crew, and at the same moment the Lord, either (*a*) on His way from the apartments of Annas across the court-yard to the palace of Caiaphas, or (*b*) thrust back into the court after His condemnation, *turned and looked upon Peter* (Luke xxii. 61).

72. *And Peter called to mind*] That glance of sorrow went straight to the Apostle's heart; all that his Lord had said, all His repeated warnings rushed back to his remembrance, and lit up the darkness of his soul. He could contain himself no longer, and

when he thought thereon] for so we have rendered the original word. Others render it (i) *abundantly*="he wept *abundantly*," as in the margin; others (ii) "*he began to weep;*" others (iii) "*he threw his mantle over his head;*" others (iv) "*he flung himself forth and wept,*"

he wept] Not with the remorse of Judas, but the godly sorrow of true repentance. Observe that the Apostle has not lessened his fault, for it is from him, doubtless, through St Mark, we are informed "that the first crowing of the cock did not suffice to recal him to his duty, but a second was needed." Lange.

CH. XV. 1—15. THE EXAMINATION BEFORE PILATE.

1. *And straightway*] As the day dawned, a second and more formal meeting of the Sanhedrim was convened in one of the halls or courts near at hand. A legal Sanhedrim it could hardly be called, for there are scarcely any traces of such legal assemblies during the Roman period. In theory the action of this august court was humane, and the proceedings were conducted with the greatest care. A greater anxiety was manifested to clear the arraigned than to secure his condemnation, especially in matters of life and death. It was enacted (i) that a majority of at

consultation with the elders and scribes and the whole council, and bound Jesus, and carried *him* away, and delivered *him* to Pilate. And Pilate asked him, Art thou the King of 2

least two must be secured before condemnation; (ii) that while a verdict of *acquittal* could be given on the same day, one of *guilty* must be reserved for the following day; (iii) that no criminal trial could be carried through in the night; (iv) that the judges who condemned a criminal to death must fast all day; (v) that the sentence itself could be revised; and that (vi) if even on the way to execution the criminal reflected that he had something fresh to adduce in his favour, he might be led back and have the validity of his statement examined. See Ginsburg's Article on *The Sanhedrim* in Kitto's *Biblical Cyclopædia*, III. 767. But the influence of the Sadducees, who were now in the ascendancy, and were Draconian in their severity, had changed all this, and it was resolved to endorse the sentence already pronounced, and deliver over the Great Accused to the secular arm.

carried him away] Either (i) to one of the two gorgeous palaces which the first Herod had erected, or (ii) to a palace near the Tower of Antonia, for hither the governor had come up from Cæsarea "on the sea" to keep order during the feast.

to Pilate] The Roman governor roused thus early that eventful morning to preside in a case, which has handed down his name through the centuries in connection with the greatest crime committed since the world began, was Pontius Pilate. (i) *His name* Pontius is thought to indicate that he was connected, either by descent or adoption, with the gens of the *Pontii*, first conspicuous in Roman history in the person of C. Pontius Telesinus, the great Samnite general. His cognomen Pilatus has been interpreted as = (*a*) "armed with the *pilum* or javelin," as = (*b*) an abbreviation of *pileatus*, from *pileus*, the cap or badge of manumitted slaves, indicating that he was either a *libertus* ("freedman"), or descended from one. He succeeded Valerius Gratus A.D. 26, and brought with him his wife Procla or Claudia Procula. (ii) *His office* was that of *procurator* under the governor (*proprætor*) of Syria, but within his own province he had the power of a *legatus*. His headquarters were at Cæsarea (Acts xxiii. 23); he had assessors to assist him in council (xxv. 12); wore the military dress; was attended by a cohort as a body-guard (Matt. xxvii. 27); and at the great festivals came up to Jerusalem to keep order. When presiding as judge he would sit on a *Bema* or portable tribunal erected on a tesselated pavement, called in Hebrew *Gabbatha* (John xix. 13), and was invested with the power of life and death (Matt. xxvii. 26). (iii) In *character* he was not insensible to the claims of mercy and justice, but he was weak and vacillating, and incapable of compromising his own safety in obedience to the dictates of his conscience. As a *governor* he had shewn himself cruel and unscrupulous (Luke xiii. 1, 2), and cared little for the religious susceptibilities of a people, whom he despised and could not understand.

2. *And Pilate asked him*] This was a private investigation within the *prætorium*, after the Jews, carefully suppressing *the religious grounds*

the Jews? And he answering said unto him, Thou sayest
3 it. And the chief priests accused him of many things: but
4 he answered nothing. And Pilate asked him again, saying,
Answerest thou nothing? behold how many things they wit-
5 ness against thee. But Jesus yet answered nothing; so that
6 Pilate marvelled. Now at *that* feast he released unto them
7 one prisoner, whomsoever they desired. And there was *one*
named Barabbas, *which lay* bound with them that had made

on which they had condemned our Lord, had advanced against Him a triple accusation of (i) seditious agitation, (ii) prohibition of the payment of the tribute money, and (iii) the assumption of the suspicious title of "King of the Jews." This was a *political* charge, and one which Pilate could not overlook. Having no *quæstor* to conduct the examination, he was obliged to hear the case in person.

Thou sayest it] St Mark does not mention here what we know from St John, (*a*) the inquiry of our Lord of Pilate why he asked the question, and (*b*) His explanation of the real nature of His kingdom (John xviii. 37, 38). He brings out our Lord's acknowledgment of His regal dignity, though Pilate could not understand His meaning.

3. *And the chief priests accused him*] After the first examination Pilate came forth to the Jewish deputation, standing before the entrance of the palace, and declared his conviction of the innocence of the Accused (John xviii. 38; Luke xxiii. 4). This was the signal for a furious clamour on the part of the chief priests and members of the Sanhedrim, and they accused our Lord of many things, of (1) "stirring up the people," and (2) "teaching falsely throughout all Judæa, beginning *from Galilee* even to Jerusalem" (Luke xxiii. 5).

4. *And Pilate asked*] These renewed accusations led to further questions from Pilate, but our Lord preserved a complete silence. This increased the procurator's astonishment, but he thought he had found an escape from his dilemma, when he heard the word "*Galilee.*" Galilee was within the province of Herod Antipas, and he sent the case to his tribunal (Luke xxiii. 6—12). But Herod also affirmed that the Accused had done nothing worthy of punishment, and Pilate finding the case thrown back upon his hands, now resolved to try another experiment for escaping from the responsibility of a direct decision.

6. *Now at that feast*] Rather, **at festival time**. There is no article in the Greek (or in Luke xxiii. 17; Matt. xxvii. 15), and the apparent limitation of the custom to the Feast of the Passover is not required by the original words, or by the parallel in John xviii. 39. It seems to have been a custom, the origin of which is unknown, to release to the people on the occasion of the Passover and other great Feasts any prisoner whom they might select. The custom may have been of Jewish origin, and had been continued by the Roman governors from motives of policy. Even the Romans were accustomed at the *Lectisternia* and *Bacchanalia* to allow an amnesty for criminals.

7 *one named Barabbas*] There lay in prison at this time, awaiting

insurrection with him, who had committed murder in the insurrection. And the multitude crying aloud began to desire *him to do* as he had ever done unto them. But Pilate answered them, saying, Will ye that I release unto you the King of the Jews? For he knew that the chief priests had delivered him for envy. But the chief priests moved the people, that he should rather release Barabbas unto them. And Pilate answered and said again unto them, What will ye then that I shall do *unto him* whom ye call the King of

execution, a celebrated bandit or robber named Barabbas. This word is a patronymic, and means (i) according to some, Bar-Abbas=*son of Abba*="son of the father," or (ii) according to others, Bar-Rabbas="*son of a Rabbi*." In three MSS. of Matt. xxvii. 16, his name is given as "*Jesus Bar-abbas*," and this reading is supported by the Armenian and Syriac Versions and is cited by Origen.

them that had made insurrection] Barabbas had headed one of the numerous insurrections against the Roman power, which were constantly harassing the procurators, and giving untold trouble to the legionary troops quartered at Cæsarea and other places. In this particular insurrection blood had been shed, and apparently some Roman soldiers had been killed.

9. *But Pilate answered them*] The proposition of the people that he should act according to his usual custom concurred with Pilate's own wishes and hopes, and he resolved deliberately to give the populace their choice.

10. *for envy*] He could not doubt who were the ringleaders in the tumultuous scene now being enacted, or what was the motive that had prompted them to bring the Accused before his tribunal—nothing more or less than envy of the influence He had gained and the favour He had won throughout the land. He hoped, therefore, by appealing directly to the people to procure our Lord's release.

11. *But the chief priests*] It was probably at this juncture that he received the message from his wife imploring him to have nothing to do with "*that just person*" (Matt. xxvii. 19) standing before him. His feelings, therefore, of awe were intensified, and his resolve to effect the release increased. But the chief priests stirred up the people, and urged them to choose Barabbas, the patriot leader, the zealot for their country, the champion against oppression. The word translated "moved" only occurs here and in the parallel, Luke xxiii. 5. It denotes (i) *to shake to and fro, to brandish ;* (ii) *to make threatening gestures ;* (iii) *to stir up*, or *instigate*. Their efforts were successful, and when Pilate formally put the question, the cry went up, "*Not this Man*," the Holy and Undefiled, Whom they had lately welcomed with Hosannas into their city, but the hero of the insurrection, Barabbas (John xviii. 39, 40).

12. *What will ye*] This question seems to have been put in disdain and anger; disdain at their fickleness, anger at the failure of his efforts to stem the torrent.

the Jews? And they cried out again, Crucify him. Then Pilate said unto them, Why, what evil hath he done? And they cried out the more exceedingly, Crucify him. And so Pilate, willing to content the people, released Barabbas unto them, and delivered Jesus, when he had scourged *him*, to be crucified.

whom ye call the King of the Jews] He may have hoped that the sound of the title might have not been in vain on the ears of those who had lately cried, "Blessed is the *king* that cometh in the name of the Lord," "Blessed is the *kingdom* of our father David" (Luke xix. 38; Mark xi. 10). But he was bitterly deceived.

13. *Crucify him*] was the cry that now fell upon his ears, prompted by the chief priests, re-echoed by the crowd. Still the procurator did not yield, though already at Cæsarea he had had proof of the invincible tenacity of a Jewish mob, whom not even the prospect of instant death could deter (Jos. *Antiq.* XVIII. 3. 1). He resolved to make another direct appeal to the excited crowd. "Why should he crucify Him?" "What evil had He done?"

14. *But they cried out the more*] "Why and wherefore?" There were no questions with them. They were resolved to have His life. Nothing else would satisfy. The cry was kept up unbroken, *Away with this man, Crucify Him! Crucify Him!* In vain Pilate expostulated. In vain he washed his hands openly before them all (Matt. xxvii. 24) in token of his conviction of the perfect innocence of the Accused. His wavering in the early stage of the trial was bringing on its terrible consequences.

15. *And so Pilate*] One hope, however, the procurator still seems to have retained. Irresolution indeed had gone too far, and he could not retrace his steps. He thought he must content the people, and therefore released Barabbas unto them. But he imagined there was room for a compromise. Clamorous as was the crowd, perhaps they would be satisfied with a punishment only less terrible than the Cross, and so he gave the order that He, Whom he had pronounced perfectly innocent, should be scourged.

willing to content the people] "willinge for *to do ynow* to þe peple," Wyclif. Here we have one of St Mark's Latinisms. The Greek expression answers exactly to the Latin *satisfacere=to satisfy, appease, content*.

when he had scourged him] Generally the scourging before crucifixion was inflicted by lictors (Livy, XXXIII. 36; Jos. *Bell. Jud.* II. 14. 9; v. 11. 1). But Pilate, as sub-governor, had no lictors at his disposal, and therefore the punishment was inflicted by soldiers. Lange, IV. 356 n. The Roman scourging was horribly severe. Drops of lead and small sharp-pointed bones were often plaited into the scourges, and the sufferers not unfrequently died under the infliction. Compare the *horribile flagellum* of Hor. Sat. I. iii. 119; and "flagrum *pecuinis ossibus* catenatum," Apul. *Met.* viii. That the soldiers could not have per-

16—24. *The Mockery of the Soldiers. The Way to the Cross.*

And the soldiers led him away into the hall, called Præ- 16
torium; and they call together the whole band. And they 17
clothed him with purple, and platted a crown of thorns, and

formed their duty with forbearance on this occasion, is plain from the wanton malice, with which they added mockery to the scourging.

to be crucified] But the compromise did not content the excited multitude. The spectacle of so much suffering so meekly borne did not suffice. "If thou let this man go," they cried, "thou art not Cæsar's friend: whosoever maketh himself a king speaketh against Cæsar" (John xix. 12). This crafty well-chosen cry roused all Pilate's fears. He could only too well divine the consequences if they accused him of sparing a prisoner who had been accused of treason before the gloomy suspicious Tiberius ("atrocissimè exercebat leges *majestatis*," Suet. *Vit. Tib.* c. 58; Tac. *Ann.* III. 38). His fears for his own personal safety turned the scale. After one more effort therefore (John xix. 13—15), he gave the word, the irrevocable word, "*Let Him be crucified*" (John xix. 16), and the long struggle was over. St John, it is to be observed, mentions the scourging as one of Pilate's final attempts to release Jesus. St Mark, like St Matthew, looks upon it as the first act in the awful tragedy of the Crucifixion. Both views are equally true. The scourging should have moved the people; it only led them to greater obduracy; it proved, as St Mark brings out, the opening scene in the Crucifixion.

16—24. THE MOCKERY OF THE SOLDIERS. THE WAY TO THE CROSS.

16. *the hall, called Prætorium*] "in to þe *floor of þe moot hall*," Wyclif. The building here alluded to is called by three of the Evangelists the *Prætorium*. In St Matthew (xxvii. 27) it is translated "*common hall*," with a marginal alternative "*governor's house.*" In St John (xviii. 28, 33; xix. 9) it is translated "*hall of judgment*" and "*judgment hall*," with a marginal alternative "*Pilate's house*" in the first passage; while here it is reproduced in the English as "prætorium." In Acts xxiii. 35 it is rendered "*judgment hall*," and in Phil. i. 13, where it signifies "*the prætorian army*," it is rendered "*palace.*" This last rendering might very properly have been adopted in all the passages in the Gospels and Acts, as adequately expressing the meaning. See Professor Lightfoot on the *Revision of the New Testament*, p. 49.

the whole band] In the palace-court, which formed a kind of barracks or guard-room, they gathered the whole cohort. The word translated "*band*" is applied to the detachment brought by Judas (John xviii. 3), and occurs again Acts x. 1, xxi. 31, xxvii. 1.

17. *clothed him with purple*] Instead of the white robe, with which Herod had mocked Him, they threw around Him a scarlet *sagum*, or soldier's cloak. St Matthew, xxvii. 28, calls it "*a scarlet robe;*" St John, xix. 2, "*a purple robe.*" It was a war-cloak, such as princes,

18 put it about his *head*, and began to salute him, Hail, King
19 of the Jews! And they smote him on the head with a reed,
and did spit upon him, and bowing *their* knees worshipped
20 him. And when they had mocked him, they took off the
purple from him, and put his own clothes on him, and led
21 him out to crucify him. And they compel one Simon a
Cyrenian, who passed by, coming out of the country, the
22 father of Alexander and Rufus, to bear his cross. And they
bring him unto the place Golgotha, which is, being inter-

generals, and soldiers wore, dyed with purple; "probably a cast-off
robe of state out of the prætorian wardrobe,"—a burlesque of the long
and fine purple robe worn only by the Emperor. Lange, IV. 357.

a crown of thorns] Formed probably of the thorny *nâbk*, which yet
"grows on dwarf bushes outside the walls of Jerusalem." Tristram's
Land of Israel, p. 429.

and put it about his head] In mimicry of the laurel wreath worn at
times by the Cæsars.

19. *smote him*] Rather, **began to smite** or **kept smiting Him**.

with a reed] The same which they had already put into His hands as
a sceptre.

did spit upon him] See note above, ch. xiv. 65.

20. *and led him out*] The place of execution was without the
gates of the city.

21. *they compel*] The condemned were usually obliged to carry
either the entire cross, or the cross-beams fastened together like the
letter V, with their arms bound to the projecting ends. Hence the term
furcifer = "*cross-bearer.*" " Patibulum ferat per urbem, deinde affigatur
cruci." This had a reference to our Lord being typified by Isaac bearing
the wood of the burnt offering, Gen. xxii. 6. But exhausted by all He
had undergone, our Lord sank under the weight laid upon Him, and the
soldiers had not proceeded far from the city gate, when they met a man
whom they could "*compel*" or "*impress*" into their service. The
original word translated "*compel*" is a Persian word. At regular stages
throughout Persia (Hdt. VIII. 98; Xen. *Cyrop.* VIII. 6, 17) mounted
couriers were kept ready to carry the royal despatches. Hence the verb
(*angariare* Vulg.) denotes (1) *to despatch as a mounted courier;* (2) *to
impress, force to do some service.* It occurs also in Matt. v. 41,
" Whosoever shall *compel* thee to go a mile, go with him twain."

Simon a Cyrenian] The man thus impressed was passing by, and
coming from the country (Luke xxiii. 26). His name was Simon, a
Hellenistic Jew, of Cyrene, in northern Africa, the inhabitants of which
district had a synagogue at Jerusalem (Acts ii. 10, vi. 9).

the father of Alexander and Rufus] St Mark alone adds this. Like
"Bartimæus, the son of Timæus," these words testify to his originality.
From the way they are mentioned it is clear that these two persons must
have been well known to the early Christians. Rufus has been identified
with one of the same name saluted by St Paul, Rom. xvi. 13.

preted, The place of a skull. And they gave him to drink 23
wine mingled with myrrh: but he received *it* not. And 24
when they had crucified him, they parted his garments, casting lots upon them, what every man should take.

to bear his cross] The cause of execution was generally inscribed on a white tablet, called in Latin *titulus* ("*qui causam pœnæ indicaret*," Sueton. *Calig.* 32). It was borne either suspended from the neck, or carried before the sufferer. The latter was probably the mode adopted in our Lord's case. And Simon may have borne both title and Cross. St Mark does not mention our Lord's words on the way to the women (Luke xxiii. 28—31).

22. *the place Golgotha*] St Mark gives the explanation of the Hebrew word "Golgotha." St Luke omits it altogether. It was a bare hill or rising ground on the north or north-west of the city, having the form on its rounded summit of a *skull*, whence its name. It was (*a*) apparently a well-known spot; (*b*) outside the gate (comp. Heb. xiii. 12); but (*c*) near the city (John xix. 20); (*d*) on a thoroughfare leading into the country (Luke xxiii. 26); and (*e*) contained a "garden" or "orchard" (John xix. 41). From the Vulgate rendering of Luke xxiii. 33, "Et postquam venerunt in locum, qui vocatur *Calvariæ*" (=*a bare skull*, "þe place of *Caluarie*," Wyclif), the word *Calvary* has been introduced into the English Version, obscuring the meaning of the Evangelist. There is nothing in the name to suggest the idea that the remains of malefactors who had been executed were strewn about, for the Jews always buried them.

23. *they gave him*] More literally, **they offered Him.**

wine mingled with myrrh] It was a merciful custom of the Jews to give those condemned to crucifixion, with a view to producing stupefaction, a strong aromatic wine. Lightfoot tells us (*Hor. Heb.* II. 366) it was the special task of wealthy ladies at Jerusalem to provide this potion. The custom was founded on Rabbinic gloss on Proverbs xxxi. 6, "Give *strong drink* to him that is perishing, and *wine* to those whose soul is in bitterness."

but he received it not] The two malefactors, who were led forth with Him, probably partook of it, but He would take nothing to cloud His faculties.

24. *when they had crucified him*] The present tense appears to be here the preferable reading, **they crucify Him and part His garments among them.** There were four kinds of crosses, (i) the *crux simplex*, a single stake driven through the chest or longitudinally through the body; (ii) the *crux decussata* (×); (iii) the *crux immissa* (†); and (iv) the *crux commissa* (T). From the mention of the title placed over the Saviour's Head, it is probable that His cross was of the third kind, and that He was laid upon it either while it was on the ground, or lifted and fastened to it as it stood upright, His arms stretched out along the two cross-beams, and His body resting on a little projection, *sedile*, a foot or two above the earth. That His feet were nailed as well as His hands is apparent from Luke xxiv. 39, 40.

they parted] i.e. the soldiers, a party of four with a centurion (Acts

25—38. *The Death.*

25 And it was the third hour, and they crucified him. And
26 the superscription of his accusation was written over, THE
27 KING OF THE JEWS. And with him they crucify two
thieves; the one on his right hand, and the other on his
28 left. And the scripture was fulfilled, which saith, And he

xii. 4), for each sufferer, detailed, according to the Roman custom, *ad excubias*, to mount guard, and see that the bodies were not taken away.

casting lots] The dice doubtless were ready at hand, and one of their helmets would serve to throw them.

what every man should take] The clothes of the crucified fell to the soldiers who guarded them, as part of their perquisites. The outer garment, or *tallith*, they divided into fourth parts, probably loosening the seams. The inner garment, like the robes of the priests, *was without seam, woven from the top throughout* (John xix. 23), of linen or perhaps of wool. It would have been destroyed by rending, so for it they cast lots, unconsciously fulfilling the words spoken long ago by the Psalmist, *They parted my raiment among them, and for my vesture they did cast lots* (Ps. xxii. 18).

25—38. THE DEATH.

25. *it was the third hour*] or nine o'clock. St John's words (xix. 14) clearly point to a different mode of reckoning.

26. *And the superscription*] "and þe title of his cause was written," Wyclif. The cause of execution was generally, as we have seen, inscribed on a white tablet, *titulus*, smeared with *gypsum*. It had been borne before Him on His way to the Cross, or suspended round His neck. It was now nailed on the projecting top of the cross over His head.

The King of the Jews] Pilate had caused it to be written in three languages, that all classes might be able to read it. The ordinary Hebrew or Aramaic of the people, the official Latin of the Romans, and the Greek of the foreign population (John xix. 20). For the endeavour of the Jewish high-priest to get the title altered see St John xix. 21, 22.

27. *two thieves*] Rather, **two robbers**, or **malefactors** as St Luke calls them (xxiii. 33). See note above, xi. 17. It is more than probable that they belonged to the band of Barabbas and "had been engaged in one of those fierce and fanatical outbreaks against the Roman domination which on a large scale or a small so fast succeeded one another in the latter days of the Jewish commonwealth." This explains the fact that we read of no mockery of *them*, of no gibes levelled against *them*. They were the popular heroes. They realized the popular idea of the Messiah. See Trench's *Studies*, p. 294.

28. *And the scripture was fulfilled*] The reference here is to Isaiah liii. 12, but the verse is omitted in some MSS.

was numbered with the transgressors. And they that passed 29
by railed on him, wagging their heads, and saying, Ah, thou
that destroyest the temple, and buildest *it* in three days,
save thyself, and come down from the cross. Likewise also 30
the chief priests mocking said among themselves with the 31
scribes, He saved others; himself he cannot save. Let 32
Christ the King of Israel descend now from the cross, that
we may see and believe. And they that were crucified with
him reviled him. And when the sixth hour was come, there 33

29. *railed on him*] The instincts of ordinary pity were quenched in the fierceness of malignant hatred and religious bigotry.
Ah] "Fyȝ," Wyclif. It is an exclamation of exultant derision = the Latin *Vah*.
that destroyest the temple] This saying of our Lord at His first cleansing of the Temple was never forgotten. Perhaps some of the false witnesses of the previous night were now present.
31. *the chief priests*] whose high dignity and sacred office should have taught them better than to descend to the low passions of the mob.
mocking said] "scornynge him, ech to oþer, wiþ scribis, seiden," Wyclif. The ordinary bystanders *blaspheme* (*v.* 29), the members of the Sanhedrim *mock*, for they think they have achieved a complete victory.
32. *they that were crucified with him*] At first both the robbers joined in reproaching Him. The word rendered here "they *reviled* him" is rendered "cast the same in his teeth" in Matt. xxvii. 44. One of them, however, went further than this, and was guilty of blaspheming Him (Luke xxiii. 39), but, as the weary hours passed away, the other, separating himself from the sympathies of all who stood around the Cross, turned in unexampled penitence and faith to Him that hung so close to him, and whose only "token of royalty was the crown of thorns that still clung to His bleeding brows," and in reply to his humble request to be remembered when He should come in His kingdom, heard the gracious words, "*To day shalt thou be with me in paradise*" (Luke xxiii. 43). Thus even from "the Tree" the Lord began to reign, and when "lifted up," to "draw" men, even as He had said, unto Himself (John xii. 32).
33. *And when the sixth hour was come*] i.e. 12 o'clock. The most mysterious period of the Passion was rapidly drawing near, when the Lord of life was about to yield up His spirit and taste of death. At this hour nature herself began to evince her sympathy with Him Whom man rejected. The clearness of the Syrian noontide was obscured, and darkness deepened over the guilty city. It is impossible to explain the origin of this darkness. The Passover moon was then at the full, so that it could not have been an eclipse. Probably it was some supernatural derangement of the terrestrial atmosphere. The Pharisees

34 was darkness over the whole land until the ninth hour. And at the ninth hour Jesus cried with a loud voice, saying, Eloi, Eloi, lama sabachthani? which is, being interpreted, My 35 God, my God, why hast thou forsaken me? And some of them that stood by, when they heard *it*, said, Behold, he 36 calleth Elias. And one ran and filled a spunge full of vinegar, and put *it* on a reed, and gave him to drink, saying, Let alone; let us see whether Elias will come to take 37 him down. And Jesus cried with a loud voice, and gave up

had often asked for a "sign from heaven." Now one was granted them.

until the ninth hour] i.e. till 3 o'clock. A veil hides from us the incidents of these three hours, and all the details of what our Lord, shrouded in the supernatural gloom, underwent "for us men and for our salvation."

34. *And at the ninth hour*] the hour of the offering of the evening sacrifice,

Jesus cried with a loud voice] He now gives utterance to the words of the first verse of the xxiind Psalm, in which, in the bitterness of his soul, David had complained of the desertion of his God, and said,

"Eloï! Eloï! lama sabachthani?"

This is the only one of the "Seven Sayings from the Cross," which has been recorded by St Mark, and he gives the original Aramaic and its explanation. Observe that of these sayings (i) the first three all referred to others, to (*a*) His murderers, (*b*) the penitent malefactor, (*c*) His earthly mother; (ii) the next three referred to His own mysterious and awful conflict, (*a*) His loneliness, (*b*) His sense of thirst, (*c*) His work now all but ended; (iii) with the seventh He commends His soul into His Father's hands.

35. *Behold, he calleth Elias*] They either only caught the first syllable, or misapprehended words, or, as some think, spoke in wilful mockery, and declared He called not on Eli, God, but on Elias, whose appearance was universally expected. See note above, ix. 11.

36. *full of vinegar*] Burning thirst is the most painful aggravation of death by crucifixion, and it was as He uttered the words, "*I thirst*," that the soldier ran and filled a sponge with vinegar, or the sour wine-and-water called *posca*, the ordinary drink of the Roman soldiers.

and put it on a reed] i.e. on the short stem of a hyssop-plant (John xix. 29).

Let alone] According to St Mark, the man himself cries "Let be;" according to St Matthew, the others cry out thus to him as he offers the drink; according to St John, several filled the sponge with the sour wine. Combining the statements, together we have a natural and accurate picture of the excitement caused by the loud cry.

vv. 38, 39.]   ST MARK, XV.   181

the ghost. And the veil of the temple was rent in twain 38
from the top to the bottom.

39—41. *The Confession of the Centurion.*

And when the centurion, which stood over against him, 39
saw that he so cried out, and gave up the ghost, he said,

37. *And Jesus cried with a loud voice*] saying, "It is finished." The three Evangelists all dwell upon the loudness of the cry, as it had been the triumphant note of a conqueror.
and gave up the ghost] saying, "Father, into thy hands I commend my spirit," and then all was over. The Lord of life hung lifeless upon the Cross. "There may be something intentional in the fact that in describing the death of Christ the Evangelists do not use the neuter verb, 'He died,' but the phrases, '*He gave up the ghost*' (Mark xv. 37; Luke xxiii. 46; John xix. 30); '*He yielded up the ghost*' (Matt. xxvii. 50); as though they would imply with St Augustine that He gave up His life, '*quia voluit, quando voluit, quomodo voluit.*' Comp. John x. 18." Farrar, *Life,* II p. 418 n.
the ghost] Ghost, from A. S. *gâst*, G. *geist*,=spirit, breath, opposed to body. "The word has now acquired a kind of hallowed use, and is applied to one Spirit only, but was once common." *Bible Word-Book,* p. 224. Compare (*a*) Wyclif's translation here, "deiede *or sente out the bre*þ;" (*b*) "*ghostly* dangers" (=spiritual dangers), "our *ghostly* enemy" (=our spiritual enemy), in the Catechism; (*c*) Bishop Andrewes' Sermons, II. 340, "Ye see then that it is worth the while to confess this [that Jesus is the Lord], as it should be confessed. In this sense none can do it but by the Holy Ghost. Otherwise, for an *ore tenus* only, *our own ghost* will serve well enough." *Bible English,* p. 265.
38. *And the veil of the temple*] the beautiful thick, costly veil of purple and gold, inwrought with figures of Cherubim, 20 feet long and 30 broad, which separated the Holy Place from the Most Holy,
was rent in twain] For the full symbolism of this see Heb. ix. 3, x. 19. For the earthquake which now shook the city, see Matt. xxvii. 51. Such an event must have made a profound impression, and perhaps was the first step towards the change of feeling which afterwards led a great number of "*the priests to become obedient to the faith*" (Acts vi. 7).

39—41. THE CONFESSION OF THE CENTURION.

39. *when the centurion*] in charge of the quaternion of soldiers. See above, *v.* 24.
that he so cried out] The whole demeanour of the Divine Sufferer, the loudness of the cry, and the words He uttered, thrilled the officer through and through. Death he must have often witnessed, on the battle-field, in the amphitheatre at Cæsarea, in tumultuous insurrec-

40 Truly this man was the Son of God. There were also women looking on afar off: among whom was Mary Magdalene, and Mary the mother of James the less and of Joses, 41 and Salome; (who also, when he was in Galilee, followed him, and ministered unto him;) and many other women which came up with him unto Jerusalem.

tions in Palestine, but never before had he been confronted with the majesty of a Voluntary Death undergone for the salvation of the world. The expression of a wondrous power of life and spirit in the last sign of life, the triumphant shout in death, was to him a new revelation.

the Son of God] In an ecstacy of awe and wonder "*he glorified God*," he exclaimed, "*In truth this man was righteous*" (Luke xxiii. 47); nay, he went further, and declared, "*This Man was a* (or *the*) *Son of God.*" It is possible that on bringing the Lord back after the scourging, which he superintended, the centurion may have heard the mysterious declaration of the Jews, that by their Law the Holy One ought to die, because He *made Himself the Son of God* (John xix. 7). The words made a great impression on Pilate *then* (John xix. 8). But now the centurion had seen *the end*. And what an end! All that he had dimly believed of heroes and demigods is transfigured. This man was more. He was *the Son of God*. Together with the centurion at Capernaum (Matt. viii.) and Cornelius at Cæsarea (Acts x.) he forms in the Gospel and Apostolic histories a triumvirate of believing Gentile soldiers. The words, *I, if I be lifted up, will draw all men unto me*, had been already fulfilled in the instance of the penitent malefactor. They are now true of this Roman officer. The "Lion of the tribe of Judah" was "reigning from the Tree."

40. *There were also women*] forerunners of the noble army of Holy Women, who were, in the ages to come, throughout the length and breadth of Christendom, to minister at many a death-bed out of love for Him Who died "*the Death.*"

Mary Magdalene] Mary of Magdala, out of whom had gone forth seven demons (Luke viii. 2). This is the first time she is mentioned by St Mark.

Mary the mother of James the less] The "Mary of Clopas" (John xix. 25) who stood by the cross, and "Mary of James the Less" (comp. Matt. xxvii. 56), are the same person; she was the sister of the Blessed Virgin, and had married Clopas or Alphæus.

James the less] James the Little, so called to distinguish him from the Apostle St James, the son of Zebedee. Some think he was so called (*a*) because he was younger than the other James; or (*b*) on account of his low stature; or (*c*) because, when elevated to the bishopric of Jerusalem (Gal. ii. 12), he took the name in humility, to distinguish him from his namesake, now famous in consequence of his martyrdom (Acts xii. 2).

Joses] See note above, iii. 31.

Salome] See note above, x. 35.

42—47. *The Burial.*

And now when the even was come, because it was the 42
preparation, that is, the day before the sabbath, Joseph of 43
Arimathæa, an honourable counseller, which also waited for
the kingdom of God, came, and went in boldly unto Pilate,
and craved the body of Jesus. And Pilate marvelled if he 44

42—47. THE BURIAL.

42. *the preparation*] i.e. for the Sabbath, which St Mark, writing for other readers than Jews, explains as "*the day before the Sabbath.*"
43. *Joseph of Arimathæa*] i.e. either of Rama in Benjamin (Matt. ii. 18) or Ramathaim in Ephraim (1 Sam. i. 1). Probably the latter. The place is called in the LXX. "Armathaim," and by Josephus "Armathia." Joseph was a man of wealth (Matt. xxvii. 57), a member of the Sanhedrim (Luke xxiii. 50), and a secret disciple of Jesus (John xix. 38), who had not consented to the resolution of the rest to put Him to death (Luke xxiii. 51).
waited for the kingdom] like Simeon (Luke ii. 25) and Anna (Luke ii. 38).
went in boldly] He is no longer a secret disciple. He casts away all fear. The Cross transfigures cowards into heroes. "It was no light matter Joseph had undertaken: for to take part in a burial, at any time, would defile him for seven days, and make everything unclean which he touched (Num. xix. 11; Hagg. ii. 13); and to do so now involved his seclusion through the whole Passover week—with all its holy observances and rejoicings." Geikie, II. 576.
craved the body of Jesus] It was not the Roman custom to remove the bodies of the crucified from the cross. Instead of shortening their agonies the Roman law left them to die a lingering death, and suffered their bodies to moulder under the action of sun and rain (comp. Cic. *Tusc. Quæst.* I. 43, "Theodori nihil interest humine *an sublime* putrescat"), or be devoured by wild beasts (comp. Hor. *Epist.* XVI. 48, "Non hominem occidi: non *pasces in cruce corvos*"). The more merciful Jewish Law, however, did not allow such barbarities, and the Roman rulers had made an express exception in their favour. In accordance, therefore, with the request of the Jewish authorities, the legs of the malefactors had been broken to put them out of their misery (John xix. 31), but our Lord was found to be *dead already* (John xix. 33), and the soldier had pierced His side with a spear, the point of which was a handbreadth in width, thus causing a wound which would of itself have been sufficient to cause death, whereupon there had issued forth blood and water (John xix. 34). Thus the Holy Body was now ready for its entombment.
44. *And Pilate marvelled*] Death by crucifixion did not generally supervene even for three days, and thirty-six hours is said to be the earliest period when it would be thus brought about. Pilate, therefore, marvelled

were already dead: and calling *unto him* the centurion, he
45 asked him whether he had been any while dead. And when
he knew *it* of the centurion, he gave the body to Joseph.
46 And he bought fine linen, and took him down, and wrapped
him in the linen, and laid him in a sepulchre which was
hewn out of a rock, and rolled a stone unto the door of the
47 sepulchre. And Mary Magdalene and Mary *the mother* of
Joses beheld where he was laid.

at the request of Joseph, and required the evidence of the centurion to assure himself of the fact.

45. *he gave the body to Joseph*] The word translated "gave" only occurs in the New Testament here and in 2 Peter i. 3, 4; "according as his divine power *hath given* unto us all things that pertain unto life and godliness;" "whereby *are given* unto us exceeding great and precious promises." It means more than simply to give, and = "*to give freely*," "largiri." The word appears to be used designedly by St Mark, implying that Pilate, who from his character might have been expected to extort money from the wealthy "counsellor," *freely gave up* the Body at his request, placing it at his disposal by a written order, or a verbal command to the centurion.

46. *And he bought fine linen*] Thus successful, Joseph purchased fine (probably *white*) linen, the original word for which has been already explained in the note on ch. xiv. 51, and then he repaired to Golgotha, where he was joined by Nicodemus, formerly a secret disciple like himself, but whom the Cross had emboldened to come forward and bring *a mixture of myrrh and aloes, about an hundred pound weight* (John xix. 39), to do honour to the Lord of life.

wrapped him in the linen] Thus assisted, Joseph took down the Holy Body, laid it in the fine linen, sprinkled the myrrh and aloes amongst the folds, and wound them round the wounded Limbs.

a sepulchre] He then conveyed the Body to a new Tomb, wherein as yet no man had ever been laid, and which he had hewn out of the limestone rock in a garden he possessed hard by Golgotha (John xix. 41). He was anxious probably himself to be buried there in the near precincts of the Holy City. Here now they laid the Holy Body in a niche in the rock, and

rolled a stone] of large size (Matt. xxvii. 60) to the horizontal entrance, while

47. *Mary Magdalene*] and Mary the mother of Joses (see note above, *v.* 40) and the other women (Luke xxiii. 55), "beheld," i. e. *observed carefully*, the place where He was laid, and where, surrounded by all the mystery of death,

> "Still He slept, from Head to Feet
> Shrouded in the winding-sheet,
> Lying in the rock alone,
> Hidden by the sealèd stone."

1—8. *The Resurrection.*

And when the sabbath was past, Mary Magdalene, and 16
Mary the *mother* of James, and Salome, had bought sweet
spices, that they might come and anoint him. And very 2
early in the morning the first *day* of the week, they came
unto the sepulchre at the rising of the sun. And they said 3
among themselves, Who shall roll us away the stone from
the door of the sepulchre? And when they looked, they 4
saw that the stone was rolled away: for it was very great.
And entering into the sepulchre, they saw a young man sit- 5

CH. XVI. 1—8. THE RESURRECTION.

1. *And when the sabbath was past*] Friday night, Saturday, and Saturday night passed away, three days according to the Jewish reckoning (comp. (*a*) 1 Sam. xxx. 12, 13; 2 Chron. x. 5, 12; (*b*) Matt. xii. 40; John ii. 19; Matt. xxvii. 63), and He, Who had truly died, lay also truly buried.

bought sweet spices] Meanwhile the holy women, whom a love stronger than death had drawn to observe the spot on the evening of His burial, had returned in order that they might complete the embalming of the Body, which had necessarily been done in haste, *as the Sabbath drew on* (Luke xxiii. 54).

2. *And very early in the morning*] while "*it was yet dark*" (John xx. 1), before the dawn streaked the eastern sky on

the first day of the week] the world's first Easter-Day, our *Lord's Day* (Rev. i. 10),

they came] or rather, **come** (observe again the graphic present of the Evangelist), **draw near**, to the sepulchre.

3. *And they said among themselves*] Unaware of the deputation of the Jewish rulers, which had gone to Pilate, and secured the sealing of the Stone and the setting of the watch over the Tomb (Matt. xxvii. 62—66), their only anxiety was, *Who shall roll away the stone from the door of the sepulchre?*

4. *And when they looked*] But as they drew nearer amidst the glimmering light, the earth quaked beneath their feet (Matt. xxviii. 2), and **looking up** they saw that all cause of anxiety was removed, for the stone was already rolled away. Observe the force of the expression "*when they looked.*" It means when they "*looked up;*" an accurate and graphic detail.

for it was very great] About this fact there could be no doubt. The stone which had closed the entrance was "*very great,*" and even at a distance on looking up to the height, on which the rock-tomb lay, they could see it was not in its place, but had changed its position.

5. *And entering into the sepulchre*] This emboldened them all to enter into the tomb, except Mary of Magdala, who, seeing in the rolling away of the stone the confirmation of her worst fears, fled away to the Apostles Peter and John; and there they saw

ting on the right side, clothed in a long white garment; and
6 they were affrighted. And he saith unto them, Be not affrighted: Ye seek Jesus of Nazareth, which was crucified: he is risen; he is not here: behold the place where they
7 laid him. But go your way, tell his disciples and Peter that he goeth before you into Galilee: there shall ye see him, as
8 he said unto you. And they went out quickly, and fled from

a young man] or as some of them may have specified, *two* (Luke xxiv. 4), sitting on the right hand. (Comp. Luke i. 11.)

clothed in a long white garment] white or "*glistering*" (Luke xxiv. 4); "hilid with a whit stoole," Wyclif. Note the word "hilid" here, from "hélan" to "cover," whence our word "hell"="*the covered place*."

and they were affrighted] On the force of the Greek word thus rendered, see above, ch. ix. 15. The sight of the heavenly visitants (Luke xxiv. 4) filled them with the utmost terror and amazement, "þei weren *abaist*," Wyclif.

6. *he is risen*] When exactly He had risen no man knoweth, for no man saw. But that it was true did not admit of doubt. When the Apostles Peter and John visited the tomb an hour or so afterwards (John xx. 3—10), they went in undismayed, but it was empty. The Holy Body was gone! There were no traces of violence. All was order and calm. The linen bandages lay carefully unrolled by themselves. The face-cloth that had covered the Face lay not with them. It was folded up in a place in the empty niche by itself. But HE was not there. He had risen even as He had said.

behold the place] where, indeed, He had been laid by kindly hands, but which did not contain Him now.

7. *go your way*] Practical action must take the place of vague astonishment. There was a message to be borne.

and Peter] No wonder it is in the Gospel of St Mark we find this wondrous touch. Who afterwards would have been so likely, as the Apostle himself, to treasure up this word, the pledge of possible forgiveness, after the dreadful hours he must have spent during Friday night, Saturday, and Saturday night? What story would he have so often told to his son in the faith either in Eastern Babylon or the capital of the West?

he goeth before you] as a true Shepherd before His sheep. It is the same word which (*a*) He Himself used on the evening of the Betrayal, "After I am risen again, I will *go before you* into Galilee" (Matt. xxvi. 32; Mark xiv. 28); which (*b*) is applied to the star "*going before*" the Magi at His nativity, and (*c*) to His own "*going before*" His Apostles on the road towards Jerusalem, where He was to suffer. See note above, ch. x. 32.

8. *they went out quickly*] At present the holy women were overwhelmed with alarm at the sight they had witnessed and the words they had heard.

the sepulchre; for they trembled and were amazed: neither said they any thing to any *man;* for they were afraid.

9—11. *The Appearance to Mary Magdalene.*

Now when *Jesus* was risen early the first *day* of the week, 9 he appeared first to Mary Magdalene, out of whom he had cast seven devils. *And* she went and told them that had 10

they trembled] Literally, **for trembling and amazement possessed them**, or as Wyclif renders it, "forsoþe drede and quakynge hadde assaylid hem." The original word = "*amazement,*" has been already the subject of comment above, ch. v. 42. The word rendered "*trembling*" occurs nowhere else in the Four Gospels.

neither said they any thing to any man] That is, on their way to the Holy City they did not open their lips to any *passers by they chanced to meet.* Joy opened them freely enough afterwards to the Apostles (Matt. xxviii. 8).

for they were afraid] In a tumult of rapture and alarm they fled back from the tomb towards the Holy City. The occurrence of the morning was so new to them, great, and unheard of, that they ventured not as yet to publish it.

9—11. THE APPEARANCE TO MARY MAGDALENE.

9. *Now when*] On this section from 9—20, see Introduction, pp. 15, 16.

he appeared first] As yet, it will be observed, no human eye had seen the risen Conqueror of Death. The holy women had seen the stone rolled away, and the empty tomb, and had heard the words of the Angels, and announced all that had occurred to the Eleven, but their words appeared to them as "*idle tales*" (Luke xxiv. 11). The Apostles Peter and John also, when they visited the Sepulchre, beheld proofs that it was indeed empty, but "*Him they saw not.*" The first person to whom the Saviour shewed Himself after His resurrection was Mary of Magdala. After recounting to the Apostles Peter and John the rolling away of the stone, she seems to have returned to the sepulchre; there she beheld the two angels in white apparel, whom the other women had seen (John xx. 12), and while she was in vain solacing her anguish at the removal of her Lord, He stood before her, and one word sufficed to assure her that it was He, her Healer, and her Lord.

out of whom he had cast seven devils] That He should have been pleased to manifest Himself first after His resurrection not to the whole Apostolic company, but to a woman, and that woman not His earthly Mother, but Mary of Magdala, clearly made a strong impression on the early Church.

10. *she went and told*] In the fulness of believing faith she hurried back to Jerusalem and recounted her tale of joy to the Eleven and the rest.

11 been with him, as they mourned and wept. And they, when they had heard that he was alive, and had been seen of her, believed not.

12, 13. *The Appearance to Two of them.*

12 After that he appeared in another form unto two of
13 them, as they walked, and went into the country. And they

as they mourned and wept] Desolate at the loss of their beloved Master, and unable to realize the wonderful accounts of His resurrection. "Weylinge and wepynge" is Wyclif's rendering.

11. *had been seen of her*] The original word here translated "had been seen" occurs nowhere else in St Mark except here in this section and in verse 14.

believed not] So incredible to them did the whole story appear.

12, 13. THE APPEARANCE TO TWO OF THEM.

12. *After that*] On the world's first Easter-Day the risen Saviour manifested Himself first to Mary Magdalene, then to the other ministering women. The Evangelist now proceeds to relate the appearance to the two disciples journeying towards Emmaus, which is more fully described by St Luke (xxiv. 13—35).

he appeared] "*he is schewid*," Wyclif. This word in the original is applied to our Lord's "manifestations" of Himself after His resurrection (*a*) by St Mark twice, here and xvi. 14; (*b*) by St John three times, xxi. 1, 14; (*c*) by St Paul to our "manifestation" in our real character at the Last Judgment, 2 Cor. v. 10 (comp. 1 Cor. iv. 5); (*d*) by the same Apostle to the "manifestation" of Christ at His second coming, Col. iii. 4. The word points here to a change in the Person of our Lord after His resurrection. He is the same and yet not the same. (*a*) *The same.* There are the well-known intonations of His voice, and the marks in His hands and feet (John xx. 20, 25); and He eats before His Apostles, converses with them, blesses them. And yet He is (*b*) *not the same.* His risen Body is no longer subject to the laws of time and space. He comes we know not whence. He goes we know not whither. Now He stands in the midst of the Apostles (John xx. 19); now He vanishes out of their sight (Luke xxiv. 31). He knows now of no *continued* sojourn on earth. He "*appears from time to time*" (Acts i. 3); He "*manifests*" Himself to chosen witnesses, as seemeth Him good.

in another form] It is plain from St Luke xxiv. 16 that He was not at the time recognised. This appearance would seem to have been vouchsafed early in the afternoon of the day of the Resurrection.

unto two of them] The name of one was Cleopas = Cleopatros, not the Clopas of John xix. 25, and another whose name is not known. Some have conjectured it was Nathanael, others the Evangelist St Luke.

as they walked] from Jerusalem in the direction of the village of Emmaus. St Luke says it was *sixty stadia* (A.V. "threescore furlongs"), or about 7½ miles from Jerusalem. From the earliest period it was identified by Christian writers with the Emmaus on the border of the

v. 14.]   ST MARK, XVI.   189

went and told *it* unto the residue : neither believed they them.

14—18.   *The Appearance to the Eleven.*

Afterward he appeared unto the eleven as they sat at 14 meat, and upbraided them with their unbelief and hardness

plain of Philistia, afterwards called Nicopolis (1 Macc. iii. 40), situated some 20 miles from Jerusalem. Afterwards it was identified with the little village of *el-Kubeibeh*, about 3 miles west of the ancient Mizpeh, and 9 miles from Jerusalem. The true site has yet to be settled.

13.   *they went and told it unto the residue*] No sooner did they recognise our Lord in the breaking of the bread (Luke xxiv. 35), and He had vanished out of their sight (Luke xxiv. 31), than they returned in haste to Jerusalem, ascended to the Upper Room, found ten of the Apostles met together (Luke xxiv. 33), and whereas they thought they alone were the bearers of joyful tidings, they were themselves greeted with joyful tidings, "*The Lord has risen indeed, and appeared unto Simon*" (Luke xxiv. 34; 1 Cor. xv. 5). When this appearance was vouchsafed to St Peter we are not told. It certainly occurred after the return from the sepulchre, but whether *before* or *after* the journey to Emmaus cannot be determined.

neither believed they them] The Ten, as we have just now seen, announced that the Lord had appeared to Simon, and this they at the time believed. When the two disciples arrive, they announce that He had appeared to *them* also. Unable to comprehend this new mode of existence on the part of their risen Lord, that He could be now here and now there, they were filled with doubts. They had refused to believe the evidence of Mary Magdalene (Mark xvi. 11), and even now hesitation possessed them, and they could not give credence to the word of the two disciples. The Evangelists multiply proofs of the slowness of the Apostles to accept a truth so strange and unprecedented as their Lord's resurrection, and that not to a continuous sojourn, as in the case of Lazarus, but to a form of life which was *manifested* only from time to time, and was invested with new powers, new properties, new attributes. The Resurrection, it is to be remembered, was unlike (*a*) any of the recorded miracles of raising from the dead, (*b*) any of the legends of Greece or Rome. It was "not a restoration to the old life, to its wants, to its inevitable close, but the revelation of a new life, foreshadowing new powers of action and a new mode of being." See Westcott's *Gospel of the Resurrection*, pp. 154—160.

14—18.   THE APPEARANCE TO THE ELEVEN.

14.   *Afterward*] That is on the evening of the day of the Resurrection, when the two disciples returning from Emmaus had recounted their tale of joy, and the others had told them of the appearance to St Peter.

as they sat at meat] On this occasion, when they were terrified at His sudden appearing (Luke xxiv. 37), and thought they were looking at a

of heart, because they believed not them which had seen
15 him after he was risen. And he said unto them, Go ye into
16 all the world, and preach the gospel to every creature. He
that believeth and is baptized shall be saved; but he that
17 believeth not shall be damned. And these signs shall fol-

spectre or phantom, He calmed their fears by (*a*) bidding them take
note of His Hands and His Feet, by (*b*) eating in their presence of
broiled fish (Luke xxiv. 41—43), and by (*c*) reiterating His salutation,
"*Peace be unto you*" (John xx. 21).

and upbraided them] Their new-born joy still struggled with bewil-
derment and unbelief (Luke xxiv. 21), and one of their number, St
Thomas, was absent altogether, having apparently thrown away all
hope.

hardness of heart] Compare His words (*a*) after the feeding of the
Five and Four Thousand, and (*b*) to the disciples journeying towards
Emmaus, Luke xxiv. 25.

them which had seen him] Of the five appearances after the Resurrection vouchsafed on the world's first Easter-Day four had already
taken place before this interview. (i) To Mary Magdalene, (ii) to the
other ministering women, (iii) to the two journeying to Emmaus,
(iv) to St Peter.

15. *And he said unto them*] St John informs us that on this occasion the Risen Saviour breathed on the Apostles, and gave them a foretaste of the bestowal of the Holy Ghost, with power to remit sin and
retain sin. St Mark tells us of very important words, which He went
on to utter, anticipating the final charge recorded by St Matthew (Matt.
xxviii. 16—20).

Go ye into all the world] Or, as it is expressed in St Matthew's
Gospel, "*make disciples of all nations*" (xxviii. 19), and comp. Luke
xxiv. 47; Acts i. 8. Contrast these injunctions with those to the
Twelve during His earthly ministry, Matt. x. 5, 6, "*Go not* into the
way of the Gentiles, and into any city of the Samaritans *enter ye not:*
but go rather to the lost sheep of the house of Israel."

every creature] i.e. *to the whole creation*, the whole world of men,
not Jews only or Samaritans, but Gentiles of all nations. Comp. Rom.
viii. 21, 22.

16. *He that believeth and is baptized*] Not faith only, but baptism
also is required by the Lord. Compare the words of Philip the deacon
to the Ethiopian eunuch, Acts viii. 37.

he that believeth not] He addeth not *and is baptized* here. This
would have been superfluous. He who refuses to believe will refuse to
be baptized.

shall be damned] See note above, ch. xii. 40. He who wilfully
rejects the Gospel message, when duly offered him, shall have no share
in its saving mercies, but shall be left to the condemnation due to him
for his sins.

17. *And these signs*] For this word applied to Miracles see
note, ch. vi. 2.

low them that believe; In my name shall they cast out
devils; they shall speak with new tongues; they shall take 18
up serpents; and if they drink any deadly thing, it shall not
hurt them; they shall lay hands on the sick, and they shall
recover.

19, 20. *The Ascension.*

So then after the Lord had spoken unto them, he was 19

shall follow] Literally, shall **proceed along with**. The same word
in the original is used by St Luke, i. 3, "It seemed good to me also,
having had perfect understanding of all things" (literally, **having carefully followed up**).
them that believe] i.e. those *that shall have believed*, shall have adopted
the Faith and been baptized.
In my name shall they cast out devils] As is afterwards recorded to
have been done by Philip the deacon in Samaria (Acts viii. 7), by St
Paul at Philippi (Acts xvi. 18) and Ephesus (Acts xix. 15, 16).
they shall speak with new tongues] as all the Apostles did on the day
of Pentecost, and the Gentile friends of Cornelius (Acts x. 46), and the
twelve disciples at Ephesus (Acts xix. 6), and many afterwards in the
Church of Corinth (1 Cor. xii. 10).
18. *they shall take up serpents*] And so we read of St Paul shaking
off the viper at Malta (Acts xxviii. 5). Comp. Luke x. 19.
and if they drink] As is related of St John that he drank the cup of
hemlock which was intended to cause his death, and suffered no harm
from it, and of Barsabas surnamed Justus (Eusebius, *Eccl. Hist.* III. 39).
they shall lay hands on the sick] As St Peter did on the lame man at
the Beautiful Gate of the Temple (Acts iii. 7), and St Paul on Publius
in the island of Malta (Acts xxviii. 8). "Gifts of healing" are mentioned both by this last Apostle (1 Cor. xii. 9) and by St James (v. 14, 15)
as remaining in the Church.

19, 20. THE ASCENSION.

19. *So then after the Lord*] Some MSS. here insert the word Jesus.
Combined with Lord, it would be a term of reverence.
spoken unto them] This does not mean immediately after our Lord
had uttered the last words, but after He had on different occasions
during the "Great Forty Days" spoken unto them of "the things pertaining to the kingdom of God" (Acts i. 3). The original word here
rendered "*had spoken unto them*" has a much wider signification. It
signifies *to teach, to instruct by preaching and other oral communication.*
Compare its use in Mark xiii. 11; John ix. 29, "We know that God
spake unto Moses," i.e. *held communications* with Moses; John xv. 22,
"If I had not come," says our Lord, "and *spoken unto* them," i.e.
preached to them. So that here it denotes after our Lord had during
the forty days fully instructed His Apostles by His oral teaching in all
things appertaining to His kingdom and the planting of His Church.

received up into heaven, and sat on the right hand of God.
20 And they went forth, and preached every where, the Lord

he was received] The original word only occurs here in the Gospels. It is applied three times in the Acts (i. 2, 11, 22) to the Ascension, and is so applied by St Paul, 1 Tim. iii. 16, "*received up* into glory."

into heaven] What St Mark records thus concisely in his short practical Gospel for the busy, active, Christians of Rome, St Luke has related at much greater length. From him we learn how one day the Lord bade His Apostles accompany Him along the road from Jerusalem towards Bethany and the Mount of Olives; how, full of hopes of a temporal kingdom, they questioned Him as to the time of its establishment; how their inquiries were solemnly silenced (Acts i. 7); and how then after He had bestowed upon them His last abiding blessing, while His Hands were yet uplifted in benediction (Luke xxiv. 50, 51), "*He began to be parted from them, and a cloud received Him out of their sight.*"

and sat on the right hand of God] The Session at the right Hand of God, recorded only by St Mark, forms a striking and appropriate conclusion to his Gospel, and "conveys to the mind a comprehensive idea of Christ's Majesty and Rule." Our Lord was "taken up," and bore our redeemed humanity into the very presence of God, into "the place of all places in the universe of things, in situation most eminent, in quality most holy, in dignity most excellent, in glory most illustrious, the inmost sanctuary of God's temple above" (Barrow's *Sermon on the Ascension*). There, having led "captivity captive, and received gifts for men" (Ps. lxviii. 18; Eph. iv. 8), He sat down on the right Hand of God, by which expression we are to understand that in the heaven of heavens He now occupies the place of greatest honour, of most exalted majesty, and of most perfect bliss, and that God hath conferred upon Him all preeminence of dignity, power, favour, and felicity. See Pearson *on the Creed*, Art. vi.

20. *And they*] i. e. the Apostles.

went forth] Not immediately. They were commanded not to "depart from Jerusalem," but to "tarry" there until at Pentecost they should be endued with power from on high (Luke xxiv. 49; Acts i. 4). But when the day of Pentecost had come, and the Comforter had been bestowed, they went forth on their career of conquest,

and preached every where] St Mark himself when he wrote his Gospel had witnessed the spread of the Church from Babylon in the distant East to the City of the Seven Hills in the West.

the Lord working with them] according to His promise, "*Behold I am with you* always, even unto the end of the world." The word translated "*working with them*" only occurs here in the Gospels, but is used by St Paul, Rom. viii. 28, "all things *work together* for good to them that love God;" 1 Cor. xvi. 16, "to every one that *helpeth with us;*" 2 Cor. vi. 1, "we then as *workers together with Him*, beseech you also that ye receive not the grace of God in vain;" and by St James (ii. 22), "seest thou how faith *wrought with* his works?"

working with *them*, and confirming the word with signs following. Amen.

confirming] The original word here employed denotes (1) *to make firm to the tread*, (2) *to make steadfast*, (3) *to establish, confirm*. It occurs nowhere else in the Gospels, but it is found five times in St Paul's Epistles, and twice in the Epistle to the Hebrews. Thus St Paul writes to the Romans (xv. 8), "Jesus Christ was a minister of the circumcision......to *confirm* the promises made unto the fathers;" and to the Corinthians (i. 8) that God will "*confirm* them unto the end, that they may be blameless in the day of our Lord Jesus Christ;" and to the same Church again (2 Cor. i. 21), "now he which *stablisheth* us with you...... is God;" and he exhorts the Colossians (ii. 6, 7), "to walk, rooted and built up in [Jesus Christ], and *stablished* in the faith." And for illustrations of the confirmation of the Apostolic commission compare (i) Acts iv. 29, 30; (ii) Acts v. 12; (iii) Acts xiv. 3.

with signs] Rather, **by the signs which followed**.

following] The original word thus rendered denotes more than merely *to follow*, and = *to follow close upon, to follow in the track of another*. St Paul uses it in 1 Tim. v. 10, speaking of the condition of a "widow indeed," "if she had *diligently followed* every good work;" and in 1 Tim. v. 24, "Some men's sins are open beforehand......and some men they *follow after*." St Peter uses the word in one place (1 Pet. ii. 21), "Christ also suffered for you, leaving you an example, that ye should *follow* His steps." The word is very expressive here, and denotes that the "signs" followed close upon, and were the immediate result of, the continued operation of Him, Who, clad in majesty ineffable, sitteth at the right hand of God, and hath promised to be with His Church "*even unto the end of the world*" (Matt. xxviii. 20). The Evangelist does not conceive of Christ's Session as a state of inactive rest. (i) As the High Priest of His Church He pleads with the Father the merits of His wondrous sacrifice (Rom. viii. 34; Heb. iv. 14, vii. 25; 1 John ii. 1, 2). (ii) As the Prophet, He teaches, inspires, and guides His Church into all truth (Deut. xviii. 15; Luke xxiv. 19). (iii) As King of kings and Lord of lords, He sways the destinies of the universe, and employs the agency of heaven and earth for the government and defence of His people, till He shall have *subdued all things unto Himself* (Phil. iii. 21), and the *last enemy*, even death, *shall be destroyed* (1 Cor. xv. 26), and the victory, for which all Creation waits, shall be finally and completely won (Rom. viii. 19—23).

Amen] This is wanting in the best MSS. For some remarks respecting the *apotheosis* of the Cæsars at the era of the Ascension, see Abp Trench's *Hulsean Lectures*, and compare the striking fact that "on public buildings at Ephesus, Augustus is found, from inscriptions on recently discovered buildings there, to have been described by the singular title Υἱὸς Θεοῦ, "*Son of God.*" With this revelation of the great Conqueror, the true *divus Cæsar*, seated at the right hand of God—of which glorious reality the divine honours paid to the emperors at the very time he was writing from Rome were the dark shadow—

the second Evangelist brings his Gospel to a close. He has portrayed the Son of Man and the Son of God as He wrought on earth, in all the fulness of His living Energy, "*going about doing good*" (Acts x. 38); He leaves us to realize, and realizing to believe in, His continued operation in the very heaven of heavens, in behalf of His Church and the Humanity He came to save.

"The golden censer in His hand,
He offers hearts from every land,
Tied to His own by gentlest band
    Of silent love:
Above Him winged blessings stand
    In act to move."

Keble's *Christian Year*. *Ascension Day*.

INDEX I.

Abiathar and the shewbread, 44
Adultery, woman taken in, 137
Agony in the Garden, 161; comparison of, with first temptation, 162
Ahimelech, 44
Alphæus, 41
Angels, at the temptation, 31; at the sepulchre, 186
Annas, some account of, 166; our Lord's examination before, 166
Apostles, meaning of word, 48; lists of, 48, 49; mission of, 69; return of, after their first mission, 75; slowness of, to believe the Resurrection, 190
Appearance of our Lord to Mary Magdalene, 187; to the other ministering women, 188; to the two disciples, 188; to St Peter, 189; to the Ten Apostles, 189
Arimathæa, site of, 183
Ascension, as recorded by St Mark, 191
Atonement, figures used to describe effects of, 117

Babylon, St Mark at, 10
Baptism, our Lord's, 29; probable locality of, 29; import of, 30
Barabbas, 172; various reading, 173; his crime, 173
Barnabas, his connection with St Mark, 9; sharp contention with St Paul on account of, 10
Bartholomew. *See* Nathanael.
Baskets, kinds of, 78; use amongst the Jews, 78
Beelzebub, meaning of, 51
Bethany, supper at, 151
Bethphage, meaning of, 120, 123; probable site of, 120
Bethsaida, western, 78; eastern = Bethsaida-Julias, 93; history of, 76
Betrayal of our Lord, 164; circumstances of, 165; planned by Judas, 154
Brethren of our Lord, 68; opinions concerning, 68

Cæsarea on the sea, 95; seat of the procurator, 171; Pilate resides there, 171
Cæsarea Philippi, 94; history of, 94; events connected with, 64
Caiaphas, 166; his character, 166, 167
Calvary, meaning of word, 177
Cana, miracle at, 87

Cananite, Simon the, 50; meaning of word, 50
Capernaum, 33; events connected with, 33
Chief priests, meaning of the name, 124; conduct of, at the Crucifixion, 179
Clement of Alexandria, testimony of, concerning St Mark, 13
Cleopas, 188
Clothes, rending of, by the high priest, 168
Cock-crowing, 150
Corn, plucking ears of, 43
Cross, form of, 177; title on, 178; our Lord's borne by Simon the Cyrenian, 176; Roman customs regarding, 178
Crown of Thorns, materials of, 176

Dalmanutha, position of, 91
Darkness, the, at the Crucifixion, 179, 180
David and the shewbread, 44
Decapolis, cities in the region of, 63
Demoniacs, healing of, 51; boy, healing of, 103; at Gadara, 60
Denarius, the, value of, 76; description of, 77; shewn to our Lord, 132
Devil, the temptation of Christ, 31
Disciples, early, call of, 32; disciples of Hillel, 110, 136
Discourse of our Lord, character of, after the Transfiguration, 101

Emmaus, doubts concerning site of, 187, 188; two disciples journeying to, 188
Ephraim, Christ retires to, 109
Eucharist, the Holy, institution of, 159
Eusebius, testimony of, concerning St Mark's Gospel, 11

Fasting, Jewish rules concerning, 42
Figs, time of, 123
Fig-tree, withering of, 125
Five thousand, feeding of, 75; site of miracle, 76
Four thousand, feeding of, 89; site of miracle, 90

Gabbatha, 171
Galilee, populousness of, 31; dialect of inhabitants of, 170; Apostles bidden to repair to, after the Resurrection, 186

INDEX I.

Garment, Christ's seamless, 178
Genealogy, none in St Mark, 16
Gennesaret, names of, 32; storm on, 59; land of, 80
Gergesa, site of, 60
Gethsemane, meaning of word, 161; our Lord's agony in, 161
Golgotha, site of, 177; meaning of, 177
Gospels, the one Gospel, 7; commemoration of, in the Gospels, 8; meaning of the word, 8, *n*.; the Gospel of Jesus Christ, 27
Grave-clothes, position of, at the Resurrection, 186
Greek language spoken at Rome, 12, *n*. 3; title on the Cross in, 178
Greeks, the enquiring, 140; brought to our Lord, 140
Guards, setting of, 185

Hell, meaning of, 107
Herod Antipas, his adultery, 72; his murder of the Baptist, 75; our Lord before, 172
Herodians, the, some account of, 46; formation of the name, 46; their hostility to our Lord, 132; their questioning of Him, 132
Herodias, wife of Herod Antipas, 72; some account of, 72; her hatred of the Baptist, 72; causes his murder, 74
High priest, the appointment of, under the Romans, 124
Hillel, school of, 110, 136; opinions of, respecting divorce, 110
Holy Ghost, the descent of, at our Lord's Baptism, 29; promised to the Apostles, 143; sin against the, explained, 52

Idumæa, meaning of word, 46; extent of, 46; multitudes from, come to our Lord, 46
Inscription, the, placed on the Cross, 178
Irenæus, testimony of, concerning St Mark, 13

Jairus, daughter of, restored to life, 66
James, St, the Great, call of, 33; named with his brother Boanerges, 49; present at the raising of Jairus' daughter, 66; at the Transfiguration, 98; his ambitious request, 115; at Gethsemane, 161; early martyrdom of, 49
James, St, the Less, call of, 30; meaning of appellation, 182
Jericho, early history of, 117; blind men restored at, 118
Jerome, testimony of, concerning St Mark, 14
Jerusalem, our Lord's triumphal entry into, 121; view of, from Mount Olivet, 122; His prophecies respecting, 141; destruction of, 146, 147

JESUS
(i) His Baptism, 29; His Temptation, 30
(ii) *Ministrations in Eastern Galilee*
Calls His first disciples, 32; cures the demoniac at Capernaum, 33; heals Peter's wife's mother, 35; cleanses a leper, 37; cures the paralytic, 38; calls St Matthew, 40; defends the disciples for plucking the ears of corn, 43; heals the man with the withered hand, 45; calls the Apostles, 47; delivers the parables, of the Sower, 53; the Seed growing secretly, 57; the Mustard Seed, 5N; stills the Storm, 59; heals the Gadarene demoniac, 60; and the woman with the issue, 64; raises the daughter of Jairus, 65; is rejected at Nazareth, 67; sends forth the Apostles, 69; feeds the Five Thousand, 76; walks on the Sea, 78
(iii) *Ministrations in Northern Galilee*
Heals the daughter of the Syrophœnician woman, 85; gradually heals the deaf and dumb, 87; feeds the Four Thousand, 89; warns His Apostles against the leaven of the Pharisees and of Herod, 91; gradually cures the blind man, 93; receives the confession of St Peter, 94; predicts for the first time His Passion, 96; is transfigured, 98; heals the lunatic boy, 103; predicts His Passion for the second time, 105; teaches His Apostles humility and self-denial, 106
(iv) *Ministrations in Peræa*
Replies to question about divorce, 110; blesses little children, 111; puts the rich young ruler to the test, 112; reveals the danger of riches, 113; promises the reward of self-sacrifice, 114
(v) *Last journey to Jerusalem and the Passion*
Predicts His sufferings for the third time, 115; rebukes the ambitious Apostles, 116; heals blind Bartimæus, 118; is anointed by Mary at Bethany, 152; enters Jerusalem in triumph, 121; declares the judgment of the barren fig-tree, 123; cleanses the Temple, 123; is questioned by the Sanhedrim, 126; replies to the Pharisees respecting the tribute-money, 132; to the Sadducees respecting the resurrection, 134; to the lawyer, respecting the Commandments, 136; puts His counter-question, 137; predicts the destruction of Jerusalem, and the end of the world, 140; prepares for the Passover, 155; institutes the Holy Eucharist, 159; endures the agony at Gethsemane,

INDEX I. 197

161; is betrayed, 164; is tried before the Jews, 166; denied by St Peter, 169; is tried before Pilate, 170; is condemned, 168; crucified, 176; dies, 180; is buried, 184
(vi) *Victory over the grave and Ascension*
Lies in the Tomb, 184; rises again, 185; is seen by Mary Magdalene, 187; by the two disciples, 188; by the Eleven, 189; gives His last charge, 190; ascends up into heaven, 191; sitteth at the right Hand of God, 192

John, St, call of, 33; account of, 49; he and his brother surnamed Boanerges, 49; at the raising of Jairus' daughter, 66; at the Transfiguration, 98; in the garden of Gethsemane, 161

John, surnamed Mark. *See* Mark

John the Baptist, his mission, 27; his appearance, 28; his diet, 28; his message, 28; its effect, 28; baptizes our Lord, 29; imprisoned by Herod, 72; his murder, 75

Jordan, the, St John Baptist at, 28

Joseph of Arimathæa, some account of, 183; assists at our Lord's burial, 184; his new tomb, 184

Joseph, the husband of the Blessed Virgin, his early death, 68

Judas Iscariot, the call of, 51; his complaints at the anointing of our Lord by Mary, 152; causes of his betrayal of our Lord, 153, 154; his compact with the rulers, 153; his movements after the Supper, 164; his betrayal of our Lord, 164

Judas of Galilee, rising of, 132

Jude, St, the call of, 50; his surname, 50; once mentioned in the Gospels, 50

Justin Martyr, testimony of, concerning St Mark, 13

Kanean or Kaneniah, 51

Kingdom of God, the, meaning of the expression, 32

Language of the Galileans, 170

Lazarus, position of family of, 151; resurrection of, 109; at the house of Simon the Leper, 151

Leper, purification of, 37, 38

Levi, identity of, with St Matthew, 41

Locusts, as an article of food, 28

Lots, casting of, at the Crucifixion, 178

Luke, St, his testimony regarding the written Gospels, 8

Magdala, meaning of word, 91; position of, 91

Magdalene, Mary. *See* Mary

Malchus, his ear cut off by St Peter, 165; healed by our Lord, 165

Mark, St
(a) *his name*, 8; changes in his name, 8
(b) *his early life*, his mother, 9; connection with Barnabas, 9; probably converted by St Peter, 9
(c) *his early activity*, with Paul and Barnabas, 9; leaves them at Perga, 9; second missionary journey, the sharp contention, 10; repairs to Cyprus, 10
(d) *his later activity*, with St Paul at Rome, 10; with St Peter at Babylon, 10; with both Apostles at Rome, 10
(e) *his death*, probably by martyrdom, 11

Mark's, St, Gospel
(i) *time* of its composition, 11; place, 11; for whom written, 11, 12; language in which written, 12
(ii) *relation of the Evangelist to St Peter;* testimony of John the Presbyter, 13; of Justin Martyr, 13; of Irenæus, 13; of Origen, 13; of Clement of Alexandria, 13; of Tertullian, 14; of Jerome, 14
(iii) *genuineness*, 15; concluding section, xvi. 9—20, 15
(iv) *characteristics*, 16; absence of genealogy of our Lord, 16; design of St Mark, 16; his testimony to our Lord's divine power, 16, 17; to His human personality, 17; graphic power of the Evangelist, 18; minute details in respect to *person*, 18; *number*, 18; *time*, 19; *place*, 19
(v) *language and style*, 19, 20
(vi) *analysis of*, 20—25

Marriage, question of the Jews concerning, 134

Mary Magdalene, healed by our Lord, 182; at His Cross, 182; at the Burial, 185; Christ's appearance to, 187

Mary, St, the Virgin, seeks our Lord, 53; at the Cross, 180; Christ's words to, 180

Mary, sister of Barnabas, 8; her house at Jerusalem, 9; receives St Peter, 9

Mary, sister of Lazarus, anoints our Lord, 152; His words respecting her, 153

Mary, wife of Clopas, at the Cross, 182; at the sepulchre, 185

Matthew, St, call of, 40; feast at the house of, 41; identity with Levi, 41

Messiah, popular expectation of, 178

Miletus, seashore of, kissing of St Paul at, 164

Miracle, words used to express, in the Gospels, 67; miracles recorded by St Mark, 26

Miraculous draught of fishes, the, 33

Mount of Transfiguration, 98

INDEX I.

Mustard Seed, the, Parable of, 58
Mustard tree, the, 58

Nathanael, or Bartholomew, call of, 50; character of, 50; incidents respecting, recorded in the Gospels, 50
Nazareth, position of, 29; Christ in the synagogue of, 67
Nicodemus, a secret disciple, 184; boldness after the Crucifixion, 184; helps at the burial of our Lord, 184

Origen, testimony of, concerning St Mark, 13

Paneas, site of, 94; meaning of, 94
Parable, meaning of, 54; use of word in Old Testament, 54; St Mark's record of, 26
Parables, scenery round the Lake suggesting, 53
Paralytic, the, healing of, 38
Passover, the first, attended by our Lord, 43; the second kept at Capernaum, 75, 80; the third, 155; as celebrated in the time of our Lord, 156
Passover, the = Paschal Victim, 155
Peræa, our Lord's tour in, 109
Perga, vacillation of St Mark at, 9
Peter, St, call of, 32; meaning of his name, 49; his wife's mother healed, 35; present at the resurrection of Jairus' daughter, 66; his confession, 95; present at the Transfiguration, 98; impetuosity of, 164; with our Lord on Olivet, 141; sent to prepare the Passover, 155; his denials foretold, 160; protestation of, 161; his fall, 169; his visit to the sepulchre, 187; appearance of our Lord to, 189; his relation to St Mark, 9, 10; John the Presbyter's testimony concerning, 13; his influence in the composition of St Mark's Gospel, 13
Pharisees, their hostility to our Lord, 45, 46; attempt to ensnare Him, 132; His counter-question to, 137
Philip, St, the Apostle, call of, 50; occasions when mentioned, 50
Pilate, early history, 171; meaning of name, 171; office of, 171; character, 171; our Lord's first appearance before, 171; His second appearance, 172; his vacillation, 171; his awe in the presence of our Lord, 173; gives the irrevocable sentence, 174; places the title over His Head, 178; consents to our Lord's burial, 184
Pilate's wife, her message to her husband, 173
Potion, the, offered to Christ, 177
Prætorium, meaning of word, 175
Prayer, posture of the Jews at, 126

Procurator, head quarters of, at Cæsarea, 171; insignia of his authority, 171
Publicans, the, office of, 41; general character, 41; present at St John's Baptism, 28; general opinion respecting, 41
Purple robe, the, of Christ, 175

Resurrection of Jairus' daughter, 65; circumstances of our Lord's, 185, 186; appearances of our Lord after, 187, 189
Resurrection-body, nature of our Lord's, 188
Rome, St Paul and St Peter at, 10; St Mark at, 10; Greek language of, 12, n. 3
Roofs, nature of, 38; breaking up of, 38
Ruler of synagogue, office of, 63

Sabbath, the, doctrine of the Pharisees concerning, 43; teaching of our Lord concerning, 44; miracles wrought on, 45
Sabbath-day's journey, a, 146
Sadducees, their doctrines, 134; their opposition to our Lord, 134; their attempt to ensnare Him, 134; their influence in the Sanhedrim, 171
Salome, mother of James and John, 115; her ambitious request, 115; at the crucifixion, 182
Salome, daughter of Herodias, 73; asks for St John Baptist's head, 74
Samaria, our Lord's first journey through, 31; second journey through, 109
Samaritan woman, our Lord's discourse with, 31
Sanhedrim, the, hostility of, to our Lord, 109, 172; resolves on Christ's death, 109; a deputation from, questions Christ, 170; assembles to try our Lord, 170; lost the power of life and death, 168; sends our Lord to Pilate, 171
Scourging by the Romans, its terrible cruelty, 174
Scribes, from Jerusalem, 51; some account of, 33; opposition to our Lord, 45, 46, 51
Shammai, school of, 110, 136; rivalry with school of Hillel, 110
Shekel, the coin, current only in the temple, 124; half, annual payment of, 106, 124
Sidon, description of, in the time of our Lord, 85
Simon of Cyrene, 176
Simon Peter. *See* Peter
Simon, St, call of, 32; explanation of his name, 49; his connection with the Sect of the Zealots, 51
Simon, the leper, entertains our Lord at Bethany, 151

INDEX I.

Son of Man, meaning of the title, 40; applied only to our Lord by Himself, 40; exception to this rule, 40
Sower, the Parable of, 53; explained by our Lord, 55
Spikenard, costliness of, 152
Stone, great, rolled against the door of the Sepulchre, 184
Sufferings, our Lord's predictions of His own, 114
Supper, the Last, celebration of, 159; our Lord's preparations for, 155; order of incidents of, 158
Swine, the destruction of, 62
Synagogue, our Lord present in, 33; miracle wrought in, 34; rulers of, 63; scourging in, 142
Syrophœnician woman, the, her petition, 86; her mighty faith, 87; her victory, 87

Temple, the, first cleansing of, 31; second cleansing, 123; Christ's prophecies respecting destruction of, 141; veil of, rent in twain, 181
Temptation, the, of Christ, 30; features of, as recorded by St Mark, 30
Tertullian, testimony of, concerning St Mark, 14
Thaddæus, 50; identity with Jude, 50
Thief, the penitent, 179
Thirty pieces of silver, value of, 154
Thomas, St, character of, 50; occasions when mentioned, 50
Thorns, the crown of, 176

Tiberias, Sea of. *See* Gennesaret.
Title, the, placed by Pilate, on the Cross, 178
Tombs, demoniacs dwelling in, 60, 61
Transfiguration, the, 98; probable scene of, 98; circumstances attending, 99, 100; significance of, 99
Treasure-chests in the Temple, 139
Treasury, the rich men casting their gifts into the, 139; situation of, 139
Tribute to Cæsar, Christ questioned respecting, 132
Triumphal entry, description of, 121; attendant circumstances, 121
Tyre, description of, 85; our Lord's journey towards, 85

Voice, the heavenly, at the Jordan, 30; at the Transfiguration, 30, 100; in the Temple Courts, 30

Watch, setting of the, 185
Watches, the Jewish, periods of, 79
Widow's offering, the, 139
Wilderness of Judæa, 27
Woman, the, of Syrophœnicia, 86; her disadvantages, 86; her wrestling with Christ, 86; her victory, 87
Woman, the, taken in adultery, 137

Zealot, Simon the, 50, 51
Zealots, the, factions of, at siege of Jerusalem, 145
Zebedee, his social position, 33

INDEX II.

WORDS AND PHRASES EXPLAINED.

Abba, 162
Abomination of desolation, 144
Affliction, 56
Again-buying, 117
Ah, 179
Alabaster box, 152
Apostle, 48
Atonement, 117

Beelzebub, 51
Beginnings of sorrows, 142
Beside himself, 51
Branches, 121
Bridechamber, children of the, 42
Bush, in the, 135
By and by, 74

Calvary, 177
Camel, 113
Cares, 57
Charger, 74
Chief seats, 138
Choke, 55
Clearly, 131
Coasts, 87
Companies, by, 77
Compel, 176
Confirm, 192
Corban, 82
Corner-stone, 131
Covenant, 159
Covetousness, 84
Crumbs, 87

INDEX II.

Damnation, 139
Den of thieves, 124
Denarius, 76, 77
Desolation, abomination of, 144
Discreetly, 137
Dogs, 86
Doubt, 125
Draught, 83

Elders, 127
Endure, 143
Ephphatha, 89
Exceeding sorrowful, 162
Executioner, 75
Exercise lordship, 117

Fat (winefat), 128
Follow, 191

Garment, 64, 119, 121
Gehenna, 107
Generation, 148
Ghost, 181
Golgotha, 177
Gospel, 8, n.
Greek, 86
Guestchamber, 156

Had a quarrel, 72
Haply, if, 123
Hardness, 45
Head of the corner, 131
Heavy, to be very, 162
Hedge, 128
Hell, 107
His (= its), 108
Hold thy peace, 34

If haply, 123

Lasciviousness, 84
Latchet, 28
Leaven, 92
Lepton, 139
Lordship, to exercise, 117
Lowring, 113

Man, Son of, 40
Mighty works, 67
Millstone, 107
Miracles, 67
Mite, 139
Murmur, 37
Mystery, 55

Naked, 166
Net, 32
New cloth, 43

Of (= by), 29

Parable, 54
Passover, 155
Penny, 76
Plagues, 47

Powers, 68
Prætorjum, 175
Presently, 123
Pride, 84
Purple, 175

Quadrantes, 10
Quarrel, had a, 72

Rabbi, 119
Rabboni, 119
Ranks, in, 77
Redemption, 117
Render, 133
Rooms, uppermost, 138

Sabbath, second-first, 43
Satan, 31
Satisfacere, 12, 174
Savour, to, 96
Scrip, 70
Seats, chief, 138
Shortened, 146
Signs, 67
Sindôn, 165
Son of Man, 40
Sorrows, beginnings of, 142
Speculator, 12, 75
Stony ground, 54
Stoolis, 138
Straitly, 37
Syrophœnician, 86

Talitha cumi, 66
Tares, 53
Testament, 159
Thieves, 178
Thieves, den of, 124
Thought, 143
Thought, 170
Toiling, 79
Tower, 129
Tradition, 83
Trespass, 126
Tribulation, 56
Trouble, to, 65

Upper room, 156
Uppermost rooms, 138

Ways, 121
Whelp, 86
Which (= who), 116
Wickedness, 84
Winefat, 128
Wist, 100
Works, 68
Worship, 112
Wound in the head, to, 130

Xestes, 12

Zelotes, 50

CAMBRIDGE: PRINTED BY C. J. CLAY, M.A. AND SONS, AT THE UNIVERSITY PRESS.

THE CAMBRIDGE BIBLE FOR SCHOOLS AND COLLEGES.

GENERAL EDITOR, THE VERY REV. J. J. S. PEROWNE, DEAN OF PETERBOROUGH.

Opinions of the Press.

"*It is difficult to commend too highly this excellent series.*"—Guardian.

"*The modesty of the general title of this series has, we believe, led many to misunderstand its character and underrate its value. The books are well suited for study in the upper forms of our best schools, but not the less are they adapted to the wants of all Bible students who are not specialists. We doubt, indeed, whether any of the numerous popular commentaries recently issued in this country will be found more serviceable for general use.*"—Academy.

"*One of the most popular and useful literary enterprises of the nineteenth century.*"—Baptist Magazine.

"*Of great value. The whole series of comments for schools is highly esteemed by students capable of forming a judgment. The books are scholarly without being pretentious: and information is so given as to be easily understood.*"—Sword and Trowel.

"*The value of the work as an aid to Biblical study, not merely in schools but among people of all classes who are desirous to have intelligent knowledge of the Scriptures, cannot easily be over-estimated.*"—The Scotsman.

The Book of Judges. J. J. LIAS, M.A. "His introduction is clear and concise, full of the information which young students require, and indicating the lines on which the various problems suggested by the Book of Judges may be solved."—*Baptist Magazine.*

1 Samuel, by A. F. KIRKPATRICK. "Remembering the interest with which we read the *Books of the Kingdom* when they were appointed as a subject for school work in our boyhood, we have looked with some eagerness into Mr Kirkpatrick's volume, which contains the first instalment of them. We are struck with the great improvement in character, and variety in the materials, with which schools are now supplied. A clear map inserted in each volume, notes suiting the convenience of the scholar and the difficulty of the passage, and not merely dictated by the fancy of the commentator, were luxuries which a quarter of a century ago the Biblical student could not buy."—*Church Quarterly Review.*

"To the valuable series of Scriptural expositions and elementary commentaries which is being issued at the Cambridge University Press, under the title 'The Cambridge Bible for Schools,' has been added **The First Book of Samuel** by the Rev. A. F. KIRKPATRICK. Like other volumes of the series, it contains a carefully written historical and critical introduction, while the text is profusely illustrated and explained by notes."—*The Scotsman.*

II. Samuel. A. F. KIRKPATRICK, M.A. "Small as this work is in mere dimensions, it is every way the best on its subject and for its purpose that we know of. The opening sections at once prove the thorough competence of the writer for dealing with questions of criticism in an earnest, faithful and devout spirit; and the appendices discuss a few special difficulties with a full knowledge of the data, and a judicial reserve, which contrast most favourably with the superficial dogmatism which has too often made the exegesis of the Old Testament a field for the play of unlimited paradox and the ostentation of personal infallibility. The notes are always clear and suggestive; never trifling or irrelevant; and they everywhere demonstrate the great difference in value between the work of a commentator who is also a Hebraist, and that of one who has to depend for his Hebrew upon secondhand sources."—*Academy.*

"The Rev. A. F. KIRKPATRICK has now completed his commentary on the two books of Samuel. This second volume, like the first, is furnished with a scholarly and carefully prepared critical and historical introduction, and the notes supply everything necessary to enable the merely English scholar—so far as is possible for one ignorant of the original language—to gather up the precise meaning of the text. Even Hebrew scholars may consult this small volume with profit."—*Scotsman.*

I. Kings and Ephesians. "With great heartiness we commend these most valuable little commentaries. We had rather purchase these than nine out of ten of the big blown up expositions. Quality is far better than quantity, and we have it here."—*Sword and Trowel.*

I. Kings. "This is really admirably well done, and from first to last there is nothing but commendation to give to such honest work."—*Bookseller.*

II. Kings. "The Introduction is scholarly and wholly admirable, while the notes must be of incalculable value to students."—*Glasgow Herald.*

"It is equipped with a valuable introduction and commentary, and makes an admirable text book for Bible-classes."—*Scotsman.*

"It would be difficult to find a commentary better suited for general use."—*Academy.*

The Book of Job. "Able and scholarly as the Introduction is, it is far surpassed by the detailed exegesis of the book. In this Dr DAVIDSON's strength is at its greatest. His linguistic knowledge, his artistic habit, his scientific insight, and his literary power have full scope when he comes to exegesis....The book is worthy of the reputation of Dr Davidson; it represents the results of many years of labour, and it will greatly help to the right understanding of one of the greatest works in the literature of the world."—*The Spectator.*

"In the course of a long introduction, Dr DAVIDSON has presented us with a very able and very interesting criticism of this wonderful book. Its contents, the nature of its composition, its idea and purpose, its integrity, and its age are all exhaustively treated of....We have not space to examine fully the text and notes before us, but we can, and do heartily, recommend the book, not only for the upper forms in schools, but to Bible students and teachers generally. As we wrote of a previous volume in the same series, this one leaves nothing to be desired. The notes are full and suggestive, without being too long, and, in itself, the introduction forms a valuable addition to modern Bible literature."—*The Educational Times.*

"Already we have frequently called attention to this exceedingly valuable work as its volumes have successively appeared. But we have never done so with greater pleasure, very seldom with so great pleasure, as we now refer to the last published volume, that on the **Book of Job**, by Dr DAVIDSON, of Edinburgh....We cordially commend the volume to all our readers. The least instructed will understand and enjoy it; and mature scholars will learn from it."—*Methodist Recorder.*

Job—Hosea. "It is difficult to commend too highly this excellent series, the volumes of which are now becoming numerous. The two books before us, small as they are in size, comprise almost everything that the young student can reasonably expect to find in the way of helps towards such general knowledge of their subjects as may be gained without an attempt to grapple with the Hebrew; and even the learned scholar can hardly read without interest and benefit the very able introductory matter which both these commentators have prefixed to their volumes. It is not too much to say that these works have brought within the reach of the ordinary reader resources which were until lately quite unknown for understanding some of the most difficult and obscure portions of Old Testament literature."—*Guardian.*

Ecclesiastes; or, the Preacher.—"Of the Notes, it is sufficient to say that they are in every respect worthy of Dr PLUMPTRE'S high reputation as a scholar and a critic, being at once learned, sensible, and practical.... An appendix, in which it is clearly proved that the author of *Ecclesiastes* anticipated Shakspeare and Tennyson in some of their finest thoughts and reflections, will be read with interest by students both of Hebrew and of English literature. Commentaries are seldom attractive reading. This little volume is a notable exception."—*The Scotsman.*

"In short, this little book is of far greater value than most of the larger and more elaborate commentaries on this Scripture. Indispensable to the scholar, it will render real and large help to all who have to expound the dramatic utterances of **The Preacher** whether in the Church or in the School."—*The Expositor.*

"The '*ideal* biography' of the author is one of the most exquisite and fascinating pieces of writing we have met with, and, granting its starting-point, throws wonderful light on many problems connected with the book. The notes illustrating the text are full of delicate criticism, fine glowing insight, and apt historical allusion. An abler volume than Professor PLUMPTRE'S we could not desire."—*Baptist Magazine.*

Jeremiah, by A. W. STREANE. "The arrangement of the book is well treated on pp. xxx., 396, and the question of Baruch's relations with its composition on pp. xxvii., xxxiv., 317. The illustrations from English literature, history, monuments, works on botany, topography, etc., are good and plentiful, as indeed they are in other volumes of this series."—*Church Quarterly Review*, April, 1881.

"Mr STREANE'S **Jeremiah** consists of a series of admirable and well-nigh exhaustive notes on the text, with introduction and appendices, drawing the life, times, and character of the prophet, the style, contents, and arrangement of his prophecies, the traditions relating to Jeremiah, meant as a type of Christ (a most remarkable chapter), and other prophecies relating to Jeremiah."—*The English Churchman and Clerical Journal.*

Obadiah and Jonah. "This number of the admirable series of Scriptural expositions issued by the Syndics of the Cambridge University Press is well up to the mark. The numerous notes are excellent. No difficulty is shirked, and much light is thrown on the contents both of Obadiah and Jonah. Scholars and students of to-day are to be congratulated on having so large an amount of information on Biblical subjects, so clearly and ably put together, placed within their reach in such small bulk. To all Biblical students the series will be acceptable, and for the use of Sabbath-school teachers will prove invaluable."—*North British Daily Mail.*

"It is a very useful and sensible exposition of these two Minor Prophets, and deals very thoroughly and honestly with the immense difficulties of the later-named of the two, from the orthodox point of view."—*Expositor.*

Haggai and Zechariah. This interesting little volume is of great value. It is one of the best books in that well-known series of scholarly and popular commentaries, 'the Cambridge Bible for Schools and Colleges' of which Dean Perowne is the General Editor. In the expositions of Archdeacon Perowne we are always sure to notice learning, ability, judgment and reverence.... The notes are terse and pointed, but full and reliable."—*Churchman.*

"**The Gospel according to St Matthew**, by the Rev. A. CARR. The introduction is able, scholarly, and eminently practical, as it bears on the authorship and contents of the Gospel, and the original form in which it is supposed to have been written. It is well illustrated by two excellent maps of the Holy Land and of the Sea of Galilee."—*English Churchman.*

"**St Matthew**, edited by A. CARR, M.A. **The Book of Joshua**, edited by G. F. MACLEAR, D.D. **The General Epistle of St James**, edited by E. H. PLUMPTRE, D.D. The introductions and notes are scholarly, and generally such as young readers need and can appreciate. The maps in both Joshua and Matthew are very good, and all matters of editing are faultless. Professor Plumptre's notes on 'The Epistle of St James' are models of terse, exact, and elegant renderings of the original, which is too often obscured in the authorised version."—*Nonconformist.*

"**St Mark**, with Notes by the Rev. G. F. MACLEAR, D.D. Into this small volume Dr Maclear, besides a clear and able Introduction to the Gospel, and the text of St Mark, has compressed many hundreds of valuable and helpful notes. In short, he has given us a capital manual of the kind required—containing all that is needed to illustrate the text, i.e. all that can be drawn from the history, geography, customs, and manners of the time. But as a handbook, giving in a clear and succinct form the information which a lad requires in order to stand an examination in the Gospel, it is admirable......I can very heartily commend it, not only to the senior boys and girls in our High Schools, but also to Sunday-school teachers, who may get from it the very kind of knowledge they often find it hardest to get."—*Expositor.*

OPINIONS OF THE PRESS.

"With the help of a book like this, an intelligent teacher may make 'Divinity' as interesting a lesson as any in the school course. The notes are of a kind that will be, for the most part, intelligible to boys of the lower forms of our public schools; but they may be read with greater profit by the fifth and sixth, in conjunction with the original text."—*The Academy.*

"**St Luke.** Canon FARRAR has supplied students of the Gospel with an admirable manual in this volume. It has all that copious variety of illustration, ingenuity of suggestion, and general soundness of interpretation which readers are accustomed to expect from the learned and eloquent editor. Any one who has been accustomed to associate the idea of 'dryness' with a commentary, should go to Canon Farrar's **St Luke** for a more correct impression. He will find that a commentary may be made interesting in the highest degree, and that without losing anything of its solid value. . . . But, so to speak, it is *too good* for some of the readers for whom it is intended."—*The Spectator.*

"Canon FARRAR'S contribution to The Cambridge School Bible is one of the most valuable yet made. His annotations on **The Gospel according to St Luke**, while they display a scholarship at least as sound, and an erudition at least as wide and varied as those of the editors of St Matthew and St Mark, are rendered telling and attractive by a more lively imagination, a keener intellectual and spiritual insight, a more incisive and picturesque style. His *St Luke* is worthy to be ranked with Professor Plumptre's *St James*, than which no higher commendation can well be given."—*The Expositor.*

"**St Luke.** Edited by Canon FARRAR, D.D. We have received with pleasure this edition of the Gospel by St Luke, by Canon Farrar. It is another instalment of the best school commentary of the Bible we possess. Of the expository part of the work we cannot speak too highly. It is admirable in every way, and contains just the sort of information needed for Students of the English text unable to make use of the original Greek for themselves."—*The Nonconformist and Independent.*

"As a handbook to the third gospel, this small work is invaluable. The author has compressed into little space a vast mass of scholarly information. . . The notes are pithy, vigorous, and suggestive, abounding in pertinent illustrations from general literature, and aiding the youngest reader to an intelligent appreciation of the text. A finer contribution to 'The Cambridge Bible for Schools' has not yet been made."—*Baptist Magazine.*

"We were quite prepared to find in Canon FARRAR'S **St Luke** a masterpiece of Biblical criticism and comment, and we are not disappointed by our examination of the volume before us. It reflects very faithfully the learning and critical insight of the Canon's greatest works, his 'Life of Christ' and his 'Life of St Paul', but differs widely from both in the terseness and condensation of its style. What Canon Farrar has evidently aimed at is to place before students as much information as possible within the limits of the smallest possible space, and in this aim he has hit the mark to perfection."—*The Examiner.*

www.ingramcontent.com/pod-product-compliance
Lightning Source LLC
Chambersburg PA
CBHW020858230426
43666CB00008B/1233